LAST WALK IN NARYSHKIN PARK

OTHER BOOKS BY ROSE ZWI

LAST WALK
IN NARYSHKIN PARK

ROSE ZWI

Spinifex Press Pty Ltd
504 Queensberry Street
North Melbourne, Vic. 3051
Australia
women@spinifexpress.com.au
http://www.spinifexpress.com.au/~women

Edited by Janet Mackenzie
Maps by Yvonne Critchell
Typeset in Adobe Garamond by Claire Warren
Cover design by Deb Snibson, Modern Art Production Group
Made and printed in Australia by Australian Print Group

National Library of Australia
Cataloguing-in-Publication data:

Zwi, Rose.
Last walk in Naryshkin Park.

ISBN 1 875559 72 8

1. Zwi family. 2. Holocaust, Jewish (1939–1945) – Lithuanian.
3. Jews – Persecution – Lithuania. I. Title.
940.5318094793

Australia Council
for the Arts
This publication is assisted by the Australia Council,
the Australian Government's arts funding and advisory body.

For my children and grandchildren

In memory of the 220 000 Jewish Lithuanians,
among them family and friends,
who were massacred in 1941 by the Nazis
and their local collaborators.

Since the fourth century after Christ, there have been three anti-Jewish policies: conversion, expulsion and annihilation . . . The missionaries of Christianity have said in effect: you have no right to live among us as Jews. The secular rulers who followed had proclaimed: You have no right to live among us. The Nazis at last decreed: You have no right to live.

Raul Hilberg: *The Destruction of the European Jews.*

"You killed my family."

"It is true. I killed your parents . . . I had orders . . . The chief of the group . . . said that if I did not kill, I would be killed."

"My father was your godfather. You were his neighbour . . . You were my friend. You were like my brother . . ."

"I never thought I would kill like that. I am Christian . . ."

Innocent Kabera, a Tutsi, accuses Jean Twagiramungu, a Hutu neighbour, of murdering his family in a Rwandan village.
Guardian Weekly, 7 May 1995.

Contents

Acknowledgements

It is impossible to acknowledge individually all the people who have given so generously of their time and memories, and without whom this book could not have been written. My heartfelt thanks to the survivors who continue to bear witness to the greatest single catastrophe of the twentieth century; to those who left *der heim* before the Holocaust with memories of a way of life which is gone forever; to the translators of Yiddish and Hebrew documents and texts from the archives of YIVO, Yad v'Shem and other libraries and museums, and to family and friends who encouraged and sustained me during the five years it has taken to research and write *Last Walk in Naryshkin Park*.

Special thanks to my aunt Leah and her family in Vilna; to Misha, who twice drove us across the length and breadth of Lithuania, and to Freda, incomparable guide and translator; to the family of the late Jack Trubik, who allowed me unrestricted use of his 1920s photographs, without which Zhager would have remained steeped in myth; and to Sharon Zwi, who not only processed Jack's photographs, facilitating their use in this book, but also contributed most of the 1993 photographs of Vilnius and Zagare.

Special thanks also to Bronye, who has given another dimension to the book by providing material to which I would not otherwise have had access.

For various reasons, some of my interlocutors have been given pseudonyms.

Rose Zwi

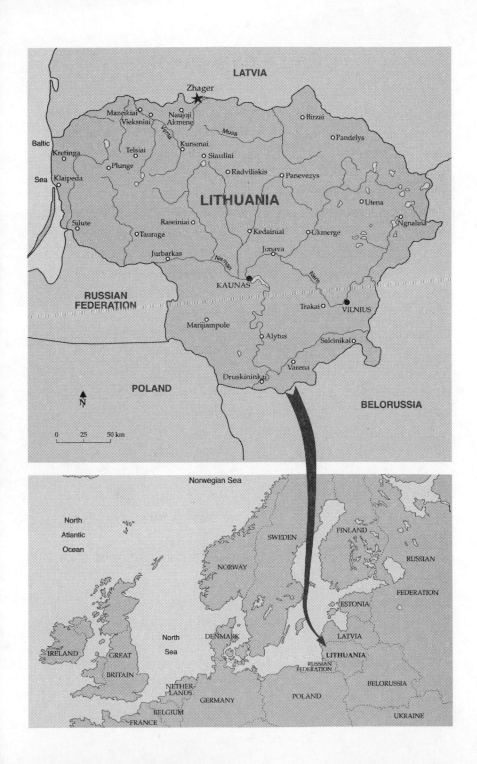

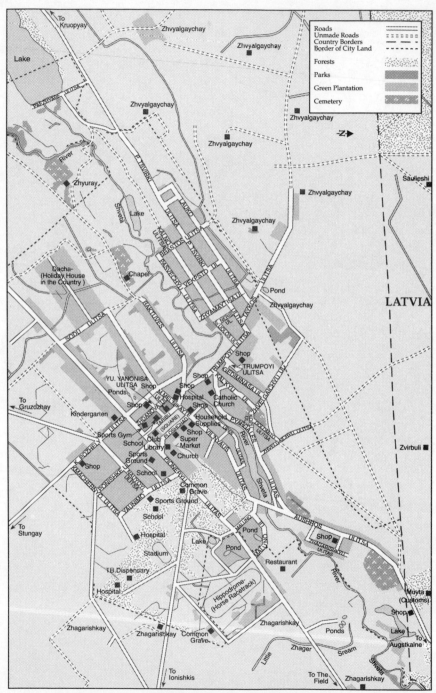

Zhager township, 1984.

PART ONE

Memorial at the mass grave in Naryshkin Park.

1

Prologue

There is a grave in Yelets, a small town on the River Don, which has not been visited in fifty years. Smothered by weeds or covered in snow, it lies among graves of other strangers. Its inscription can only be imagined: Leib Simonovitch Yoffe, 1909–1943. What more can be written over a war grave?

Leib Simonovitch's mother, younger sister and brother lie in the mass grave in Naryshkin Park, Zhager, a small town on the Lithuanian–Latvian border, about 2000 kilometres north-west of Yelets. The fate of another brother and sister and their families is not known.

A rough-hewn obelisk, about 1.5 metres high, was erected over the Zhager grave by survivors of the massacre. Only the line beginning "Here lie . . ." remained visible after the Soviet authorities overlaid the Yiddish inscription with a plaque in Russian:

Three thousand Soviet citizens, victims of Fascism, were massacred in this place on 2 October 1941.

After Lithuanian independence in 1990, the word "Soviet" was roughly chiselled out, leaving a pale wound. Two years later, the Soviet plaque was removed, the obelisk cleaned up, and three metal plaques were riveted into the stone, with an epitaph in Lithuanian, Yiddish and Hebrew.

In this place on 2 October 1941 the Hitlerist murderers and their local helpers massacred about 3000 Jewish men, women and children from the Shavel District.

The grave is visited once a year by a dwindling group of survivors living in Vilna and Kovno. They come together on Yom Kippur, the Day of Atonement, to mourn and to remember. The number of victims, some say, is closer to 7000 than 3000.

Only two members of Leib's family of eight died in their own beds: his father Simon, in the early 1920s when such deaths were still common among the Jews of Zhager, and Lcib's older brother Gershon, my father, who left Lithuania in 1927. Gershon died of a broken heart, misdiagnosed as a coronary, at the age of fifty-eight, in the heart of Africa.

It is almost too late to reconstruct the catastrophic events behind the Zhager memorial and thousands like it in Eastern European cities, towns and villages; in dense forest and alongside deep ravines. Haunted, ageing, dying, the survivors have long fled their blood-soaked homelands. The perpetrators, feigning amnesia, denying guilt, walk free over killing fields sealed with shady parks and gardens.

Had my parents remained in Lithuania, we too might have lain in the mass grave in Naryshkin Park. Gershon never forgave himself; he had abandoned his family and survived. I am heir to his guilt and to his unfulfilled desire to propitiate the dead. Survival imposes obligations. But how does one appease the unquiet spirits? Prostrate oneself before the grave and swear vengeance? Plead that Gershon had been overtaken by history? How can one avenge murders that harrow up the soul and freeze the blood? I borrow words to express the horror; the Holocaust is beyond ordinary language.

My spirits do not demand revenge for murder most foul; they ask only for remembrance; memory is vengeance. If they are forgotten, they are doomed to wander through history, over the killing fields of crazed ideologues and warlords, grieving for the massacre of other innocents, despairing at the hatred and destruction. Remember us.

As though one could forget.

The Holocaust had dominated my childhood and adolescence, suppurating like a neglected wound. Vacillating between dreams of utopia and the depths of despair, I had joined movements and left movements, but finally understood that the solution, if indeed there were a solution, lay at unreachable depths, where the struggle for justice and the desire for a better world seems irrelevant. The Holocaust belongs in the realm of evil, and it is not possible to legislate against sickness of the soul, demonic hatred or the primeval passions which produced such a tragedy.

Over the years phrases like Six Million, Final Solution, Mass Graves, Gas Chambers, Cattle Trucks, have become terrible clichés that distance the horror and armour the emotions. By following the fate of six – not Six Million – people, one might catch a glimpse into the human dimensions of the tragedy, and in doing so, propitiate the unquiet spirits, my father's among them.

Thus it is that I add my pencil mark to history. Little remains of a way of life that has vanished forever: tales told by survivors, faded photographs, songs, stories. Had Leib lived to tell his own story, we might have known more. But as "facts", over the years, fade into myth, we are left with a few fragmented images with which to stitch a patchwork quilt, not a tapestry. Remembering may not be enough, but to forget is unconscionable.

2

Exile to Eden

Naryshkin Park, 1920s.

Growing up among immigrants whose songs and stories were steeped in nostalgia for "*der heim*", Lithuania inevitably became my "home" as well. But their stories were not only of forests and fields, sledge rides and strawberry picking. When my parents spoke about the time *ven men hot unz arausgeshikt*, when we were deported, I experienced the trauma of exile with them: the clank of the cattle trucks in the long journey through the steppes; the heat, the hunger, the thirst; the crush, the fear of an unknown destination. Box cars have never lost their horror for me.

Gershon, my father, had been twelve, my mother Sheva a few months younger, when World War 1 broke out. As the German army advanced on Lithuania in 1915, the Tsarist regime, which had ruled Lithuania for 120 years, decreed that Jewish Lithuanians from all front-line towns and villages be deported; they were regarded as potential collaborators, particularly as they spoke Yiddish, a language based on medieval German. Ethnic Lithuanians were not exiled.

The Jews had suffered greatly under Tsarist rule. During the reign of Nicholas I from 1825 to 1855, over six hundred anti-Jewish laws had been enacted. They ranged from expulsions from towns and villages where Jews had lived for generations, to a conscription edict issued in August 1827, making Jewish communities responsible for delivering up young males between the ages of twelve and eighteen for twenty-five years' service in the Tsar's army. If they proved tardy in carrying out this pernicious law, press gangs – *khappers* – descended on them, kidnapping youths at random, often netting children as young as eight or nine. The *Nikolaiyevske soldaten*, as these pitiful Jewish boy-warriors were called, were seldom seen again. They either died before they reached the furthest outposts of the Russian empire, or were forced to convert to Christianity.

Stories are told about a rabbi in Zhager, Eliyahu Schick, who literally took up arms against forced conscription in the nineteenth century.[1] A vigorous defender of the poor and the powerless, he objected when the local Jewish council handed over children from poor families to the Tsar's officers, and protected the sons of the rich. Once, on hearing that certain children had been captured and locked up in the *kahal shtiebl*, the community centre, he took up a hatchet, assembled a group of poor Jews, and stormed the centre, freeing the children. He hid them in his own house until the recruiting agents left town.

Towards the end of the nineteenth century, less stringent conscription laws were introduced, requiring one son from each family

---

1 Kagan, *Yiddishe Shtet, Shtetlech un Dorfishe Yishuvim in Lite*, p. 157.

to serve in the army. Breadwinners and only sons were exempted. My paternal grandfather fought in the Russo-Japanese war in 1904. My maternal grandfather, on the other hand, became an only son when his older brother was "adopted" by a childless aunt. Many young men emigrated before reaching military age. After Lithuanian independence, however, they served willingly in the national army.

Given their history under the Tsars, it is not surprising that Jewish Lithuanians, in 1915, were overwhelmed by fear and anxiety when they were ordered to assemble at their nearest railway station within twenty-four hours. The night before, Gershon and his younger brother Leib dug a hole in the half-frozen earth of the back yard, where snow still gleamed in dark corners. Freyde, my grandmother, wept as she placed into the shallow pit her copper pots, samovar, pestle and mortar and brass candlesticks, wondering whether they would ever return to their home.

The next day over 5000 Jews from Zhager made their way on foot or by cart to the railway station. Randomly herded onto cattle trucks that would take them to different destinations deep into the Russian interior, mothers were sometimes separated from children, husbands from wives, the young from the old. Most families were reunited after the war; some never met again. Many died from typhus and other illnesses on their long journey south-east to the Ukraine.

After weeks of travelling under gruelling, insanitary conditions, they arrived, exhausted and disorientated, in Berdyansk, a port city on the Sea of Azov. Situated in a prosperous wheat-growing area, it was a popular seaside resort linked to the rest of the Russian Empire by a large network of railway lines that carried tourists to its famous mud baths on the salt lagoons. This time the trains brought refugees, not holiday makers. As they stumbled out of the cattle trucks with their families of half-starved, crying children, they saw both pity and revulsion in the eyes of the reception committee.

The Russian-educated Jews of Berdyansk had nothing but religion in common with their shtetl brethren. Although they had retained their religious and cultural identity, they had integrated into the thriving commercial life of the city. From the outset, the refugees felt ambivalent towards their benefactors who dispensed charity without warmth.

My father and his family had been housed in a disused army barracks; my mother's family was crowded into a communal hall with other refugees. Soup kitchens were set up and clothing and bedding distributed. *Bezhintzes*, their Berdyansk co-religionists called them; refugees. A new word to add to their limited Russian vocabulary. They spoke Yiddish, prayed in Hebrew, knew enough Lithuanian to deal with the peasants in the market-place, but understood little Russian. What education they had, had been acquired in the traditional Hebrew study houses of the shtetl.

Just as jokes are anonymously spawned, so were songs composed, describing the misery and hardship of the refugees. In his low, rather croaky voice, Gershon used to sing a song based on a nineteenth-century folk song about a Jewish recruit in the Tsar's army. It contrasts the hardships of exile with the warm security of home life, the glow of sabbath candles and the traditional sabbath meal. Both soldier and *bezhintzes* had eaten the bread of affliction.

> ... *Fraytig tsunacht derlangt men di lokshn,*
>   *Oy vey gevalt!*
> *Undz traybt men arum azoy vi di oksn,*
>   *Oy vey gevalt!* ...
> *Fraytig tsunacht derlangt men dem tsimes,*
>   *Oy vey gevalt!*
> *Undz traybt men avek in vayte medines,*
>   *Oy vey gevalt!* ...

After a few weeks, some artisans found employment in their trades; the rest took whatever work was available. Gershon's family moved out of the barracks into lodgings in the poorer quarter of town and, like most other people, lived one family to a room. *Nisht onkumen on shtetl* was the imperative; not to be dependent on the town, on charity.

Food, in this warmer, fertile land, was abundant. Grapes, oranges and tomatoes, luxuries of the rich in the shtetl, were inexpensive in season, as were watermelon and black bread. Booten, a type of flounder fished in the Sea of Azov, was also plentiful. The children thrived. In the shtetl the staple diet had been herring and potatoes, often potatoes without the herring. The diet had varied only on the sabbath and during religious festivals when, Gershon said, you might have potato pudding. And for this too there was a song.

> *Zuntig bulves, muntig bulves,*
> *Dinstig un mitvoch – bulves,*
> *Donershtig un fraytig – bulves*
> *Shabes in a novine, a bulve kugel . . .*

The children adapted to exile more readily than their parents. Berdyansk opened up a new, exciting world for them. They went to secular schools where they learned to read and write Russian. As they walked along the shaded streets, breathing in the perfume of the *byela* acacia trees, they never spared a thought for the home they had left behind, except to compare its wooden houses and muddy streets to this metropolis of stone buildings and paved avenues. Overcoming their initial timidity, the children ventured beyond their own neighbourhood into areas that filled them with wonder. They watched stevedores loading wheat onto steamers in the port; stared at elegant tourists coming and going into the grand hotels which lined the sea front; gaped into shops filled with luxuries they could not name, and marvelled at the horseless carriages that glided along the tree-lined streets.

"Only once before," my mother told me, "had we seen a motor car. As it drove through Raktuvegass in Zhager, all the children had chased after it, shouting, *A meshugener vogen! A meshugener vogen!*" A mad waggon indeed, a magical waggon, one which could move without horses.

Awed at first by the seemingly endless inland sea which flowed into the Black Sea through the straits of Kerch, they soon made it their playground. In summer they disported themselves on the beaches and in the water; between December and March they skated on its frozen surface.

Like goyim, their parents said as the children lost their pale complexions and shtetl timidity, and grew confident, sturdy and rosy-cheeked. Few of the older people could speak or read Russian. The eggs are teaching the chickens, they said when the children became their interpreters in necessary but unwelcome dealings with the Tsarist bureaucracy. They had well-grounded fears of government officials, soldiers and police. *Kneppeldikke* they called these threatening figures of authority who wore uniforms with shiny buttons, *knepplech*, and who wielded arbitrary power over their lives.

"Little was achieved without a bribe," Gershon recalled. "We even paid for the privilege of being driven into exile." He told the story, possibly apocryphal, of how, on a stiflingly hot day, the train had stopped suddenly in the middle of the endless Russian steppes. Released from the overcrowded trucks, they had watched the train driver walking alongside the train, tapping the wheels with a hammer.

"What's the problem?" they asked.

Jack Trubik

Zhager, 1920s.

"The wheels won't turn," said the driver. "They need grease."

"*Az men schmirt, geit es,*" the refugees sighed, and proceeded to collect money for a bribe. If you smear, it moves.

Poverty cut short the carefree period of childhood. After bar mitzvah, the boys were apprenticed to tailors, barbers, shoemakers or carpenters. The girls helped their mothers with the younger children, or became learner dressmakers, knitters or milliners. At twelve, Gershon was working in a barbershop after school; Itze, my mother's older brother, made a suit for his own bar mitzvah. Few could afford further schooling. But exposed to a wide, vibrant world, they eagerly took what it had to offer.

In the evenings, they either attended study circles arranged by the Bund, the General Jewish Workers' Alliance, or joined Zionist groups which ranged from the most extreme religious sects dedicated to ushering in the millennium, to the far left factions, which preached redemption through work on the land in Palestine. The Bundists dismissed Zionism with contempt. The only solution to the Jewish question, they believed, was socialism, which would restore dignity and equality to the downtrodden of the world, among whom were the Jews.

Gershon and his peers went to night classes in Russian literature and history, sang in choirs, and revelled in the atmosphere of impending change which pervaded the wider society. They had no doubt that the old repressive system was on its way out, and that a new equitable society would be ushered in, with their invaluable help.

Gershon spent all his free time at the Jewish Workers' Club, reading in the library, or attending lectures. When his father, Simon, found revolutionary pamphlets under Gershon's mattress, he burned them. "Do-you-know-what-happens-to-people-who-make-revolutions?" he shouted as he landed blows on whatever part of Gershon's anatomy he could reach.

Simon knew what happened to people who made revolutions. He had fought in the Russo-Japanese war in 1904, an unpopular war which had contributed to the outbreak of the October Revolution in 1905. Among the uprisings which had occurred throughout the Russian Empire was one in Zhager, where local revolutionaries, many of them Jews, had set up a short-lived Zhager Republic. The Tsarist government's response had been immediate and brutal. It sent in General Orlov and his Cossacks, who destroyed Jewish homes and beat up hundreds of people. The men were locked into a synagogue, and threatened with torture and death if they did not reveal the hiding place of the revolutionaries. Nobody spoke. They had been freed only after the community paid a fine of 4500 rubles. The revolutionaries suffered a worse fate. Zemach Essin, a tailor, was shot; a socialist called Ritter was killed in a Riga prison, and the others were either tortured to death or exiled to Siberia. Only a few succeeded in escaping over the border. Among them was a woman, Rifka Kreiger, who had embroidered the flag of the Zhager Republic.[2] "You'll be shot and we'll be exiled to Siberia," Gershon's mother cried, begging Gershon to end his socialist activities. But neither his father's beatings nor his mother's pleas had kept Gershon from Bund meetings. He comforted her, then hid his political tracts in a safer place. Leib, six years younger than Gershon, hero-worshipped him.

Exile, for the first two years, had protected the refugees from the war. It would soon catch up with them. When Tsarist Russia was defeated by Germany in 1917, the country was plunged into revolution. The Ukrainians, taking advantage of the internal chaos, declared an autonomous Ukrainian Republic. It did not last long. After the peace agreement was signed, the German army withdrew, and the new Communist government, like the Tsarist regime before it, refused to relinquish hegemony over the bread-basket of the region. After many battles, in one of which Poland, a former enemy, fought on the side of the Ukraine, the Red Army overcame all resistance, and in December 1919, the Ukrainian Soviet Socialist Republic was established. But the war between the Red Army and

---

2 Schoenburg, Nancy and Stuart. pp. 283–5.

the White Army raged on, and soon the sound of battle was heard on the outskirts of Berdyansk.

Overcoming the reluctance of the youth to leave, the refugees applied for permission to return to Lithuania. "If the Bolsheviks win, we'll be shot as capitalists," they argued. "And if the White Army wins, we'll be strung up as Bolsheviks."

"I might have defied my parents and remained on," Gershon told me many years later, "but at the age of sixteen, I was suddenly thrust into the role of breadwinner. My father had throat cancer, and my mother was pregnant with her sixth child."

As soon as trains for civilians became available, they left Berdyansk, ending their four-year exile in Eden.

3

Waiting for the Revolution

Left to right: Gershon Yoffe, his sister Henke, and brother Leib, 1920s.

Vu zayt ir alle, mayne chaveirimlech
Tzu lebt ir, tzu vandert ir,
Tzu zayt ir shein teit?
Zingt mir a liedala, zingt mir a liedala,
Zingt mir fun Yiddishen neit . . .

Are you alive, the song asks of absent friends who have not returned to their *heimen shtetala*; or are you dead? Are you still wandering, and will you ever come back?

When the Jews returned from exile they found their homes in ruins, their possessions stolen, their livelihood destroyed. Their non-Jewish neighbours, with whom they had only poverty in common, were sullen, resentful at their return. And once again songs were sung of hardship, loss and sorrow.

The Yoffes' house, on the slopes near the River Shvete, was half-demolished. The floor boards had been ripped up for firewood, the windows smashed, the roof tiles broken. And as my grandmother Freyde dug up her copper pots, the brass candlesticks, samovar and pestle and mortar, she wept again. Simon was dying, the children were young and dependent, and Gershon, at sixteen, was supporting the family.

With a resilience drawn from years of adversity, the Yoffes, like the other exiles, began to rebuild their lives. Some emigrated to America; the rest remained in their shtetlech, repaired their homes, reopened the study houses, returned to their workshops, and renewed trade with their neighbours. The youth, however, was restless and rebellious. Exile had opened a new world for them. They could not return to the traditional values and life of the shtetl. If you will it, one of their culture heroes had said, it is no myth. So they set about transforming their particular myths into reality.

Ethnic Lithuanians, too, were rediscovering their myths. Until serfdom had been abolished in 1861, the peasant had not raised his head from the plough. By the 1880s a fragile Lithuanian intelligentsia of peasant origin had emerged, and with it, the first stirrings of Lithuanian nationalism. By the end of World War I, they were in a turmoil of nationalist fervour, reasserting their right to govern themselves, and to establish their long-suppressed cultural identity. Jewish Lithuanians empathised with these aspirations. They had been living in the country since the fourteenth century and spoke of themselves as Litvaks. Freed from Tsarist repression, they hoped to live in peace, with dignity, under an independent Lithuanian government.

During its occupation of Lithuania in 1917, the German government had permitted the establishment of a Taryba, a twenty-man council. In February 1918, the Taryba proclaimed an independent Lithuanian state, which Germany recognised. By November that year, a government was formed. Both the Bolsheviks and the Poles had sought hegemony over the tiny country of three million people, but neither had been strong enough to impose their will on the Lithuanians. Political and military scuffles continued until 1921, when Lithuania was accepted as a member of the League of Nations. It suited the Great Powers to have an independent buffer state.

Jewish Lithuanians, especially the younger generation, were drawn into the heady days of early Lithuanian independence. Despite the poverty and general economic depression in the country, hopes had been high when Lithuania became a signatory to a League of Nations' document for the protection of linguistic, racial and religious minorities.[3] A Ministry of Jewish Affairs and a Jewish National Council had been set up in Kovno; Jews served in the Lithuanian administration, in Parliament, and as officers in the army. Hebrew street signs even appeared in Kovno. Some envisaged another Golden Age for the Jews. Others hoped for a revolution that would usher in a socialist utopia in Lithuania. But neither millenarian dream was shared by those with longer historical memories who had no trust in the altruism of host countries. A Jewish national home, they were convinced, was the only solution to centuries of persecution.

In Gershon's barbershop, opposite the market square, young working-class intellectuals argued passionately about their beliefs and aspirations. Freyde could not understand why her son was not making a better living when his barbershop was always crammed with customers. "We're planning a better life," Gershon told her, "not a better living."

After independence, three kinds of Jewish schools had been set up, in addition to general state schools: Zionist-oriented Tarbut

---

3 League of Nations, *Document for Protection of Linguistic, Racial and Religious Minorities by the League of Nations.*

schools, which taught in Hebrew; Yavneh religious traditional schools, whose medium of instruction was Hebrew; and Yiddish-language elementary schools. The latter were established by the socialist-oriented Kulturlige, which wished to make secular education available to the majority of Jews whose language was Yiddish. Teachers and lecturers were brought out to Zhager in 1919, where, in addition to the elementary schools, the Kulturlige also set up a library and night schools for the working people.

"That was our university," Gershon used to recall with pride, "the university of the working youth."

Hungry for knowledge, young men and women flocked to the night classes of the Kulturlige. A large library was gradually built up, and study groups ranged from Russian and German literature to Marxism and Darwinism. Gershon's prize possession had been a three-volume Yiddish edition of Charles Darwin's *Origin of Species, Di Afshtamung fun Menschen.* The books now stand on my bookshelf, their ochre covers faded to pale brown. On the front cover is a picture of Darwin; on the back, a drawing of a Neanderthal family.

Jack Trubik

The English class.

It is illustrated with drawings of fish and birds, antelopes and apes. As he prepared talks for his study group at the Kulturlige, Gershon could not have imagined that within two decades, his own family would fall victim to distorted theories of evolution, and would die a terrible death through unnatural selection.

The youth of the shtetl flourished. The Kulturlige attracted not only the autodidacts; it also drew young people to its social activities, the most popular of which was the choir. Sheva, my mother, sang in the choir. So did Leib. The songs they sang reflected the revolutionary spirit of the time. Even non-political young women like Sheva were urging the poor and the suffering of all nations to slough off oppression, and become masters of their own fate.

> *Un du akerst, un du zeist,*
> *Un du fiterst, un du neist,*
> *Un du hammerst, un du shpinst,*
> *Zog mir mein fraynt vos du fardinst?*
> *Gling, glang, gling, glang,*
> *Zingkt der hammer mit zayn gezang, gling, glang . . .*

You plough and you sow, tend flocks and sew, hammer and spin, but live in poverty as your hammers sing their song: gling, glang, gling, glang.

Impressed with his musicality, the choirmaster taught Leib the rudiments of music. When he became Gershon's apprentice, Leib saved every hard-earned kopeck to buy a trumpet. "One day," he told his mother, "I'll be a real musician."

"Such ambition," she scoffed. "Better a barber than a gypsy."

Had the trumpet been the only available instrument Leib could afford at the time? Or had it appealed to his sense of drama? The trumpet, after all, is an instrument of celebration, an instrument with which to reach The People, to alert them to danger, to sound the call to freeedom, to herald in a new age. Had he been the son of rich parents, he might have chosen the violin or the cello. He would have taken lessons in one of the larger towns, in Riga perhaps, and become a professional musician; his talent and inclination certainly lay in that direction. As it happened, the circumstances of his life drew him in a different direction.

At sixteen, Leib joined the band of the local fire brigade. In a small town like Zhager, where most houses were built of wood, the fire brigade had depended on the voluntary services of the residents. To attract supporters, it organised parades and performances by the band. The Pizharniks wore peaked helmets, and a uniform with two rows of shiny buttons, giving them the appearance of a *kneppeldikker*, an official with authority, but not the power. When a fire broke out, the trumpeter alerted the residents. *"Pizhar! Pizhar!"* the cry would ring through the shtetl. Their fire-fighting equipment was crude: barrels on wheels, drawn by horses brought to the scene by anyone who owned a horse; the fire brigade had none of its own. While the flames leapt from house to house, volunteers filled the barrels from street pumps, or drew water from the River Shvete with hand pumps.[4] The fire of 1881, when 400 houses had been destroyed, and that of 1902, when nearly all of Old Zhager had burned down, were always recalled with awe. In his youth, it has been said of Leib, he was devoted to putting out fires. In later years, he stoked them.

While Leib, as an apprentice, swept up hair cuttings, scrubbed combs and stropped razors, he listened intently to the debates in the barbershop. By the time he was cutting hair and shaving beards, including his own, he was participating in the discussions. At first, like Gershon, he became a member of the Bund, the General Jewish Workers' Alliance. After Gershon left Lithuania, Leib joined the underground Communist Party. Poverty and the desire for a better world had radicalised him. Many years later, an acquaintance of Leib's, a Zionist, said it had been difficult, even dangerous, to argue with Leib.

"There I was, stretched out on the barber's chair, my hands immobilised under a white sheet, while he stood over me, brandishing a razor. He had, so to speak, persuasive arguments in hand."

---

4 Fedler, *Shalecheth*, p. 41.

During this brief flowering of democracy, the Jewish youth, with the Kulturlige at the heart of the community, had studied and debated, danced and sung, fallen in love and married; life had returned to normal. On Saturdays they had dressed in their sabbath best and strolled through Count Naryshkin's Park. Despite the difficult times, they had great hopes for the future.

"Who wears sabbath clothes throughout the week?" was a riddle Leib used to ask. The answer could have been given by anyone in the shtetl. "He who does not have sabbath clothes."

Gershon, at the age of twenty-two, fell in love with the teacher of Russian literature. She was an educated woman from Riga, several years his senior, who had helped organise the Kulturlige. Their love affair lasted almost a year, during which time he learned a lot of Russian. "What do you expect, with all those extra lessons," was Sheva's comment. "I can't imagine what he saw in that old maid." The teacher, whose name is lost, must have been about twenty-eight at the time. "She was plain, had no dress sense, her skirt hems were uneven, and her stockings twisted around her ankles." This says more about Sheva, perhaps, than about the teacher. Gershon always spoke about her with admiration, tinged with regret.

Sheva was the sister of Gershon's friend, Itze Reisen. She had been a beautiful woman in a shtetl renowned for its good-looking women and clever men, a dichotomy no one questioned. Her good looks and vivacity had attracted many admirers. "Before I married," she used to reminisce, "I got more *sekretkes* at our dances than anyone else. *Sekretkes?* They were cards you bought when you went to a dance, on which you wrote a secret message to someone you liked. You folded it over, wrote his or her name on it, and the person in charge would act as postman. Flying Post, we called it. We were modern already; we wouldn't go to a *shadchan*. We made our own matches. In this way even a shy, unattractive girl could contact a young man, discreetly. But it was mostly the men who sent the *sekretkes*. You just wrote something like, would you like to walk with me in Naryshkin Park on Saturday? The rest followed. I burned all my *sekretkes* when I married."

Sheva fell in love with one of her admirers. For two years they strolled arm in arm through Naryshkin Park. When he left for South Africa with his family, he promised to send for her. She never heard from him again. Gershon comforted the desolate sister of his friend Itze, and within a few months, the teacher of Russian literature returned to Riga.

In the meantime, the democratic process in Lithuania had stalled. Lithuanian politics, after independence, had been pluralistic and multi-party, but conflicts between the parties had made it impossible to form stable governments. A *coup d'état* in 1926 brought an extreme nationalist government to power. Antanas Smetona and his young officers and intellectuals abolished opposition parties, curtailed civil liberties, executed a few Communists, and imprisoned a number of socialists, social democrats and Christian democrats. Parliament was dissolved in April 1927, and a temporary constitution was promulgated which abolished the most important democratic principles of the original constitution. The rights of the Jews and other minorities had been eroded before the coup; the Golden Age had lasted from 1919 to 1922. By 1924 the Kulturlige and some of its most important institutions – the elementary schools, evening classes and libraries – had been closed down.

Economic anti-Semitism was also growing. As peasants moved into urban areas, they faced competition from the established Jewish, German and Polish traders and artisans. An organisation known as the Verslininkai – skilled workers – adopted as its slogan "Lithuania for the Lithuanians", reverting to an insular policy which discriminated against the minorities in Lithuania. The ethnic Catholics had never really accepted the Jews as fellow Lithuanians; it had been expedient to enlist their cooperation during the struggle for independence. After centuries of residence, the Jew remained the Other, the Stranger. Although they stopped short of pogroms, anti-Semitic demonstrations occurred from time to time, often stoked by the Church which fulminated against the "Christ slayers" from the pulpit.

Gershon eventually despaired of any meaningful political change in Lithuania. With a strong right-wing government in power, it seemed the revolution would never come. Sheva's twin brother Bentze had been urging them to join him in Mexico where he had immigrated a few years previously. "Enough of the poverty and pogroms of the Old World," he wrote. "There is no anti-Semitism in Mexico. They don't even know what Jews are." Sheva was enthusiastic about the idea. She wanted to begin married life in a new country; Zhager held too many unhappy memories. Your family will join us in Mexico once we're settled, she said to Gershon, echoing the intentions of other migrants.

"There's no future for the Jews in Lithuania," Gershon told his family soon after the wedding. "Sheva and I will go to Mexico first, and when I've saved enough money for sea fares, I'll send for you. We'll soon be together again." His family, he rationalised, would manage without him for a few years. His sister Henke was sewing and embroidering bed and table linen, and her work was in great demand; Leib was a fully-fledged barber, with his younger brother Faivke as his apprentice. Only the two younger children were still at school. With their earnings and the money he would send from Mexico, the family would be cared for.

When Leib heard of Gershon's plan, he was devastated. Gershon, who had always confided in him, had not even hinted at his desire to emigrate. "Sheva is leading you by the nose," he said in a bitter confrontation with Gershon. "You're abandoning family and ideals for a pretty face."

"I am abandoning neither," Gershon argued. "I'm conflicted about being a revolutionary in an anti-Semitic milieu. Look at the Populists. They justify pogroms against the Jews on the grounds that such outbursts express the legitimate resentments of the peasants. 'What are we to do when they beat up the Jews?' they ask; 'defend them?'"

"You sound like a Zionist," Leib said, delivering the ultimate insult.

In their barbershop on the market square, he had listened with delight as Gershon had demolished Zionist arguments with a snip of the scissors, religious mysticism with a scrape of the razor, utopian dreams with an incisive word. Yet he had never been Gershon's unquestioning acolyte. He had sided with younger Jewish populists and Marxists who criticised the Bund for getting bogged down in parochial matters. Although he understood the conflicts of Jewish revolutionaries, indeed, had experienced them, he rejected the doubts that had made his brother a renegade. The Revolution, he insisted, would resolve such problems; all men would become brothers. He refused to take leave of Gershon.

Gershon's other siblings were sad and bewildered, especially Shmulke, his youngest brother, for whom Gershon had been a surrogate father. Hardest of all had been parting from his mother. The image of Freyde and her children, huddled outside their little wooden house on the Shvete, mute with misery as he embraced them for the last time, was to remain with Gershon for the rest of his life.

Despite increased responsibilities, and his distress at Gershon's defection, Leib was eager for life. He was young and handsome, and loved music and dancing. The young women in the shtetl fell in love with him, and he with them. With the benefit of hindsight, some claimed that Leib had played the shtetl Don Juan to conceal the depth of his political involvement; others suggested that his air of mystery attracted women.

Gershon's youngest brother, Shmulke, in 1927 when Gershon left Lithuania for Mexico.

Philandering and politics, however, are not mutually exclusive. What everyone is agreed on, however, is his passion for music. He played on every possible occasion, in any milieu. After Gershon left, he formed a band, and played with non-partisan enthusiasm at socialist, religious and even Zionist functions. Music, for him, was the great equaliser.

"Leib Yoffe the musician?" people still say. "I remember him well. When Leib stood up to play solo, everybody stopped dancing or romancing, and listened."

They may remember him well, but they remember him differently, with horns or with a halo; as a gifted musician or as a mere village barber, blowing his trumpet wild; as a dedicated idealist or a party *apparachnik*; as a caring human being, or one who loved The People, not people; as a tender lover, or an arrogant Don Juan. Because he encapsulated the spirit of his age, he became the stuff of local myth. Even his role in the days preceding the German occupation of Zhager in 1941, and the circumstances of his death, two years later, remain unclear.

It was not until after the war that Gershon learned anything more about Leib's life and his death. Leib wrote to him only twice; soon after Gershon left Lithuania, then again in 1943, when Leib lay dying from his war wounds. The first letter had plunged Gershon into a deep depression; the second, fortunately, never reached him.

4

Oaxaca, Mexico

Oaxaca, 1928. View of town.

Bentze, Sheva's twin brother, had originally planned to go to the United States, not Mexico. By the time he was ready to depart, the immigration quota for Lithuanians had closed. Fascinated by the cornucopia-shaped landmass south of the United States, with the Pacific Ocean to the west and the Gulf of Mexico to the east, he noted the arbitrary line dividing the two countries: one continent, no seas to cross. He would start off in Mexico and work his way north. Aquatic skills acquired in the River Shvete and the Sea of Azov, he said, had prepared him for crossing any river in the world, including the Rio Grande.

He might have become the first Jewish-Lithuanian wet-back in history. Instead, he remained in Oaxaca, a beautiful colonial town 450 kilometres south of Mexico City, which stands in a fertile valley, on a high plateau, surrounded by mountains. The weather is mild, he wrote home, and the natives are friendly. When he foolishly mentioned the black-eyed Spanish beauties of Oaxaca, his mother began a search for a bride, preferably a young Jewish orphan whose relatives (or lack of relatives) would not be a financial drain on him.

Gershon also fell in love with Oaxaca. Here he lost his urgency to create a better world; none could be more idyllic. He could understand why Cortes had chosen Oaxaca above all other places as his own province. The gold was in the long summer days, if not in the surrounding mountains. And the natives, as Bentze had written, were indeed friendly, the climate mild. Gershon learned Spanish quickly, made easy contact with the people, and enjoyed the spicy dishes and the new rhythm of life. Only in Berdyansk, his other Eden, had he felt so free. He assuaged his guilts by writing regularly to his mother, sending her a portion of his earnings, and putting aside what he could for sea fares. Life in Lithuania, his mother wrote, was more difficult than ever.

"Our neighbours don't know we're Jewish," Bentze told them soon after they arrived. "They think we're German."

Sheva's enthusiasm faltered. "Why pretend? Are they anti-Semitic?"

"They don't even know what Jews are."

"Are they Catholic?" Sheva persisted. In the shtetl the Catholic priests had stoked the incipient anti-Semitism of the peasants.

"Those who aren't pagan," Bentze admitted, "are Catholic."

"Then they know what Jews are. For this we had to travel in *d'rerd oifen dek*, to the rooftops of hell? We had enough Jew haters at home."

"Don't worry. The Mexicans are easy-going people. Everything is *mañana* and *siesta*." Bentze showed off his Spanish. "Nothing bothers them. Except the earthquakes . . ."

"Earthquakes?"

"Little tremors. They occur very seldom," he added quickly. "You get used to them."

"I want to go home," Sheva had wept that night and on many following nights. "Everything's so different, so strange. The people are too dark, their clothes are too bright, the food's too spicy, the climate's too hot. And I'll never learn their language."

She was lonely. The few Jews who lived in Oaxaca had integrated into Mexican life. Two of them had married local women, and the others no longer observed Jewish festivals, customs or rituals. Sheva lit candles every Friday night, kept a calendar of the Jewish holy days, and prepared special dishes associated with the festivals, just as she had done in the shtetl. The idea of eating pork or mixing meat dishes with milk dishes was abhorrent to her. The only time she ate meat was when Bentze, on a business trip to Mexico City, brought back a kosher chicken.

Gershon was often away from home. He and Bentze travelled to outlying villages, selling cloth and other manufactured articles, and bringing back village crafts and the black pottery for which Oaxaca was famous. They planned to rent a shop in town when they had saved enough money, and take turns to travel into the country.

Oaxaca, 1929. Sheva with Rose and Hinde, Gershon, Bentze, Joel.

Sheva hated to be left on her own, especially after she fell pregnant. The only neighbour with whom she had contact was their landlady Juanita, a jolly, middle-aged woman who lived on the same square as her tenants. Juanita took pity on Sheva. She taught her some basic Spanish, and took her to the market, where she persuaded Sheva to buy different kinds of fruit and vegetables. Under Juanita's tutelage, Sheva learned enough Spanish to conduct simple conversations with the stallkeepers and with her neighbours. She was beginning to settle in.

"When the tremors begin," Juanita told Sheva one day, performing appropriate actions, "stand under the lintel of the main doorway and wait for it to pass. Don't run outside. But don't worry. The big quakes don't come often."

They came one day when Gershon and Bentze were out of town. The floor seemed to tilt, furniture slid around, glasses and crockery crashed down from the shelves, and the windows rattled in their frames. Sheva was about seven months pregnant, alone at home, and she panicked. She ran into Juanita's house, and together they stood under the lintel, holding on to one another. For once, even Juanita was silenced. She clung to Sheva, releasing her only to cross herself. A great deal of damage was done to the town, particularly to the 200-year-old Catholic church opposite their house.

"If this can happen to the Catholics," she cried when Gershon returned home later that evening, "imagine what's in store for the Jews! I want to leave! I want to go home!"

This was 1928, and there was no question of going "home". The extreme Lithuanian nationalists had entrenched themselves in power, the rights of minority groups had been further eroded, and Leib, at one stage, had had to go into hiding. Gershon was putting money aside as fast as he could. He had to get his family out of Lithuania before Leib, hothead that he was, was sent into exile. Or worse.

As the time drew nearer for Sheva to give birth, Juanita took her to the only doctor in town, a heavy drinker. Juanita extracted a promise from him to remain sober until the baby was born. He kept his word until the pregnancy went two weeks beyond term. Hauled out of a bar by Juanita and Gershon, he could barely stand on his feet as he breathed tequila fumes over her. In vain she called for Mother and Home. Impatient with the pace of the birth, the doctor used forceps.

Sheva, at the end of the long, painful labour, looked at the bloodied face of the child whose forehead had been dented by the forceps, and cried, "It is better she should die than be an imbecile!" The birth trauma would be dredged up whenever I displayed what my mother considered aberrant behaviour. Her worst fears were realised when, in my teens, I joined a Zionist-Socialist movement and announced that I was going to live on a kibbutz.

As an infant, however, I had not shown any signs of brain damage. The only fair-skinned, blond, green-eyed child in the district, I became a favourite with the neighbours, who drew us into the community. Bentze's mail-order bride arrived soon afterwards from Lithuania, together with Sheva's younger brother Joel.

By this time Bentze and Gershon had opened a shop in the town, and Joel, after he had learned a little Spanish, travelled into the countryside. Sheva was beginning to enjoy life in Oaxaca when, one afternoon, she was woken from her siesta by the sound of shooting and shouting. Grabbing me from the cot, she rushed into the courtyard to find a crowd gathered around a grotesque papier-mâché figure of a man with an enormous nose and horns. The men were shooting into the air, yelling, and throwing up their sombreros. The women were ululating and shaking their fists at the papier-mâché figure.

"What's happening?" Sheva asked Juanita.

"Today we celebrate a great religious holiday," Juanita explained. "Today is the day we kill the Jews."

"Have you ever seen a Jew?" Sheva clutched me to her breast.

"God forbid!" Juanita crossed herself. "That," she pointed to the evil-looking figure at the centre of the incensed crowd, "is a Jew."

Gershon, finally, gave in to Sheva's pressure to leave Mexico. Not even Bentze's entreaties could persuade Sheva to remain in a country where Jews were shot in courtyards. First papier-mâché Jews, she said, then real ones. She wanted to go to South Africa where her mother, sister and two other brothers had settled.

So it was that three years after their arrival in Mexico, Bentze accompanied them to the port of Veracruz, where they embarked for South Africa. Gershon never ceased to hanker after Oaxaca. Worse: in order to make the move, he had used up the savings with which he meant to bring his family out of Lithuania.

We arrived in South Africa in 1930, in the middle of the Depression. Unable to find work in Johannesburg, Gershon took a job in Shabani, a small mining town in Rhodesia, where we lived for two years. Only then did he have enough money to open a barbershop in Johannesburg.

"How is it possible," Leib wrote, breaking his silence of several years, "to live in the *goldene medina*, the golden country, and not have enough money to send to your mother? You are no doubt supporting the whole of Sheva's family."

"On the contrary," Gershon replied. "It is only by living with them in a cramped little house, that we are able to make ends meet. The streets of Johannesburg, contrary to rumour, are not paved with gold. Last month I had to borrow money to pay the rent."

Most Jewish immigrants, he explained, had neither money nor language. They tried, with mixed success, to find a place for themselves in a society which divided English-speakers from Afrikaners, and the blacks from everyone else. "For once, the Jews are not at the bottom of the social pile. If you are white, you are automatically privileged. Jews react to this evil system in two ways: we can't solve everyone's problems; we can barely cope with our own. Or: this is how the Jews were treated for centuries; what can we do to alleviate the lot of the blacks?" Gershon did not say which option he had chosen. Leib would not have understood that his political beliefs had been compromised by his need to survive. Leib did not reply to his letter.

From his mother, Gershon received a letter with the words of "*A Brivale di Mammen*".

> *A brivale di mammen,*
> *Zolst du mayn kind nisht farzamen,*
> *Shrayb geshvind, liebes kind,*
> *Shenk ir di nechome.*
> *Di mamme vet dayn brivale lezn,*
> *Un zi vert genezn,*
> *Heilst ir shmerts, ir bitter herts,*
> *Erkvikst ir di neshome . . .*

Write a letter to your mother, grant her this comfort. Her bitter heart will be comforted, her pain assuaged, her soul refreshed.

The song concludes with the son receiving news of his mother's death. Her last request had been that he should say the prayer for the dead.

Gershon had no defence against this kind of letter. He had no money to send, nor much prospect of earning enough to bring them to South Africa. His letters, consequently, trickled down to one or two a year, with an occasional enclosure of a small sum of money. With the outbreak of war in 1939, it was already too late to write a letter to his mother, a *brivale di mammen*. It would soon be time to say the prayer for the dead.

5

Questions

Shabani, Rhodesia, 1932. Gershon, Rose, Sheva.

Gershon never became the rich man of Leib's fantasy. The mythical land of gold-paved streets barely yielded a living in the early years. There was unemployment in the urban areas, and starvation on the farms. Drought, cattle disease and mismanagement were driving farmers off the land. Thousands flocked to the cities where they had to compete for unskilled jobs with poverty-stricken blacks.

With Hitler's rise to power, the Afrikaner nationalists, under D. F. Malan, openly allied themselves with Nazism. They were racist and fiercely nationalist, and blamed their economic misfortunes on the blacks and the Jews. Jewish involvement in commerce, Malan said, must be checked. Until Afrikaners could compete in the business world, the "poor white" problem would persist. And immigration had to be stopped. When Jews constitute more than 4 per cent of a country's population (the South African figure was 4.52 per cent of the white population), they create a Jewish Problem.

"This time I'm not running," Gershon told Sheva. "It's the same everywhere. In *der heim* it was Lithuania for the Lithuanians. After centuries of living there, we hadn't qualified as Lithuanians. We ran from Oaxaca because they shot papier-mâché Jews. And here the Blackshirts and the Greyshirts desecrate synagogues and clamour for a halt to Jewish immigration. Everyone's got a 'Jewish Problem'. But what's the solution?" A homeland of one's own, I argued with my father when I was growing up. Utopian fantasies, was his predictable response.

My parents and I shared a house with my maternal grandmother, her sons Itze and Hille, who had a tailoring workshop in town, and her younger daughter Hoda, a dressmaker. I was particularly close to my grandmother, whom I called Bobbe, with whom I shared a room, and to Hoda, whom I never called aunt. We lived near a large mine dump which, in the windy month of August, shed its fine yellow sand all over the houses and the people. The River Shvete and the fragrant pine and birch forests of *der heim* were a world away. But for me they were more real than the mining suburb in which we lived.

Tell me about *der heim*, was my constant request. As they spoke, I visualised the low wooden houses that lined the cobbled streets, the market-place, the River Shvete which divided Old Zhager from New Zhager, the Mill Hill, the woods and, best of all, Count Naryshkin's Park, where trysts were kept and hearts were broken.

Gershon talked about *der heim*; Sheva sang about it. Her songs encapsulated the life of the shtetl. Orphans walked barefoot in the snow, and parented children chanted the aleph-beth at the rabbi's hearth; fathers sought a living in the New World, abandoning families in the Old; mothers waited for letters from sons, and widows comforted babes, promising a future selling raisins and almonds. Some ambition, Gershon would mutter when Sheva sang *"Rozhinkes mit Mandlen"*. And there were songs about pogroms and burning villages, exile and desolation. Her favourite songs, however, were about star-crossed lovers:

> *Vie ken ich in finstern vald,*
> *Fargessen die liebe zu dir,*
> *Dermon ich mir dein geshtalt,*
> *Ervekt zich a veitik in mir . . .*

> How can I in this dark wood
> Forget my love for you
> Your image haunts my memory
> Awakening the pain in my heart.

My father, who sang out of tune, recited poems about workers who built palaces for the powerful and themselves lived in hovels, who sewed for the rich and wore rags, who tilled the soil but went hungry. His favourite poem, set to music, is by Abraham Reisen, no relation to my maternal grandfather who bore the same name. It is about a man who has nothing by which to measure his years. The rich man measures his days by his money, the happy man by the passing hours. If misery were the measure of life, he would be ancient; if happiness is, he is not yet born.

> *Eib leben heist laiden, dan leb ich shein lang*
> *Dan hob ich genug shein die yahren,*
> *Eib leben heist heren fun glick chotz ein klang*
> *Dan bin ich noch gornisht geboren . . .*

Why, I wondered in retrospect, had they been so nostalgic for the shtetl? But the question came long after the stories, the poems and the songs had imprinted themselves deeply on my mind and heart.

There were also happy songs. Like the one Leib's widow Leah

would sing, many years later, on our way back from Zhager where we had visited the mass grave in Naryshkin Park. "The living", she said, "must go on living. Otherwise the victory is theirs. Do you know the song about the cat's wedding . . . ?"

I was told stories about Rosa-di-meshugene who went mad when her illegitimate child was taken from her; Benna-der-haiker, a hunchback who had been the butt of nasty jokes; Yekke-mit-di-medallen, a returned soldier who had hung bits of metal, cloth and paper on his chest, and boasted of the heroic deeds which had earned him these "medals".

"Most people lived narrow, constricted lives," Gershon used to tell me, "and showed little tolerance for the mad, the eccentric, non-conformists or rebels." But pride in his birthplace sometimes eclipsed his criticism. He would intone the names of Zhager's writers: Avram Zakesh, Yakov Dineson, Shmuel Zanger, Yehoshua Magach, and Arye, Benjamin and Yosef Mandelstam. And those of the scientists, the scholars and the secular educators. At the top of his list was Sydney Hillman who, in 1906 at the age of nineteen, had been jailed for advocating labour reforms. On his release, he had immigrated first to England, then to the United States, where he became a celebrated labour leader. "We also had famous rabbinical scholars like Salanter," he would add grudgingly. "And others."

I was deprived of one of my story sources at the age of six, when my brother was born. Go pester your Bobbe, my mother would say. So I hung around the kitchen and while my grandmother cooked and baked, she told me about life in the shtetl, and how the ice floated down the Shvete in spring, and which berries grew in the forest in summer. My aunt Hoda was another captive storyteller. While fitting my dresses, she would remove the pins from between her lips and tell me about the Naryshkins, the absentee Russian landlords, who spent the summers on their Zhager estate. Repetition never dulled my pleasure. Tell me the one about the Countess and the sweets, I would request.

Modulating her voice to story-telling mode, Hoda would begin at the beginning. "*Amol iz geven* . . . Once-upon-a-time, there was a famous Russian general who was a favourite of Catherine the Great. In recognition of his loyalty and his services to the crown," – I was too young to detect *double entendre* – "Catherine presented him with the beautiful estate of Zhager. When he died, Zhubov left the estate to his daughter's son, the Graf Naryshkin, and the Naryshkins have owned it ever since. Their palace was surrounded by beautiful gardens and woods, and part of it was opened to the people of Zhager, who to this day stroll there on the sabbath."

"Are there swings and slides and roundabouts in the Park?" I knew the answer; I had heard the story before. But I kept hoping such essential equipment would one day appear in the story.

"It's not that kind of park," Hoda explained patiently. "It's more like a very big garden or a wood. At the beginning of summer, the Naryshkins and their friends and their servants used to arrive in magnificent carriages, and the whole shtetl would turn out to watch. The Countess waved to the people, and threw bonbons through the carriage window, all wrapped up in little papers with pictures of fruit on them. And we, silly children, would rush into the street to pick them up. Just like little black children do in South Africa."

Sheva never admitted to such undignified behaviour. "My father", she said, "used to lease the Count's orchards when the trees were in blossom, and throughout summer we'd live in the orchards, in shelters, and help the hired workers pick the fruit. Zhager cherries were famous throughout Lithuania. My father would take the fruit to larger towns in Lithuania and Latvia, and bring back manufactured goods, which he sold to the peasants."

"Like other Jews in Europe, Litvaks were always the middlemen," my uncle Itze would interject. He and my father never talked down to me; a six-year-old should know such things. "In most places they were not allowed to own land, so they leased it."

My Bobbe nodded as he spoke, gazing with admiration at her eldest son, understanding as little as I did. "Such a mind," she would say in the privacy of our room. "If he'd had the opportunity to study, he'd have become an *avocade*." She never learned to distinguish between the fruit and the profession.

"Tell me more about *der heim*," I would ask her.

"It wasn't an easy life." She sighed. "But those were the good years, when we were all together. When Avrome died I was only forty, with seven children to support . . . As Sheva said, in summer Avrome rented orchards and we slept under the stars, breathing in the sweet smell of hay drying out in nearby fields. One summer," she added shyly, "the Count came on his white horse to visit your grandfather in the orchard. He smiled at me, then said something to Avrome in Russian. 'He said I had a beautiful wife,' Avrome told me afterwards. 'Hide yourself if he comes again. You never know with these aristocrats.'"

"Did he come again?" I asked.

"No," said my grandmother. Among the songs she sang was one about a prince who falls in love with a simple village girl, wins her love, then deserts her for a beautiful princess.

Part of Naryshkin's estate, 1920s.

> *Zog mir, du meidala, vos tust du aher,*
> *Binst shein vi a malach, un rein vi a trer,*
> *Ich leb do nit vayt mit mayn fotter in einem,*
> *Keiner ken mir, un ich ken do keinem . . .*
> *Er hot zich bakent mit a sheine Princessen,*
> *Di oreme meidala ingantzen fargessen . . .*

"Your grandfather", Gershon told me another time, "was known as Avrome der Ugerke, Avram the Cucumber. In addition to the orchards, he also rented fields from the Count, and employed local peasants to plant and harvest cucumbers. Then he marketed them. Always the middleman, as Itze says."

My mother glared at him. "Only stupid, envious people called him Avrome der Ugerke. Everyone had respect for Avram Reisen, unlike . . ."

"Naturally." My father turned back to the *Forwerts*, the American Yiddish workers' newspaper he had borrowed from the Workers' Club.

"When we returned from exile in 1919, things were different," my Bobbe told me. "Avrome couldn't hire fields or orchards any more, so he bought goods in the big cities, and traded with the peasants. After he died, may he rest in peace, your uncle Bentze, your mother's twin brother, took over the business until he left for Mexico. He never writes, Bentze. Perhaps he had too much responsibility when he was young. A *brivale di mammen*, a letter to his mother . . ."

"The *Internationale* of Jewish motherhood," my father muttered.

"Have you got a family?" I asked my father, aware of an imbalance in our kinship system.

"Of course I've got family," he assured me. "A mother, three brothers and two sisters. My father died a long time ago, before you were born. But they live far away, in Lithuania. Lietuva in Lithuanian, Litva in Russian, Lita in Yiddish. Depends which language you're speaking. Your other Bobbe is a lovely, kind lady. She's short, stout, with big brown eyes and pink cheeks. She's had a hard life."

"Didn't my Zeide work for the rent?" I was not sure what rent was, but had overheard my parents quarrelling over it. How can you send money home when you haven't got enough to pay the rent, my mother had said. Gershon held me close. Time passed before he was able to speak again.

"Where is Lithuania, Lita?"

"Lithuania", he said, "is one of the Baltic states, a small country which used to be ruled by Russia, Russland in Yiddish." He never patronised me. I might have understood more if he had. But I kept asking questions, many answers to which I only understood as I grew older.

Russland, Russia. All the people I knew came from Russland; it was the place they called *der heim*. In winter they skated on the frozen river, and in summer they walked through pine forests, gathering wild strawberries and mushrooms. I yearned for *der heim*. In dreams I slid down the Mill Hill on a sled, over dazzling white snow. In our mining suburb we slid down acrid-smelling mine dumps on sheets of corrugated iron. There were no fragrant forests here, only bluegum plantations and a smelly slimes dam. A young boy had once been sucked into the dam and was never found again. It became forbidden territory, hence our secret playground.

There were few trees in our suburb where numbered avenues crossed numbered streets. In addition to the eucalypts, there were a few peppercorn trees whose seeds we shot at one another through pea-shooters, and plane trees which produced dangling seedboxes, known to us as itchy balls. The gentile children picked the itchy balls in autumn, and forced their furry seeds down our backs, chanting, "Ikey is a Bolshie! Ikey is a Bolshie!"

"What's a Bolshie?" I asked my father. I guessed "Ikey" described our foreignness.

"Bolshies are Bolsheviks, people who live mostly in Russia. Don't feel insulted if they call you a Bolshie. Some of the nicest people I know are Bolshies."

I was confused. I thought only Jews lived in Russia. "Are Bolshies Jews, then?"

"Some are," he replied, compounding my confusion. To my mortification, he repeated this conversation to Uncle Itze. "Such questions she asks," I overheard him say.

It was hard to be a child of immigrant parents.

"Show me a picture of my other Bobbe and Zeide," I demanded of my father. I expected them to be among my mother's sepia-coloured photographs which she kept in shoe boxes at the bottom of her wardrobe. They always smelled of naphthalene.

"I have none," he said. "My parents' generation only got photographed for their passports. And as you know, they never left Zhager."

I glanced up at the enlarged photograph of Avram the Cucumber which hung on the lounge wall. My father shrugged. Some questions, I was learning, were too difficult to answer.

He did, however, show me photographs of three of his siblings: Henke, his older sister; Leib, the brother to whom he was very close; and his youngest brother Shmulke, at the age of three. He had none of Faivke or Bryna. Most of my parents' photographs had been taken against tasteful backdrops in the studio of Shabselban, the town's photographer. The rest were taken in Naryshkin Park. Dressed in their sabbath best, everyone looked grave, unsmiling, into the eye of the camera.

When Gershon spoke about his family, his eyelids grew pink and his voice choked up. Freyde, my grandmother, was a misty figure for me. The only thing I knew about her was that she was kind, hard-working and had a round face and dark sad eyes. I had a clearer, perhaps inaccurate, picture of grandfather Simon. He had apparently been tall and handsome, much like Leib, except that he had reddish hair. I imagined Simon with a wild, red beard; piratical. All I learned about him was that he had fought in the Russo-Japanese War, and that he had spent little time at home. None of his children had been close to him. My mother never answered questions about Grandfather Simon. When my father mentioned him, she would say, "Hardly a subject to discuss with a child."

My brother was named Abraham Simon, after both his grand-fathers. He was never called Simon. When he misbehaved, our mother would shake her head and say, guess who he takes after. Only once, when grown up, did I surprise my aunt Hoda into indiscretion.

"Why doesn't anyone ever speak about Simon?" I asked.

"They say he had a Lithuanian mistress," she replied, off guard. "But who knows? It must've been very lonely travelling such long distances over bad roads, through snow and in all kinds of weather. Perhaps that's why he took this woman along with him. Or perhaps she was his translator. In the travel business you need to know other languages. He had red hair, you know," she added thoughtfully, as though this might explain his aberrant behaviour.

Red hair, in the shtetl, was considered as great an affliction as a squint or a limp. She's got red hair, people would say, but otherwise she's quite good-looking. Or: he's a redhead, but good-tempered with it. When my father grew a moustache, it was red. His younger sister Bryna had red hair. Henke and Leib were dark. I never learned what colour hair Faivke and Shmulke had.

"Travel business indeed," my mother said when I confronted her. "Simon was a *proster furman*, a simple carter. He owned a few horses and a cart and transported people, sometimes goods, from Zhager to the larger towns in Latvia and Lithuania. Sometimes even to Koenigsberg." She ignored my questions about the Lithuanian mistress.

"Whatever one may say about him," Gershon said, confirming there was more to be said, "he was an educated man. He could speak, read and write Lithuanian and Russian, in addition to Yiddish and Hebrew. He helped arrange his passengers' travel documents with border guards and customs, and acted as a translator for them. In my father's day, the nearest port was in Riga, the capital of Latvia, and the nearest railway station was about 25 kilometres from Zhager, in a place called Benen. From there we left for exile in Berdyansk in 1915." Not a word about the Lithuanian mistress. He emphasised the historical, evaded the personal.

When I visited Zhager in 1992, I walked through the bleak, wind-swept cemetery, in search of Simon's grave. I found only overturned tombstones with faded inscriptions, and mounds whose memorial stones had been ripped up for paving by the local population. Simon remains as evasive in death as he had been in life. Nothing more will ever be known about him. A most unlikely candidate for such a death, he, at least, died in his own bed.

6

Di Deutschen Kumen!

Mining headgear, Johannesburg.

Like the Kulturlige of an earlier time, the Jewish Workers' Club in Johannesburg became the focus of cultural and social life for many Jewish immigrants. Although it had a distinctly pro-Soviet orientation, it attracted people of all political persuasions. The life of an immigrant is difficult enough without ideological conflict. Here they met with old friends and spoke Yiddish freely, unselfconsciously. They flocked to the plays, socials, dances and picnics, if not to the lectures and study circles. The choir had such a reputation for excellence that even the conservative South African Broadcasting Corporation invited it to perform on radio. They sang "The Red Flag" in Yiddish, to much acclaim.

Gershon and Itze were members of the club. Sheva, a star of the Zhager Kulturlige choir, never joined. That's for young people, she said. She was thirty at the time. Musical, sharp-witted, a talented mimic who, for want of a larger audience, had inflicted her frustrated dramatic gifts on her narrow circle of friends and relatives, she could have been an actress or a singer. It did not strike anyone to lament her wasted talents as they had her brother Itze's, the *avocade* of my grandmother's imagination.

Although the club never had more than 300 paid-up members, its impact on the Jewish community, and the country as a whole, was out of proportion to its numbers.[5] But as its members integrated into their adoptive country and became part of the larger society, some drifted away. Immigrant tailors, woodworkers, shoemakers and other artisans opened small factories or businesses, and gradually moved out of the immigrant suburbs in the south of the city, into the tree-lined suburbs of the north. In a country where social mobility depended more on skin colour than on class or culture, they increasingly saw South Africa as a land of opportunity.

There were others, however, whose political experience and class origins thrust them into positions of leadership within the new industrial unions. The once closely-knit community was splitting up along class lines. As whites, however, they remained among the privileged. After the signing of the Nazi–Soviet Pact on 23 August 1939, Gershon stopped going to the club. The rhetoric of the ideologues who were toeing the Party line had become too strident for him. Relations between Gershon and Itze, long-time friends, cooled.

"Stalin knows what he's doing," Itze insisted. "It's a ploy. He's playing for time."

"He's betraying the Revolution."

---

5   Adler, "History of the Jewish Workers' Club in Johannesburg." Unpublished paper.

"You're naive," Itze retorted. "He's got no alternative. The Western powers would crush him if they could. He hates Hitler and Nazism as much as you or I do. He'll strike when the time's right."

They barely spoke to one another until Germany invaded Russia in 1941.

On Sunday afternoons we had open house. Friends would drop in for lemon tea with strawberry jam, and stay till evening for hot brisket on rye. Among them were lonely young men whom Gershon or Itze had befriended at the club, who worked as shop assistants in concession stores on the gold mines. They lived in back rooms off the main premises, and worked long hours for little pay. Immigrants without language or a trade, they had few employment opportunities. In *der heim* some of them had been rabbinical students, or had worked in family businesses.

The concession stores were leased from mining companies by *kafferitniks* – the pejorative term for the concessionaires – who generally exploited salesmen and miners alike. As the black miners could not leave the mine compound without permission, they were forced to buy from the concession stores, which stocked anything from bicycles and blankets to trinkets and bread. The miners were captive customers, the shop assistants captive employees, and the only language they had in common was Fanagalo, a mixture of Zulu, Afrikaans and English.

The white Miners' Union protected its members from competition from cheap black labour by reserving skilled work for whites only. The blacks, most of whom were contract labourers from neighbouring countries, were not permitted to form unions. And unlike the blacks, who lived in single-sex hostels on the mine compound, the white miners lived with their families in semi-detached cottages on mine property. Even in poverty the whites were privileged.

Among my uncle Itze's friends was Issy H., who worked as a concession store assistant for some years. It was he who told us about the appalling conditions under which the black miners lived. They slept eight to ten in small, bare rooms on concrete bunks, or fifty to a hundred in large, bleak dormitories, without facilities for storing their meagre possessions. The food, served out of huge drums, was basic, and their pay for working long hours underground was shilling a day. Their ablution blocks – a few showers and rows of unpartitioned toilet bowls without seats – robbed the men of their last shred of privacy and dignity.

Issy H. had been radicalised by his contact with the mine workers. He would one day be jailed for refusing to give evidence against another anti-apartheid activist. Some salesmen went on to lease concession stores themselves.

"How can we fail to recognise our own lives in those of the black people?" Gershon said. "Leib wouldn't have stood by idly. He'd have been in the forefront of the labour movement."

Gershon finally abandoned the idea of bringing his family to South Africa. What could he offer them? A struggle like his own, in a country whose racism was worse than Lithuania's? Besides, Leib would never leave Europe; he was waiting for the Revolution. Henke had married and Faivke had married. She was living in Riga, he in Shavel. Shmulke, the youngest, was now working in the barbershop with Leib, and Bryna had a job as a knitter in a small workshop. All three lived at home with their mother. Gershon sent money whenever he could. But neither reason nor rationalisation could quell his conscience; he had broken his promise to his mother.

As the 1930s drew on, the conversation on Sunday afternoons turned on pogroms, deportations, window smashing and desecrations. Our visitors outdid one another with gory details of persecution and oppression in Germany. Every sentence seemed to begin with "*Di Deutschen . . .*" No one noticed the wide-eyed child listening intently to their tales of horror.

My dreams and waking hours became obsessed with fear of the Deutschen. At night I dreamed about mobs of wild men, armed with sticks, smashing windows, breaking through doors, bearing down on us with sharp weapons. During the day I walked along pavements, careful not to stand on lines between flagstones. If I could make it to the end of the block without stepping on a line, the Deutschen would be kept at bay. The fate of the entire community lay in my hands. Or in my feet. I could not relax my vigilance for one moment.

Long after the death of my parents, Issy H. restored a childhood memory which for years had hovered on the verge of consciousness, but which I had been unable to dredge up. One Sunday afternoon, he told me, he had been visiting my family when I rushed into the house, screaming, "*Di Deutschen kumen! Di Deutschen kumen!*"

Everyone hurried outside to see which "Germans" were coming. I clung to my mother, and refused to leave the house.

About a block from our house a group of black men, dressed in three-quarter length trousers, shod in sandals made from old motor-car tyres, and wearing red bandanas around their foreheads, were stomping from one foot to another, chanting in unison, and brandishing wooden knobkerries, as they made their way down our street towards the veld.

"They were probably a group of mineworkers on their day off," Issy told me, "or Amalaitas, stick fighters, who usually wore three-quarter trousers, on their way to a drinking party in the veld. Who'd have thought you'd heard of Deutschen, let alone black ones!"

I could not recall the actual incident, but recognised the stuff of my nightmares.

Everyone's nightmares were soon realised. With the outbreak of war in September 1939, the immigrants lost contact with their families in Europe; all communication was abruptly cut. Gershon removed the pictures of water-waved ladies and Brylcreemed gentlemen from a wall in his barbershop, and replaced them with a large map of Europe. With growing dismay, he followed the rapid advance of the Wehrmacht into Europe.

"They're getting closer to Lithuania," he reported. "Where will they run, how can they save themselves? Why didn't I bring them out while there was still time?"

Then, for a short time, he regained hope. Forgetting his anger over the Nazi–Soviet Pact of the previous year, he rejoiced when the

Red Army "liberated" Lithuania in June 1940. Not only would they defend the Jews against the Nazi hordes, he said; the long-awaited Revolution had come at last, without bloodshed.

"I should've been there," he said with deep regret. "Leib was right to remain in the old country; he had faith. All my life I have waited for this moment, and where am I when it comes? Deep in the heart of this strange dark continent."

How would he have felt had he witnessed the revolution and experienced its aftermath? Leib's wife Leah provided a partial answer when I met her in 1992.

"The revolution? Gershon did not miss much. A single tank rumbled through the streets of Zhager, and from the balcony of our house, which faced onto the market square, a Russian officer addressed the people who had gathered there. 'You are now part of the Soviet Union,' he told us. The people dispersed, wondering what new *tzores* lay in store for them."

Rumours of Nazi atrocities began filtering through to the West in the wake of the Wehrmacht's storming of Eastern Europe. There was talk of mass killings, of concentration camps, of slave labour. Gershon read every newspaper, listened to every news broadcast, and haunted every communal body which might have news of what was happening behind German lines. He plotted the movements of the German army on his map in the barbershop, and became increasingly frantic as they swarmed over Lithuania in their push north-east towards Moscow. The Red Army was being routed on all fronts. The fate of civilian populations remained shrouded in darkness.

Having exhausted his earthly investigations, Gershon went in search of the occult. On the other side of the railway line lived a well-known medium called Mrs Ritchie. People from all over Johannesburg consulted her about anything from love affairs to business ventures. For weeks there had been hushed arguments between my parents, during which the name of Mrs Ritchie often came up. Tension in the house increased, and all conversation stopped mid-sentence when either my brother or I came into the room. Knowing which subjects caused most pain, I refrained from asking my father too many questions. But my delicacy stopped short of eavesdropping at every possible opportunity.

One Wednesday, "half day", when all shops closed in the afternoon, I overheard my mother pleading with him not to go out.

"How do you think we feel about my sister Faigita and her family in Riga?" she said. "But we don't mess around with ghosts and spirits."

Who said we didn't mess with ghosts and spirits? They were my Bobbe's constant companions. They appeared in her dreams, advised her, cautioned her. She even set them on the coal man when he delivered one sack short. But she didn't think they were fit companions for children. When I whistled at night, or sat on the table, swinging my legs, she would order me to stop; I was summoning the *saidim*. I whistled secretly at night, but all I could summon was the dog.

Knowing nothing of Mrs Ritchie's profession at the time, I was puzzled about my mother's agitation. After my father left, she spoke in whispers to my grandmother, whose response was a series of distraught *Gottinkes!* and *oy veys!*

Gershon returned a few hours later, pale and distraught. My mother helped him to bed, and shunted my brother and me out of the house. I lingered under their bedroom window, suppressing my panic with difficulty.

"I told you not to go." In distress, she scolded. "It's all nonsense anyway. When you're dead, you're dead. Spirits indeed. You scoff at my mother for being a superstitious old woman. How could this Ritchie woman have known your uncle's name? She got it out of you somehow, hypnotised you. These *macheshaifas*, these witches, have ways of extracting information."

"I told her nothing," he said wearily. "She took me into a darkened room and we sat at a round table. She was quiet and I was quiet. Then she went into a trance and started mumbling words I could not understand. I heard other sounds, felt disturbances in the air.

She sighed and moaned and seemed to be warding off something with her hands. I can't remember how long this went on. I myself seemed to be in a trance. My heart was banging and my mouth felt dry. I got a pain in my chest and arm, and found it difficult to breathe. Some time later she came out of her trance, looking very exhausted. Her voice trembled when she said, 'Benjamin is weeping. He has a message for you. The news is bad . . .'"

"Fetch water!" my mother shouted. "Mamma, quick! He's fainted!"

I sat under the window weeping, too afraid to move. After a long silence I heard my father's voice.

"The family, everyone," he said softly, haltingly. ". . . a horrible death . . . blood in the streets."

"Your whole family wasn't living in Zhager any more. Your mother wrote that Henke had married and was living in Riga, and Faivke and his family were in Shavel. That Mrs Ritchie doesn't know what she's talking about. Rest now. Forget that nonsense. She's probably an anti-Semite who knows what would cause you the greatest grief."

That night my father suffered his first coronary.

Soon after he recovered, my grandmother urged him to take a loan for a deposit on a house in a "better" suburb. "All our *landsleit* are moving out, and the girl's growing up. She must meet nice Jewish boys, not climb trees and mine dumps and run wild with the *skotzim* and *shikshes* in our street. You know what can happen . . ."

Balancing pride against his daughter's ruin, my father took a loan and we moved into an orange-brick house in the north-eastern suburbs of Johannesburg. We had not been living there long when a cousin of my mother's wrote that a small café in an inner city suburb of Durban could be acquired for a negligible amount of goodwill. Come, she urged. Business is booming in Durban. The city's teeming with seamen on their way to various theatres of war.

"Vultures," my father said, but moved to Durban with my mother and brother. I remained in Johannesburg with my grandmother and Uncle Itze; Hoda had married by then, and my uncle Hille had moved to Pretoria. I was reluctant to leave friends and disrupt my first years at high school.

"That I should be making a good living while people are dying," Gershon wrote from Durban. "Such an irony. Now I would've had the means to bring them to South Africa. God alone knows what is happening. What has happened." He never mentioned Mrs Ritchie again.

He continued plotting the course of the war on his map. He also kept on writing to the Red Cross and other organisations, all of whom replied that it was impossible to get news from occupied Europe. When the war drew to an end, and the Allies uncovered the unspeakable atrocities, the first films of the death camps reached South Africa. There was no longer any doubt about what had happened behind enemy lines.

By this time my parents and my brother had returned from Durban. Gershon insisted on seeing the films. I might recognise someone, he said. Recognise someone? Sheva said. You'll have another heart attack. He could not be dissuaded from going. My brother was deemed too young for such horror, but I was reluctantly allowed to accompany them to the local cinema.

For one and a half hours we sat in frozen silence. Death camp after death camp. Pyramids of corpses piled outside charnel houses. Stick figures lying in hastily dug mass graves. Dazed, skeletal survivors shuffling among their liberators, their huge, dead eyes unseeing, too weak for joy. We came out of the cinema wordless, avoiding one another's eyes.

"You shouldn't have come," Gershon said to me, slipping a pill under his tongue. "For me, it's different. I have to know."

"I also have to know! I'm not a child any more. I'm seventeen!" I wept with rage and despair. "Don't protect me. At my age you were supporting your whole family."

After Gershon gave up the search for his family, his physical appearance began to change. He put on weight, his face grew puffy, and his walk became slow and deliberate, as though he were testing the ground with each step. He seemed always to be holding his breath, suppressing sobs. And just as he began to settle into stunned acceptance, he learned more about the fate of his family.

A few months after the war ended, a countryman of my parents, with his wife and two children, arrived in South Africa from a Displaced Persons' Camp in Italy. They had survived the Holocaust. They spent the first few months of freedom telling their story to anyone who would listen. One Sunday afternoon, they brought their terrible tale to us.

Shortly before the war they had moved from Zhager to Shavel, a larger town about 70 kilometres away, which had better educational facilities for their children. When the Germans overran Shavel, they massacred the old, the sick and the very young, and penned the rest of the Jews into a ghetto. The able-bodied men and women were put to work as labourers in essential industries. Late in October 1941, Dovid, the father, had been repairing a ghetto fence, when a peasant he had known in Zhager passed by. All the Jews of Zhager have been massacred, he whispered as he walked past. Dovid had not believed him.

As the war drew to an end, the inmates of the Shavel ghetto had been sent to death camps. The daughter had been transferred to one camp with her mother, the son to another with his father. Miraculously they all survived months of fear, torture and hunger, which they described in chilling detail. They eventually found one another through a refugee agency.

Before they left Lithuania, they went to Zhager in search of family. They found only four or five Jews who had survived by escaping into Russia just ahead of the German invasion. After the war they returned to Zhager and reclaimed their homes from hostile neighbours. They confirmed the peasant's account: all the Jews in the shtetl had been massacred.

They told Dovid that on the night before the Germans took Zhager, there was great confusion in the shtetl. The Russian troops had retreated, and the Lithuanian militia, flexing its muscles, had closed the border between Lithuania and Latvia, cutting off escape. Two nights previously, Leib and Leah had arrived in a large truck from Shavel intending to drive their families into Latvia, then over the border into Russia.

The shtetl elders had accused Leib of being a rabble-rouser. You have come to sow panic among our people, they said. We remember the Germans from World War I, and do not believe we're in any danger from them. It was Leib's Russian *yovanim* who had robbed and killed and deported. They threatened to hand Leib over to the Lithuanian militia unless he left the shtetl immediately. They would not allow him to take his family or Leah's family with them. That, they said, would create panic and chaos.

The militia had allowed Leib and Leah to leave, but without their families. Dovid did not know whether any of them had survived. He only knew that all the Jews in Zhager had been massacred and buried in a mass grave in Naryshkin Park. Neither did he know anything about Sheva's sister and family in Riga. Those who had survived, he said, were now living in larger towns like Kovno and Vilna.

Later that evening Gershon had another coronary, and was confined to bed for six weeks. Even if it had struck him that it was Leib, finally, who had "deserted" his family, it would have given him no comfort.

Some weeks later a misaddressed letter arrived from my mother's sister. They were all alive, she wrote. They had escaped on the last train out of Riga. She and her husband had spent the war years on a kolkhoz, a communal farm, in Russia, and their three children had enlisted in the Red Army. They were now living in Vilna. As she had addressed the letter from memory, she was uncertain whether it would reach us.

Gershon regained hope. Had they come across any members of his family, he wrote from his sickbed. Yes, she replied. Leib's widow and child. Tragedy and joy in four words.

Contact was established, and letters with *pinktalech*, dots, began to arrive from his sister-in-law Leah in Vilna. "We are as well as can be expected . . ." she wrote. That is, our expectations are not high. She had survived by remaining on the kolkhoz where she and Leib had taken refuge after their escape from Zhager. She had been three months pregnant when he joined the 16th Lithuanian Brigade of the Red Army in 1942. He was killed in 1943 at the front in Orel. After the war she had returned to Vilna with the child Leib had never seen.

Gershon now knew the fate of his family. At last he was able to mourn.

The correspondence between Gershon and Leah continued until his death in 1961. I was no longer enquiring into the contents of their letters. After the war I had taken a deliberate decision to cut myself off from the past, from the shtetl, from the centuries of oppression and suffering. I no longer sang the Yiddish songs about orphaned, starving children; burning shtetlech; deserted families; exploited workers. I joined a left-wing Zionist movement which had two anthems: "The Internationale" and "*Hatikvah*", Hope. We sang about making the desert bloom, and about days of labour and nights of song and dance. It would be a hard life but a joyous one. On our kibbutz, my comrades and I would slough off our bourgeois lives, become workers, own no private property, and build a society of such strength and virtue that our model would spread throughout the world. At eighteen, everything seemed possible.

Gershon could not be talked out of his antipathy to Zionism.

"We'll make a home for the survivors of the Holocaust," I told him, "and ensure that such a tragedy never recurs . . ."

"And what of the Arabs who are already living in Palestine?"

"We won't displace them. We'll live in peace, in a bi-national state."

When he responded with the inevitable "utopian fantasies", I tried a lighter tone.

"Someone has to maintain the struggle for a just society. One uncle died in the war, another is a dyed-in-the-wool Stalinist, and you lost direction on the journey to the Revolution. Now it's up to my generation."

Which didn't do so well either.

After three years in Israel, I returned to South Africa. When Gershon died, some years later, I maintained intermittent contact with Leib's wife Leah and my cousin Freda, but never learned much about their lives. The *pinktalech*, the dots, in their letters, told a story of unease. I watched Freda grow up in photographs: a lively child in school uniform, a university student in Leningrad, an actress in the Urals, a cultural worker in Vilna. Then marriage, the birth of a child with large brown eyes, like Freda's, like Leib's. It never occurred to either of us that we would one day meet.

PART TWO

7

Going Home

Shops on the market square, Zhager, 1920s.

My desire to visit *der heim* lay dormant for years. The land of my forebears had become a desert of graves, curtained by iron. With Lithuanian independence in 1991, however, it became not only possible but imperative to go "home". There were unquiet spirits to appease. Don't mess with spirits, my mother would have said; look what happened to your father. Despite his searing brush with the occult, Gershon would have understood the need for propitiation, whatever form it took. Don't whistle in the dark, my grandmother used to warn; she had always had a healthy respect for the spirits. I had now come full circle, whistling in the dark.

With the Holocaust as my touchstone, I had grappled unsuccessfully with other kinds of racism and oppression. Despairing, finally, of change in the seemingly monolithic apartheid structure in South Africa, we moved to Australia in 1988. Eighteen months later, Nelson Mandela was released from jail. It was a moment of great joy and great personal regret. Like my father, we too had been overtaken by history; the revolution had happened without us.

Freda is overjoyed when we leave South Africa. Now we can communicate freely, she writes, urging me to come to Lithuania. We'll go to Zhager together. I'll come, I reply, but first I have to disentangle the stories, myths and songs of my childhood from the "facts", and these I hope to find in the archives of YIVO in New York, and Yad v'Shem, in Jerusalem.

When I write to YIVO, a major source for Eastern European Jewish history, the chief archivist replies that there are fifteen folders on Zhager for the period 1919–1925 which will be made available to me if and when I come to New York. Yad v'Shem presents a more complicated picture. There are many eye-witness testimonies by survivors of the Holocaust on microfilm, but I shall have to work through them to find references to Zhager. Most of the testimonies are either in Hebrew or in Yiddish, I am told, both of which I read with difficulty.

While I plan my journey, I read Jewish and Lithuanian history. I also begin contacting *landsleit* in Israel, South Africa and Australia. When I tell Gerty and Jack Trubik, family friends living in Australia, of my projected visit to *der heim*, Jack shows me photographs which he and a sister had taken in Zhager in the 1920s.

As I look through the album of sepia-coloured photographs, I am jolted into reality. The photos are utterly unlike those my mother had kept in a naphthalene-saturated shoe box in her wardrobe. Hers had been studio photographs of people in their sabbath best, or of unsmiling family groups about to part forever, or of young people posing on the grassy verges of Naryshkin Park, unaware that they are sitting on the site of their grave.

Childhood fantasies, fed by nostalgia and myth, evaporate as I look at Jack's photographs: people in everyday clothes standing in front of their cramped shops and houses, pushing their way through the crowded market-place, walking along muddy streets, crossing the bridge over the River Shvete, or watching a parade of Lithuanian nationalists who would soon be chanting, "Lithuania for the Lithuanians!" There is also a photograph of the border post between Lithuania and Latvia, a mere boom across a country road. Only those who managed to escape over the border in 1941 had had a chance of survival.

When I comment on the high standard of the photography, Jack tells me he had learned the craft from the town photographer, Shabselban, to whom he had been apprenticed for some time. Jack had grown up in an affluent but troubled home. His father, a businessman and philanthropist, had been a respected member of the community who campaigned tirelessly for the creation of a Jewish homeland. Their home had been the hub for gatherings of the intelligentsia in Zhager, but when his mother, a beautiful, gentle woman, suffered a stroke while still young, the family's happiness had been blighted. To compound their sadness, a younger brother died at the age of twenty. Jack's sisters eventually immigrated to Palestine. He left for South Africa in 1927 where, like so many other young men, he could find work only in the mine concession stores. Only his brother Meyer'l remained in Lithuania with their elderly father.

Jack weeps as he shows me photographs of Meyer'l, his three sisters, and one of himself, with a violin tucked under his chin, a dreamy look in his eyes.

"Just before the Germans entered Zhager in 1941," Jack says, "Meyer'l's friends urged him to flee across the border with them by bike, but he refused to leave our aged father. They were massacred, with everyone else."

Shabselban

Jack Trubik, aged 17.

"He gets too emotional when he speaks about Zhager," Gerty whispers to me. I have known Gerty and her family since I was a child; their house had been a second home for me. It was her older sister Rosie who had taken me to school on my first day, not my mother who had been ashamed of her fractured English.

"We'll come again," I say to Jack when we leave. "There's so much I want to know about *der heim* and your photographs."

There is to be no other time. Jack, who was in his eighties, died several weeks later. And Gerty, who had left Zhager at an early age, remembers very little about the shtetl. I now understand that if anything is to be retrieved from the past, I shall have to act swiftly. Research in libraries and archives will have to wait; people are ageing, forgetting, dying.

South Africa, the home from home of the Jews of Lithuania, seems the most logical place to begin my quest. I have a strong desire to return "home", to rejoice with friends over the end of apartheid, to witness the beginning of a new society, but dread being an outsider, looking in. Unlike the exiles who have come back after a long absence, I no longer know where home is; they, surely, do. Yet what of those who have spent more time in exile than in the country of their birth? Will Soweto, or Johannesburg, or Nelspruit feel like home to them?

On arrival in South Africa, I drive past houses I had lived in as a child, and the house in which my children grew up. They evoke some memories and a little emotion; bricks and mortar alone do not constitute home. Songs, stories, guitar studies; frost on the veld, koppies, mine dumps – these do. And not for the first time I grapple with the meaning of home. Is it the place where you were born, where you grew up, where the landscape is familiar? Is it the light, the air, the sunsets? Or is it the place you yearn for when you're away from it?

But now it is my parents' *heim* I am concerned with; their life in the shtetl, not mine in the suburbs. Armed with Jack's photographs, I hope to evoke memories and get answers to questions I never asked them. I visit an elderly couple, *landsleit* of my parents, who are living in a home for the aged.

"That's the German's brewery," the wife pronounces, holding up a photograph of a Tudor-style building in front of which some young people are standing.

"No, that's Graf Naryshkin's *haif*, his palace."

"Palace! What are you saying? Naryshkin's palace was five times as big. If it's not the brewery, it could be the Graf's servants' quarters."

"Pass me the magnifying glass," her husband says, "I think the girl with the plaits is my cousin Brochke."

I phone Rachel, a school friend whose parents had been active in the Zhagerer Society in Johannesburg until the outbreak of World War II.

"Don't despair," she consoles me. "I know other *landsleit* who have clearer memories of Zhager. My father wrote a memoir before he died. Come over for tea."

"Me and the other woman?" I recall a joke our families had shared.

Chaya Fedler, her late mother, had been a poet and a great wit. Many years ago, she had dropped in to visit my mother. "Shevke," she said, "I'm hot and tired and dying for a nice cup of tea." She drank it with gusto, then held out her cup. "I feel like another woman," she said, "and now the other woman would like a cup of tea."

Chaya would have told me about Zhager, warts and all. She might even have told me about my grandfather Simon, if I'd had the sense to ask. I had missed out by about forty years.

"You remember Luba," Rachel says, triggering a concatenation of contacts which I shall follow up in the coming weeks. "She and her family survived the concentration camps. She may have been too young to remember Zhager, but she has a large network of friends. She'd put you in touch with other *landsleit.*"

It was Luba's father Dovid who had told us of Leib's vain attempt to save his family.

When we part, Rachel gives me a copy of *Shalecheth*, her father's family memoir, in which he describes life in Zhager.

Luba is hospitable and friendly, but remembers very little about Zhager. Her family, she reminds me, had moved to Shavel when she was a child.

"But I have a friend in Israel who was very close to Leib," she says. "She shared a room with our family in the Shavel ghetto, and often spoke about him. To keep our spirits up, we recalled the good things in our past life." She looks at her watch. "This would be a good time to phone her."

A few minutes later I am speaking to Leib's friend, whom I shall call Mierke.

"Leibke Yoffe!" she cries. "You are his niece? *Er iz doch geven mein geliebter!*" He was my lover.

I shall be in Israel in a few weeks' time, I tell her, to look for *landsleit* and to do research at Yad v'Shem.

"Come visit me. Luba will give you my address."

I am delighted. Who better to speak to than a lover with happy memories of my elusive uncle?

Luba also suggests I contact Max B., whom I remember as a frequent visitor to our home.

"How time has flown," he says when I phone him that evening. "Only the other day I was thinking about Gershon."

We are not able to meet as he is leaving for Cape Town the following morning, but we have a long conversation on the phone. He recalls the early years in Mayfair, and the tightly knit immigrant community which was to splinter as each family either prospered or struggled, moved into "better" suburbs or remained where they were.

"I think of the good old days with great affection," he says.

"In Mayfair," I remind him, "the good old days meant those spent in Zhager. The Park, the Mill Hill, the snow, wild strawberries, that sort of thing. Mayfair, then, was the bad present."

"Indeed. It's a human failing never to recognise the good old days while we're actually living them."

"I know so little about my father's family, how they lived, how they died," I say.

"I can't tell you much about them. I left *der heim* soon after we returned from exile in 1919, and although I was friendly with Gershon, I rarely visited his home. I never knew the rest of his family. Not even Leibke, who must have been seven or eight years younger than me. But my youngest brother Shlomo knew him well. They were in the army together during World War II. Not only does he know how Leibke lived, he also knows how he died."

My father must have known how Leib died. By then, however, I had stopped asking questions. There had been no time to mourn; a new world was waiting to be built.

Max gives me his brother's address and phone number. Shlomo, he assures me, will be happy to tell me about Leib.

With two important links to Leib, I am now impatient to leave for Israel, another place I once called home. But there are a few more sources to be tapped in South Africa, a few more squares to add to the barely existing patchwork quilt. Some will be short and broad, others long and narrow; they will be patches of varying design, texture and colour, but they are my only hope of finding a pattern in the chaos of that era.

Ada Strul is one of these sources. My uncle Itze had carried her photograph around in his wallet until she married someone else.

"How long it's been, Raizala," she says when I visit her a few days later at her daughter's house where she has been living since her husband died. "I haven't seen you since you were a child."

After we catch up on the missing years, Ada tells me she visited Zhager in 1960, with her husband and daughter.

"We travelled from Riga to Zhager by car, a mere two-hour journey. It seemed a world away when we were children," she says.

Their first stop had been at the Old Zhager cemetery where, among neglected and vandalised graves, Julius had found the graves of his mother and brother who had died before the Holocaust. From there they had driven to Naryshkin Park where the Russians had put up a memorial plaque commemorating the massacre of "3000 Soviet citizens".

"Not Jews, mind you; Soviet citizens. They'd been murdered because they were Jews," she says indignantly.

"We heard that two Jewish families, the Zlots and the Beitlers, had resettled in Zhager after the war. The men had fought in the 16th Lithuanian Brigade of the Red Army and one of them eventually become mayor of Zhager. Mayor of 3000 dead Jews and a town full of hostile Lithuanians. It was bizarre. We were directed by sullen-looking people to Zlot's shop. His wife was standing in the door-way. When she saw Julius – you know, he was all dressed up in a suit and shirt and tie, like a real South African – she cried out, 'Oy, Strul! From Alt-Zhager!' They locked the shop and took us to their house in Nai-Zhager. The Beitlers joined us, and as we sat around the table drinking tea with strawberry conserve, they told us what had happened to the Jews of Zhager."

After the Germans took Zhager, Ada was told, they had installed the Lithuanian militia in power and were not seen again until the massacre, in October. The Jews had been driven into the market square, slaughtered, then buried in the mass grave in Naryshkin Park. She knew no details. On their return from the war, Ada's hosts had heard about the massacre from local Lithuanians who protested they were innocent, or had been following orders, or had been out of town when it happened. How can you live here, Ada asked them. This is our home, they said, and we won't be driven out of it.

"We talked and cried, cried and talked. The men walked to the bridge over the Shvete, opposite their house, and stood there, reminiscing. A Lithuanian woman in a black dress – I can see her now – ran up to Julius, grabbed hold of his lapels, shook him, and shouted excitedly in Yiddish, '*Yudke! Yudke! Du binst doch Yudke Feiga-Riva's!*' You are Feiga-Riva's son. Julius didn't remember her. '*Ich hob doch far dein mammen ves gevashen.*' She had done washing for his mother. Beitler put a finger to his lips. Julius was polite, asked after her family, and evaded her questions. As soon as they could, they returned to the house.

"The less one talks to people, the better, our hosts told us. They invited us to sleep over. I took Julius aside and said, '*Ich vel do shloffen af di blutike erd?*' I couldn't bear the thought of sleeping on that blood-soaked soil. We remained for a few hours, then returned to Riga. I didn't sleep all night. I wrote a long letter to my children and covered it with more tears than words."

A few weeks later they received a letter from ex-mayor Zlot. The day after their visit, he wrote, the military police had questioned him and his wife about the "foreigners" who had visited them. They weren't foreigners, Zlot told the police. They were Zhagerer who now lived in Riga. They had come to visit the graves of their family.

"The washerwoman who had seemed so pleased to see Julius," Ada says, "must've run straight to the police to report the presence of foreigners in town. We got out by the skin of our teeth."

Ada recognises no one, nor any place, when I show her Jack's photographs. "I was only four or five when my parents left Zhager. You remember my Orkin cousins," Ada says. "Leah Yudeikin, the eldest, was nearer your parents' age. She'd be able to identify the photographs. She'd certainly know more about Gershon's family."

She gives me Leah's address and phone number. "Send her my

love," she says when I leave. "Neither of us gets around much any more."

I do not visit Leah for some days; there are places to see, friends to speak to, graves to visit. South Africa, after all, had been my home most of my life. Home, *Der Heim*. For my parents it had been forests and rivers, Naryshkin Park and the crunch of snow underfoot; a sense of community they never found again. For me it's highveld mornings, bushveld sunsets; woodsmoke and giraffe; the song of the barbet, the white-browed coucal, and the grey loerie whose call I finally heeded: go 'way! go 'way! go 'way!

8

First Witness

Lithuanian Independence March, Zagare, 1920s.

The Orkins had been our neighbours in Johannesburg for many years. Their widowed mother, a warm, simple woman, had denied herself whatever pleasures Zhager had to offer in order to provide for her three daughters and two sons. She had never been to the movies until she arrived in South Africa. When she was taken to see a cowboy film at the local cinema, she had coughed throughout the film. "It's all that dust the horses are kicking up," she is supposed to have said. She fed me delicious tit-bits whenever I visited, which was only when her daughters were at work. I had been terrified of their long, red nails which looked as though they had been dipped in blood.

As I shake hands with Leah Yudeikin, the oldest of her daughters, in the lounge of her residential hotel, I involuntarily glance down at her hands. Her nails are painted a modest shade of red, and are considerably shorter than they used to be. Or so it seems to me.

Again the ritual recall of names as we warm to the subject of Zhager. She is excited with Jack's photographs.

"That's Taitchsegass! I recognise the buildings. But who are those people marching down the cobbled street? Wait, there's a band leading the marchers. Perhaps the Zhager Fire Brigade? Your uncle Leib used to play in the band. But there are also women in uniform. And the spectators don't look Jewish. Perhaps it's a church parade. They used to have them before Easter."

I later discover it was a parade of Lithuanian Nationalists, either demanding independence or celebrating it, depending on when the photograph was taken.

"Just around that corner," Leah trains her magnifying glass on another photograph, "Avram Broide the *gevir*, the rich man of the shtetl, had a big store . . . That's in Nai-Zhager, New Zhager, where the shops were. The cinema was in Nai-Zhager. How we children loved to go to the Kino. Pola Negri, I suppose you've never heard of her, was a wonderful actress, my favourite. Zhager was more a shtot than a shtetl, a big place. Cinemas, shuls . . . That's the church. It was near the market-place. That's where my mother bought eggs, butter and vegetables from peasants on market days . . . That's Meishke Strul's mill. I think he was a cousin of Yudke's. There were two mills in Zhager . . . Ah, yes. Naryshkin Park. It was so beautiful. All the young couples used to stroll there. And before you got to the Park, you walked through the *vald*, the forest. We picked wild strawberries and *agresin* there. I don't even know how you say *agresin* in English. They're berries that grow only in Europe . . ."

She speaks with *pinktalech*, dots; much is left unsaid.

"How the years have flown. We were driven out of Zhager in

1915. In exile, in Russia, we worked very hard. But in 1921 we sold everything and returned to Lithuania. For two months we travelled on the train. There were thirty-five people in our truck, men, women, children, and we all slept on the floor. When we returned, we found our house had been burned down. If it hadn't been for the parcels we received from America, we'd have died of hunger. And there were so many beggars in Zhager after the war. We never had much, my mother was a widow, but every Friday she baked extra to give to the beggars . . .

"Your father's family? Gershon, Henke, Leibke, those were the ones I knew. Henke was a beautiful girl and the boys were handsome and clever. Your grandfather Simon was a tall man with red hair, but I didn't really know him. He didn't mix too much in the community. I didn't know your grandmother. She was always busy at home with the children.

"I knew your mother's family better. Especially Itze. He was great friends with my brothers. Pity he never married. He had lots of girlfriends in Zhager, but we were an unsettled generation. Everyone

Friends and relatives in Naryshkin Park, mid-1920s.
Back row from left: Unknown, unknown, Gershon, Sheva,
Leah Orkin, Uncle Hille, unknown, Hoda, Leib.

was always moving away somewhere else, and the greatest romances came to nothing. Itze wanted to marry Ada, whom you visited the other day. They were in love. But my aunt interfered, *zi hot geshtert.* She said he was too old for her. Such a lovely man. She was twenty-two at the time, and he was thirty-five. *Azei geit es,* so it goes . . .

"Let's go to my apartment, it's impossible to talk down here." She gestures towards the other elderly people in the lounge who all seem to be speaking at the same time, loudly. "I've just remembered something that might interest you."

In the apartment, she phones through to the switchboard. "Please put me through to Mrs Judaken," she says.

I begin to wonder how much of the information she has given me is reliable.

"There are two Mrs Yudeikins in the hotel," she explains belatedly, putting her hand over the mouthpiece. "We never know which of us is being paged, though the spelling is different. Her husband came from a small shtetl near Zhager, and she told me the other day that someone in their family has written a book about Zhager . . . Ah, Mrs Judaken . . ."

When Leah tells the other Mrs Judaken why I have come to South Africa, she invites us up to her apartment. We are introduced to her son who is on a visit from the United States. A cousin, he tells me, has done a great deal of research on the history of their family, tracing the Judeikins, spelt in at least six different ways, from their earliest days of settlement in Lithuania through to the Holocaust. He shows me a forty-page family memoir which the author has distributed among members of the Judeikin clan.[6]

"There are many references to Zhager. A member of the family was actually imprisoned in the Zhager ghetto. You are welcome to make a copy of it," he says.

I am delighted with this unexpected source of information,

---

6 Yodaiken, "The Judeikins: A Lithuanian Jewish Family in Dispersion" (unpublished version), p. 27.

which will provide my first eye-witness account of life in the Zhager ghetto, prior to the massacre on Yom Kippur 1941.

Bertha Taubman, a member of the Judeikin family, had lived in Shavel with her husband and child before the war. After Shavel was bombed, they took refuge with her family in Papiljan, a shtetl not far from Zhager. On 22 June 1941, four German officers captured the Papiljan railway station, and handed over control of the population to Lithuanian militiamen and partisans who treated the Jews with great cruelty.

They began by humiliating the Jews publicly in the market square. They pulled out hair by the handful from the rabbi's and other men's beards while their gentile neighbours stood around, laughing and jeering. Worse was to follow. A few days later, all the intellectuals, Communists and community leaders, Bertha Taubman's husband among them, were rounded up and driven to a forest near Kudziai, where they were forced to dig their own graves, then shot. The dead had been buried with the dying.

The rest of the Jews were made to walk through the town carrying portraits of Lenin and Stalin while the residents shouted insults at them. They were then transported to a farm about 10 kilometres out of town, where the men were separated from the women. Three days later, a group of drunken Lithuanians arrived from Papiljan and other villages. All the remaining men, from sixteen years up, were driven to a nearby forest where they too were shot. Mrs Taubman's brother Itzhak had been among them.

Only the women and children now remained on the farm. The physically fit women worked in the fields, while the old women and children remained in the camp. They lived under near-starvation conditions until 25 August, when they were loaded onto carts and taken to Zhager under armed guard. On arrival, they were addressed by a Lithuanian militiaman called Stankas. "You should have been shot like dogs a long time ago," he told them, "but if you behave yourselves and work hard, you will be given food. If you don't, you will be shot."

". . . we were put into a small synagogue lit by a few candles," Mrs Taubman writes. "There we met Jews from the Siauliai [Shavel] area but only the remnants of large families. The faces of the Jews were pale and fearful. They walked like living dead, helpless and hopeless. During the day and night groups of Latvian and Lithuanian partisans came and took groups of Jews and executed them by shooting in the nearby forest."

They were then moved to the Zhager ghetto, which was in the process of being fenced off with barbed wire.

"There were about 9000 people there," Mrs Taubman writes. "I remained there about 10 days and most of the time I hid like the rest of the women and young ones. The partisans robbed, bullied and raped many. We prayed to God that they would finish fencing off the area and that it would be declared a ghetto by the Germans . . . Many of the Jews went mad and wandered helplessly around the streets. Some of them also committed suicide."

The Jewish population of Zhager had been swamped by Jews from Kurshjan, Akmean, Vekshine Kadosh and others. Many of the Jews from Radviliski had been murdered by the Lithuanian partisans as they passed through a forest on their way to Zhager.

Through a Lithuanian partisan named Vazis, a coffin-maker who had been a client of her late husband's, Mrs Taubman obtained documents allowing her and her daughter to return to the ghetto in Shavel. The rest of her family had not been permitted to leave.

"At our parting," Mrs Taubman writes, "I embraced my mother and sister and Joseph'la for the last time, with a heavy heart. A few weeks after we left Zagare, the Germans partitioned off the Jewish quarter. All those able to work were organised to do so and received bread rations (that much my mother managed to inform me). My mother even regretted that . . . we travelled from there because the situation had improved a little, though not for long.

"One fine morning, Wednesday 5 October, a band of incited Lithuanians – animals in human form – arrived and brought all the Jews to the market square. They searched their clothes and loaded them onto trucks which brought them to a park where 9000 people were killed during a period of three days. They were our loved ones, brothers and sisters, the sons of our people that were slaughtered like beasts. My daughter Rive'la and I were the only ones who were saved from the 9000 slain on Yom Kippur, 7 October 1941."

She had worked in Frankel's munition factory in the Shavel ghetto from 1941 to 1944, barely surviving on the meagre rations. On 5 November 1943, the elderly and the children were rounded up and transported to Auschwitz. Ukrainian soldiers and Lithuanian partisans had participated in this *Aktion*.

"It was a Friday," Mrs Taubman writes. "The workers were taken to the factory as usual and the old people and children were loaded into wagons, brought to the railway station, thrown into the trains and transported to Auschwitz to be gassed. When we returned from work, the murderers stood at the gates of the camp and caught the few remaining children that had managed to escape and go off with us to work.

"I turned to the commanding officer named Forster . . . a tall man who had headed the *Aktion* against the children. I begged him to return my daughter to me and then take both of us. His answer was, you have to work and we will take care of your daughter.

"It is hard to think back on the misery, mourning and depression which I went through."

As the Russians advanced on Lithuania, the Germans herded all the surviving Jews in the area into the Shavel ghetto, where Bertha Taubman met up again with a few surviving members of her family. With the help of a Lithuanian Communist nicknamed Wowa, who had saved many Jews from certain death, they prepared an underground bunker in which to hide. But they were caught and shortly afterwards marched to the Stutthof concentration camp where they were put to work in a munitions factory. After terrible suffering and hardship, she and other survivors were liberated by the Russians on 10 March 1945.

The Judeikin memoir provides me with a terrible context in which to imagine the fate of my grandmother Freyde and her family. They die many times as I read about the death of other grandmothers, aunts and uncles, parents, sisters and brothers. Freyde, a frail, sick woman, might have died of grief after Leib's futile attempt to rescue her, or fallen by the wayside as the Jews were driven into the ghetto. I also imagine Freyde clinging to Bryna as they are herded into the market-place, thrown onto trucks and driven to Naryshkin Park where they are shot and buried, alive or dead. Shmulke digs his own grave in the forest, and is shot and buried in a mass grave . . .

When I take my leave of Leah Yudeikin a few days later, I tell her I don't understand how their gentile neighbours could have turned on the Jews after all those years of living together.

"How did you get on with your gentile neighbours when you lived in Zhager?" I ask.

Leah shrugs. "There was little contact between us in those days, except in the market-place. Their dogs barked at us when we passed their houses on the outskirts of town. Like dogs bark at black people in the white suburbs of South Africa. We were strangers. Perhaps it's easier to kill strangers."

Perhaps. Later that week, when I speak to survivors of the Holocaust now living in Israel, I shall learn how "good friends" of the Jews became their executioners.

9

Mierke

Zhager with market-place at centre.

Israel, the *heim* where exile was meant to end. For those truly in need of a home, it became one: for Mierke, for Shlomo, for other survivors; for idealists and perhaps for realists. For the rest, the search goes on, with doubts about its existence.

I contact Mierke on arrival in Israel. After our telephone conversation from Luba's house, I hope for a continuation of the story about her *geliebter*, Leib. She is friendly, but restrained, formal. She invites me to lunch. Bring your husband, she says after enquiring whether I am travelling alone. I hesitate. Interviews, I am discovering, are better conducted in private. But she insists he comes.

I also phone Shlomo. I explain my relationship to Leib Yoffe. "Your brother said you knew him well and suggested I contact you."

"An emissary from my brother who wants to know about her uncle Leibke Yoffe? I shall be delighted to meet you."

I feel uneasy about his ironic response, but brush it aside. As Mierke and Shlomo live within a short distance from one another, I arrange to meet him after our visit to Mierke.

A large, dignified woman greets us at the door. Mierke is wearing a shirt-dress, with sleeves turned up, as though in preparation for some task. She is regretting her spontaneous outburst, I guess as we follow her into her impeccably kept apartment. Her grey hair is still liberally streaked with blond, her lips are drawn into a straight line, and only her green eyes, couched between slightly swollen lids, show signs of sadness. Leib would have been eighty-three; she must be in her mid-seventies. It is possible neither would have recognised the other.

"Whatever else I've forgotten – or don't wish to remember," she says leading us to a table laden with delicacies, "my Litvak hospitality is still alive. We'll eat before we talk. My husband – my first husband died at the start of the war – will join us shortly. He's a survivor from another shtetl, but knows the story of Zhager and its inhabitants all too well."

Gefilte fish, chopped herring, pickled herring, potato pancakes, followed by cheese blintzes, establish our common origins. Throughout the meal she speaks of everyday matters, asks about mutual friends in South Africa, and about our life in Australia. She tells us she was born in Zhager but was educated in Shavel, where she eventually married and settled. Like many others, she had survived because workers had been needed in Shavel for industries like the Frankel tanneries, the Bata shoe factories, and the Wehrmacht engineering corps. Zhager had had nothing to offer the war machine.

After we have eaten, Mierke invites questions. I ask about the Yoffe family. Leib, Henke and Faivel, she says, had been tall and beautiful people, socially at ease in any company. She had not known the two younger children well. Henke had been in love with Bentze Tanchel for many years, and he had been in love with her, but they never married.

"Let me explain how things worked in the shtetl," she says. "You married off your daughters before your sons. Why do you think Leibke didn't marry all those years? Faivke, his younger brother, broke away, like Gershon. But Leibke remained unmarried. Someone had to look after the family. Henke had been courted by Bentze for about eight years, from the age of sixteen. He worshipped her very shadow, as the saying goes. But Bentze had three unmarried sisters. You'll remain an old maid if you wait for him, Leibke told her. An old maid indeed. She was twenty-four then. Leib arranged a match for Henke with a very nice man from Latvia. You look surprised," Mierke says. "But that's how things were done. *Ein breira*, Leib had no alternative. He had sole responsibility for the family. In those days, there was no place for love. One had to be realistic. Bentze never married. Henke was murdered in Latvia, and Bentze was killed together with his unmarried sisters in Zhager. Even in death they weren't together."

"What about the rest of the family?"

"I never knew your grandfather. He died a few years after World War I. Your grandmother was a courageous woman. You wouldn't have guessed what a struggle she had when you saw her neatly dressed children, all of whom went to school. She, Bryna and Shmulke, the youngest children, were either killed in the Zhager massacre, or while trying to get out. You must have heard how Leib tried to rescue them. He himself was killed at the front in 1943. Faivke also died in action . . . You heard he'd been killed in Zhager? Perhaps. Everyone has a different story. Things were very confused then.

"Faivke had also been a musician. He played the trombone. He looked like the other Yoffes, but he was a little shorter than Leib.

The youngest, Shmulke, looked just like Gershon. Same face. They were all lovely people, but Leib was extraordinary, a *bezundere zach*. Whenever he came to Shavel, he visited me. A cousin of my first husband's lived on the ground floor of our building. 'He's so good-looking and charming,' she used to joke, 'that I'm reluctant to let him go upstairs.'" Mierke smiles, for the first time.

Mierke does not mention the word *geliebter*. Perhaps *geliebter* means beloved, not lover. Yiddish, after all, is the language of my early childhood, when such nuances were not easily discernible. I write Yiddish ungrammatically, read it with difficulty, especially in script, and speak an anglicised version which must either grate on the ears of real Yiddish speakers, or evoke silent mirth. But I am grateful for the little I know; it links me to my heritage, to the past I am attempting to disinter.

I am beginning to wish I had refused Mierke's Litvak hospitality. I would have preferred to meet her alone, in a café, without an audience, when I would have felt freer to ask questions.

"I hear Leib worked in Shavel after the Russians annexed Lithuania in 1940," I say. I do not quote my source. My cousin Freda, in a recent letter, had mentioned this.

Mierke looks surprised. "Perhaps." She furrows her brow. "He was a very secretive person. He was a left-winger, but I never knew to what extent he was involved. He didn't talk about his political life. All I know is that he had more friends from the left than among the Zionists in Zhager. That's more or less how opinions were divided. You're mistaken," she adds, her voice strong and sure. "It was Faivel who lived in Shavel, not Leib. Had he lived in Shavel, he would have contacted me. He always did."

She changes the subject. "Have you heard how Leib died? Strul told me. No, not Yudke; his cousin, who was also a musician. He'd been in the orchestra of the 16th Lithuanian Brigade with Leib. There had been a big battle and their battalion had taken territory back from the Germans. They went to rest in a house which they thought was empty. A German had been hiding in the attic, and while they were sleeping, he came downstairs and hit Leib over the head. He died immediately. *Un dos is dos* . . . And that is that." Mierke's husband, a pleasant, unassuming man, comes into the apartment at this point. Mierke serves tea, continuity is broken, and the conversation takes a different turn.

"While I studied in Shavel," she says, "I returned to Zhager every summer and every Yomtov. The fields, the river, the forest, what a beautiful place it was . . . Zhager had one of the oldest Jewish communities in Lithuania, and produced famous scholars, writers and rabbis. *Chachmei Zhager*, they were called; the wise men of Zhager. Take the rabbi of Nai-Zhager, for example, Israel Riff. Even if you weren't religious, you had to respect him. He was a wise man who never interfered in people's lives, as the religious fanatics do today. *Kinderlech*, he used to say to the youth of the shtetl; go to dances, enjoy yourselves. But remember, the dangerous part is after the dance." She smiles. "You've heard of Naryshkin Park, the trysting place of young lovers. Nu. It's a story of romances that never worked out . . .

"I was telling you about the rabbi. His older son was the rabbi of Alt-Zhager. I was friendly with another of his sons, also a rabbi. Before the Germans arrived, the Lithuanian militia, a band of robbers and murderers, stripped old Rabbi Riff naked, and chased him across the market square, shooting at him as he ran. And all our gentile friends and neighbours stood around, laughing. This was described to me after the war by a gentile woman who used to work for my mother. I can't bear to think about it, even now; *mir klempt di hartz as ich dermon zich* . . .

"One week before the Germans invaded Lithuania, on 14 June 1941, the Bolsheviks began sending people to Siberia. My first husband's whole family were deported. Thousands were exiled, Jews and gentiles alike. If you were an intellectual or had two *kopekes* to rub together, the Bolsheviks condemned you as a capitalist. The Nazis and their Lithuanian henchmen, on the other hand, killed Jews for being Bolsheviks. What chance did we have? People began to flee when the

Germans bombed Shavel, just one week after the Russian deportations. We had nowhere to run. We got as far as the border but were
turned back by the Lithuanian militia; they had other plans for us."

Within two weeks of the German invasion, Mierke tells us, two
ghettoes had been set up in Shavel. Living conditions became
unbearably crowded. When the Judenrat, the Jewish council,
complained to the German authorities, they were told that they were
being isolated from the general community for their own safety;
they might otherwise come to harm at the hands of unruly elements.
It was a temporary measure, they said, which would only last for the
duration of the war. In fact, the Einsatzgruppen had been issued with
instructions not to interfere with any pogroms or disturbances that
might be initiated by local anti-Communist or anti-Jewish elements.
On the contrary, they were to be encouraged. The Lithuanian press
and the gentile Lithuanians as a whole supported the German
policies, Mierke says, and were only too happy to take over the
houses and possessions which the Jews had been forced to leave
behind when they were crowded into the ghettoes.

"In the ghetto," Mierke says, "we lived in the same house as
Luba's family. We had survived until then because they needed our
labour in the factories. Zhager, you see, was a small town, not
industrialised, and the Jews were expendable. But when the tide of
war turned against Germany, we were sent off to Stutthoff, the
sorting house to the death camps. It was there that I was separated
from those of my family who had survived thus far. My husband had
been killed, my whole family murdered, my child taken away . . ."

She stops, takes a deep breath and says, "I don't cry any more.
There is no relief in tears . . .

"I went back to Zhager after the war in the hope that I'd meet up
with survivors. There were none. But I met this woman who used to
work for my family. She told me that the Lithuanian militia had
closed the border after the Russians had retreated. Only a few people
managed to escape. Five thousand people had been massacred, from
Zhager and the surrounding shtetlech. She described how the Jews

had been driven into the market-place and killed. The blood, she said, had run down the small alleys that lead down to the river. The Shvete, once a fast-flowing river, had turned red and was drying up. It's all that blood, she kept saying as she wept; it's all that Jewish blood.

"She also told me about a teacher I had known who had married a certain man against her parents' wishes. He escaped before the Germans arrived. She couldn't run, she was heavily pregnant. Who can judge? They may have decided it would soon be over, or that they wouldn't harm a pregnant woman, or that he, at least, should get out . . . The will to live is strong and I am the last person to judge, I, who survived . . . The teacher gave birth at the edge of the mass grave in Naryshkin Park. The child was thrown into the grave, alive, after they shot its mother. I know what they did with children. With my own child . . .

"Yes, I can speak about it. It was a Thursday night, 4 November 1943. The Germans entered the Shavel ghetto with large empty trucks. Loudspeakers boomed out orders that all children were to be placed aboard. They tried to calm us. We were told the children were being taken to Riga, to a resort where they would be looked after. Some of us tried to climb aboard with the children. Terrible scenes. Loud music drowned out the screams of the children, the barking of the dogs which were sniffing out hidden children, attacking them. They took away 720 children. My son was seven years old . . ."

In Masha Greenbaum's *The Jews of Lithuania* I was later to find more information about the *Kinderaktion* in the Shavel ghetto. Through gentile Lithuanian contacts, some Jewish parents had received advance knowledge of the *Aktion*. In a desperate effort to save their children, drastic means had been resorted to. Small children had been drugged and placed in sacks and rubbish bins that were removed daily from the ghettos. Lithuanians had been bribed to rescue them once they were outside the ghetto gates. Other parents had hurled their children over the ghetto fences, into the arms of Lithuanians with whom an arrangement had been made. The chief of the Jewish police in the Shavel ghetto, Ephraim Gens, a former Lithuanian army officer and a university graduate, believed in the German military code of honour, and had trusted the Lithuanians with whom he had grown up. He had been convinced that neither the Germans nor the Lithuanians would harm innocent children. He was the first to surrender his own young daughter, and encouraged other parents to follow his example.

"After the war," Mierke continues her terrible tale, "I was working for a Russian captain who asked me to tell him my story. Have you any idea what happened to your son, he asked. I had no idea. The children, he told me, had been taken to a military hospital in Riga where they'd been killed. I only half-believed him. About three years later I read in an official report that the Germans had needed blood for transfusions for their soldiers. *Far dos iz Yiddishe blut geven gut...* For this Jewish blood had been good. They had taken the children to this hospital in Riga where they were drained of their blood. I have lived with this knowledge all my life. A day doesn't pass . . ."

I forget the questions I wanted to ask about Leib, and apologise for evoking her grief.

"It eases the heart to talk," she says. "While I live, I must remember."

When we leave, I tell her we have an arrangement to meet Shlomo and his wife Chana.

"They were the fortunate ones," she says without bitterness. "They got away in time. Chana and Shlomo were very friendly with a gentile Lithuanian called Edvard, I forget his surname. *Men flekt zich kuschen oifen gass*, they used to kiss one another in the street. Unlike our parents, our generation had had social contact with gentile Lithuanians. This same Edvard, this great friend of the Jews, later became one of the main murderers in Zhager."

We take our leave of Mierke's husband, who has been very quiet throughout our visit. Mierke gives us directions on how to reach Shlomo's home.

"And if you want to know more about Leib," she smiles wryly as she shakes hands with us, "ask Chana. She knew him very well."

10

Leib – A Hero?

Leib, second from right, with his band, 1920s.

Mierke's light-hearted, spontaneous response to my call from South Africa, and her apparent willingness to talk about her *geliebter* Leib, had not prepared me for that descent into the depths of her sorrow. What right has one to pry into the heart of a stranger, to evoke such pain? But how else can one get an insight into that catastrophic era? I knock on Shlomo's door with trepidation. Who knows what traumas lie behind his laconic manner.

Chana, his wife, invites us in, and leads us directly to yet another table laden with Litvak hospitality. In her round, cheerful face, the features of a shtetl beauty are still discernible. Shlomo, slightly stooped, his dark hair greying at the temples, joins us at the table.

The conversation is stilted, but the naming of friends and relatives helps dissolve generational and culture differences.

"When I was a child," I tell Shlomo, "your brother was one of the many *landsleit* who visited us on Sunday afternoons."

"I never knew my brother," Shlomo says in his staccato manner. "He was fifteen years older than me. He left for South Africa when I was about three or four years old. We met after the war, when Chana and I came to live in Israel."

There is a hint of impatience in Shlomo's voice as he answers my questions: what can these *Aingelshe chayas*, these English-speakers, understand about our lives?

Indeed, ours had been the fortunate generation; we had not suffered war, exile, death camps or starvation. Our parents might have felt alien when they landed in Cape Town; we accepted our salubrious, privileged lives as our due. While the Jews in Europe were being hunted, persecuted and exterminated, we were entering high school, and playing hockey, tennis or rugby. Our contribution to the defeat of Hitler had been to knit ill-fitting socks and balaclava caps for our troops in North Africa, or to organise cake and candy sales for the Governor-General's National War Fund. We could plan our future with a reasonable degree of certainty. We were able to decide what we were going to do when we grew up. Not if we grew up.

Shlomo is dark and thin, and his large brown eyes are shadowed by beetling brows which often meet over an aquiline nose in barely disguised irritation. We communicate in Yiddish when we speak about the shtetl, in Hebrew when we speak of other things. I know enough of both languages to ask questions and understand the answers.

I explain why I am seeking out survivors. I also tell him what I know about Leib's dash to Zhager from Shavel.

"We didn't have to wait for Leib to tell us the Germans were coming," Shlomo says. "We weren't idiots. We knew what was going on in the world. The difficulty was getting out of Zhager. Even Leib, who had transport, couldn't save his family."

"Everyone says he was a caring person. And a sincere idealist." I stop short. I am supposed to be an objective interlocutor, not a defender of Leib's honour.

"Undoubtedly," he says in a way which invites serious doubt. "But that didn't help him cope with the terrible hardships we experienced on the front later on. Many big idealists broke down. People from places like South Africa or Australia, who've never experienced war, can't possibly understand. My brother, for example, left Zhager in the 1920s and has not been hungry since."

The brother-who-got-away syndrome; echoes of Leib's resentment of Gershon. There seems little point in saying, we try to understand, even if we've led privileged lives. Our parents grieved and agonised over the fate of their families before, during and after the war, and we, their children, have internalised their guilt and anxiety.

What Shlomo sees is two decent-enough people, remote from tragedy and want, who after fifty years of apparent indifference, have suddenly discovered the past.

"Leib", he moderates his tone, "was thirteen years older than me. I started going to his barbershop once a week, then twice a week, *dem bord tzu raziren*, to have a shave. And to have my hair cut. I knew him very well. He tried to talk me over to the Communist cause. He was an interesting man. And an excellent musician. He played many instruments, and took part in all the concerts and celebrations in the shtetl."

The Zhager youth had been working class, intellectual, vigorous, Shlomo says. In their search for a solution to the Jewish problem, they had gone in two directions. A minority had looked to Communism; the rest had been Zionists. He himself had been in Hashomer Hatzair, a left-wing Zionist movement.

He raises his eyebrows when we tell him that we too had been members of Hashomer Hatzair.

"In South Africa? Who would've thought . . . As I was saying, there weren't many Communists in Zhager, but those who belonged to the Party, illegal in my day, had been ardent believers. They thought Communism was the panacea for all ills, including the sickest of the lot, anti-Semitism. They had a library of about 6000 books, one of the largest in Lithuania, bigger even than that of the Kulturlige. As Zhager only had a Lithuanian-language pro-Gymnasium, these libraries had been our main source of education. Few of us could afford to go to a larger city to study."

Anti-Semitism, Shlomo says, had increased dramatically after the Russians annexed the country in 1940, mainly because there had been a disproportionately large number of Jews in the Communist Party. The Jews constituted 7 per cent of the total population, and 15 per cent of the Party, the 15 per cent representing a membership of about 450 people, very few of whom had held high positions in the Party.

"However, all the Jews were labelled Bolshevik, and were blamed for the deportation of 33 000 Lithuanians to Siberia. What is never mentioned is that about 7000 of these deportees had been Jewish Lithuanians, yet another disproportionate figure. But then our *tzores*, our troubles, have always been disproportionate to our numbers."

Much of what Shlomo tells me is borne out by an article I shall later read in *Jerusalem in Lithuania*. Information gleaned from the archives of the Ministry of Internal Affairs of the Republic of Lithuania, and two other Lithuanian sources, reveals that the mass deportations of 14–15 June had been carried out by a central committee, with the aid of local committees.[7] There had been no Jews on that central committee. And of the 77 members on the local committees, only four or five had been Jews. There had been few Jews in the repressive bodies of the Soviet regime. For example, the People's Commissar of the NKVD in 1940–41 had been an

---

7 *Jerusalem in Lithuania*, May–June 1993, "Anti-Semitism: A Problem of all Lithuania"; References from Archives of the Ministry of Internal Affairs of the Republic of Lithuania; A. Damusis, *The Victims and Losses of the Inhabitants during the War and Post-war Times (1940–1959)*; and L. Truska, *Lithuania: The Years of the Violence of the Bolsheviks and Nazis*.

ethnic Lithuanian; the deputy commissar, a Russian; and two deputy commissars, ethnic Lithuanians. All district chiefs and their deputies had been ethnic Lithuanians, and of the 279 NKVD employees, excluding typists, drivers and cleaners, 20 had been Jews.

"The Zhager Communists", Shlomo says, "didn't benefit in a material way from the annexation by the Soviets. They were overjoyed that their ideals for a just society would be realised. To say they were naive is to put it mildly."

"I've heard that shortly before the Russian annexation, Leib had been arrested after a scuffle in the market-place," I say.

"Leib was never in jail." Shlomo is emphatic. "He might have been detained, but was never jailed. A man nicknamed Der Sheps was sentenced to eight years in jail. Not Leib. But let me tell you what happened on the eve of the German invasion. The night after Leib fled from Zhager, my mother and three sisters and I made our way to the border, together with many other people. It was Thursday, a week after the war started. The Lithuanians were already celebrating the Germans' victory. The Jews realised it would not be safe to remain in the shtetl. Everyone wanted to flee. When we got to the border, the *shlagbome* was down, and we were not allowed to cross.

"Obedient as always to authority, we turned back. Idiots that we were. All we needed was to walk another 100 metres to the left, out of sight of the drunken border guards, and we'd have been in Latvia. Not that that would've helped. The Latvians were rabid anti-Semites as well. Anyway, the old and the very young wouldn't have made it to Riga on foot. Riga was the destination. From there you could board a train direct to Russia.

"Next morning the *shlagbome* was up. I set out on my bicycle together with ten or twelve others . . . That's right. My friend Meyer Trubik wouldn't join us, wouldn't leave his father behind. Boris Kalmanowitz, Boruch der Reiter he was called, came to my mother and said, 'Sheina, *farvos lost ir em forren?* Why are you letting him go? He won't make it to Lettland.' He must go, my mother replied, and we went."

"And your family . . . ?"

"Murdered. My mother, three sisters, a brother-in-law, two grand-children. Everyone . . ."

"Have another cup of tea." Chana breaks the silence.

"The road was difficult," Shlomo continues. "We were bombed by German planes, and the Latvians sniped at us all along the way. Someone's bicycle broke, so I rode with him on the crossbar for 40 kilometres. When we arrived in Riga, the Latvians fired at us as we crossed the bridge. They shot the bell off my bicycle."

Chana, who has been listening in silence, nodding as Shlomo speaks, takes over. "I lived in Taitchsegass," she says. "That's the road that leads to the Latvian border. Shlomo stopped by our house to say he was leaving. If he's going so am I, I told my family. I organised transport and we all left: my mother and father, brother and sister-in-law and their three children. They'd opened the border that morning. There was no army, no government, nothing. The Germans arrived the day after we left."

When Shlomo and his friends arrived in Riga, they went to his cousin's house which was about 400 metres from the railway station. From time to time one of the group would crawl through the long grass to check whether the train to Russia had arrived. Conditions at the station became chaotic as more and more people joined the crush to get onto trains, and amid the noise and confusion, the Latvian militia continued sniping. When the train finally arrived, Shlomo was still urging his cousin, her husband and their young daughter to join them.

"How can we leave our house, our business, our possessions," they said. "For you it's different. You've nothing to lose."

"They lost everything, including their lives," Shlomo says. "The train was almost full by the time we got to the station. Latvian police tried to prevent us from boarding. They were armed, but we were young – I was twenty – and desperate. We grabbed the guns out of their hands and got onto the train. There was a woman and her child on the platform. We brought them in through the window. The mother went mad on the journey. Just one of the tragedies we were to witness.

"The train pulled out and we were on our way to Russia. We wandered around from place to place until the end of summer 1941. When it grew colder, we moved to Uzbekhistan where we were conscripted into the 16th Lithuanian Brigade. Most of the soldiers in this brigade were eventually killed. We'd been in very heavy battles . . .

"I met up with Leib soon after we went into the army. In the beginning things weren't too bad. But soon the situation became *shreklich*, terrible. Those who survived the fighting suffered from hunger. We were always hungry. We got a little bread, a little water and nothing else. When I met Leib a few months later, he was in a very pessimistic mood. '*Vi kenst du dos aushalten?*' he asked me. How can you bear it? '*Vet zein bashert, vet men lebben,*' I answered. '*Anit, vet men geharget verren.*' If it is our fate to live, well and good. If not, we'll be killed. 'I can't take it any more,' Leib said. 'I have no strength left.' He was very depressed. Some of us", Shlomo concludes, "broke down under the stress. Others didn't. Who can blame those who did?"

Chana nods. Shlomo emerges stoic, philosophical, brave. I recall Mierke's cryptic remark, "Ask Chana about Leib. She knew him very well." She has said nothing about Leib; Shlomo has done most of the talking. At the age of seventy Shlomo, it seems, is still reassuring Chana that she made the right choice. If indeed she had a choice. Shlomo is the first person I have spoken to who diminishes Leib's "hero" status.

"Then the really big battle began," Shlomo continues. "Near Orel. Leib was killed in a village called Nikolsk. We entered the village, were repulsed, then entered a second time. I asked someone if he'd seen Leib. He's been killed, he told me. After the battle, in a state of exhaustion, he'd gone into what seemed an empty house in the village. He had a drink of water, then lay down on a bed. There were Germans in the attic. They came down, saw a Russian soldier asleep on the bed and shot him. He was killed on the spot. *Azei geit es.*" So it goes.

Mierke had told us that Leib had been hit over the head by a German hiding in the house. I am to hear many versions of Leib's death over the next period.

"As for the massacre in Zhager . . . I heard that about 7000 men, women and children had been killed. There'd only been one German in town at the time. Our fellow Lithuanians did all the killing, with great enthusiasm and hatred. It's hard to imagine. People who'd been our friends, our neighbours . . . They killed off the leaders of the community first, Rabbi Riff among them. He'd been a very tall, strong man, a giant, but had bad eyesight. When he wanted to see something, he had to lift his eyebrows and open his eyes wide. The Lithuanian militia inspanned him like a horse to a cart, filled it with huge stones, then ordered him to pull it. As he pulled it, they shot at him, but he didn't fall, he just kept going. Everybody dispersed in fright. They thought he was indestructible. He wasn't."

After the war, Shlomo, like other survivors, had returned to Zhager to look for family. He found none. In 1946, he and a few others ordered a large memorial from a stonemason and brought it by waggon to Zhager. The Russian wife of a Jew called Mendelson kept the memorial site clear of weeds. Some time later, the Zhager municipality took responsibility for it.

"Until we left for Israel," Shlomo says, "we used to travel to Zhager from Vilna every year between Rosh Hashana and Yom Kippur, for *kaiveroves*, the memorial service. I hear that fewer and fewer people attend *kaiveroves* these days. Most have left for Israel and other places. Those who remain in Vilna are ageing, haven't much money, and are weighed down by their problems. In a few years' time, there'll be no one left to remember, to mourn."

I show Shlomo and Chana Jack's photographs. Is that the Old Zhager or the New Zhager mill, they ask one another. Who are those marchers? They recognise no one in the photographs. They must have been three or four years old when the photographs were taken.

We part from Shlomo and Chana on a more relaxed, friendly note than the one on which our visit began. I promise to write to them after I have visited Zhager. In their telling, neither Shlomo nor Chana had mentioned Edvard, who, according to Mierke, had been a close friend; Edvard, who had spoken Yiddish and mixed in Jewish circles, Edvard, who had become a mass murderer after the Germans entered Zhager in 1941. How would Edvard have acted had he faced Shlomo and Chana at the open pit in Naryshkin Park, gun raised?

I find a possible answer several days later at Yad v'Shem, in the testimony of Yehezkiel Fleischer.[8] Standing at the edge of an open pit in the Kurshan forest, a young man named Tchernikovsky recognised among the shooters a gentile Lithuanian whom he had known since childhood. "Adulas!" he called out. "Aim well, so that I won't suffer long."

Adulas obliged.

---

8 Yehezkiel Fleischer, Testimony taken by the Historical Commission in the Displaced Persons' Camp, Feldafing, 28 October 1947.

11

The Destruction of Zhager

Jack Trubik

Market day in Zhager, 1920s. On 2 October 1941, the Jews
were massacred in this market-place and in Naryshkin Park.

"Leib Yoffe?" all my interlocutors have said. "I knew him well." The
musician, perhaps; the lover, occasionally; the idealist – or Party
apparachnik – seldom. As the images proliferate, the man grows
more elusive. But through the mists of myth, a faint outline
emerges, splintered and flawed though it is. An idealist – a deluded
idealist, Shlomo would have it – who believed Communism was the

panacea for all the ills of the world; a hero – a disheartened, weary man, Shlomo insists – who died fighting the Nazis; a devoted son, who had had to abandon his family. Who can judge? Certainly not Shlomo or the other young men who had fled without their families.

Less is known about the rest of the family. After Henke had been married off to a "very nice man", she lived in Riga. It is unlikely that she survived the slaughter of 65 000 Jews in Latvia.

Some say that Faivke, his wife and child, after fleeing from Shavel with Leib, had been trapped in Zhager and massacred. Others report seeing him on the road out of Zhager the day before it fell to the Germans. Mierke claims he was killed in battle. No one knows what happened to his wife and child.

My grandmother and Bryna and Shmulke must have suffered the same fate as the other Jews of Zhager. Shmulke, who had been about twenty-two at the time, might have been among any of the groups of young men who had been shot by the Lithuanian militia prior to the final massacre.

My interviews and social visits over, I spend the rest of my time in Israel searching for "objective" information in the libraries and archives of Bet Hatfutsot in Tel Aviv, and Yad v'Shem, the Holocaust centre in Jerusalem.

Bet Hatfutsot, the Museum of the Diaspora, where I had hoped to find information about life in Zhager prior to the Holocaust, yields only a thirty-line print-out, most of which is devoted to the scholars and rabbis of the nineteenth century. I shall have to wait until I have access to the archives of YIVO in New York for information about Jewish life in pre-war Eastern Europe in general, and Zhager in particular.

At Yad v'Shem, I follow every mention of Zhager in the archives, on microfilm and in books. I eventually find two testimonies and one eye-witness account about the destruction of the shtetl Zhager. In *The Einsatzgruppen Reports*,[9] a selection from the despatches sent

---

9 Arad *et al.*, *The Einsatzgruppen Reports*, p. 278.

by the Nazi death squads to Gestapo headquarters in Berlin in which they report on their extermination activities, I find a fourth account which corroborates much of the information in the testimonies.

Of the three witnesses, only Jacob Kagan had actually lived in the Zhager ghetto. He claims to be the only person who survived the massacre. Although Yehezkiel Fleischer and Ber Peretzman had connections with Zhager, they had been confined in the Shavel ghetto at the time of the destruction of Zhager.

Fleischer had been a native of Kurshan, a small town about 50 kilometres south-west of Zhager.[10] Prior to the capture of the town, he had attempted to escape, but had been caught and sent to the Shavel ghetto. He learned about the fate of the Jews of Kurshan and Zhager from two letters from his mother and sister which a peasant had smuggled into the Shavel ghetto.

When the Germans entered Kurshan, they ordered the Jews to bury the dead Russian soldiers and their horses and to clear the roads of arms and ammunition. They did not provide proper implements for either task, but beat up the Jews for working inefficiently. Shortly afterwards, all males over twelve were rounded up and held under Lithuanian guard in the synagogue. Invalids and psychiatric cases were taken away and never seen again.

A week later, the men had been herded onto trucks and driven into a forest about 3 kilometres out of town where pits, 15 metres long, had already been prepared. Fleischer's brother, who had been among them, jumped off the truck and hid out in the forests around Shukvan, Popilan and Shavel. For a while he kept in contact with his mother and sister, then was never heard of again.

In their second letter, Fleischer's mother and sister wrote that, together with all the women and children of Kurshan, they had been transported to the Zhager ghetto. They worked in the vegetable gardens of a Zhager peasant who was paying them in kind. A few weeks later, the peasant sought Fleischer out in the ghetto and told

---

10 Fleischer, Testimony.

him that all the Jews in Zhager had been massacred. Fleischer himself managed to escape from the Shavel ghetto during the chaos created by the *Kinderaktion* in 1943. He survived by hiding out amongst Lithuanian peasants in various villages.

In his testimony he describes his visit, after the war, to the mass grave in Naryshkin Park where his mother and sister are buried. "It is 120 metres long and the width of two people," he writes. Local people had told him that at least 6000 people were buried there.

Ber Peretzman, whose testimony, like Fleischer's, had been taken at the Displaced Persons' Camp, Feldafing, in 1947, was a native of Zhager.[11] He had been incarcerated first in the Shavel ghetto, then in the Stutthof, Dachau and Uting concentration camps.

Soon after the Germans took Zhager in June 1941, Peretzman states, edicts signed by the head of the Lithuanian partisans, Edvard Ikwild Boumaister, appeared throughout the shtetl. Jews had to wear a yellow star on the chest and the back of outer garments; they were not allowed to walk on the pavements, to open the shutters of their homes, to take water from wells not belonging to Jews, or to show smoke from their chimneys. It was also forbidden to sell bread to Jews. The only place they could buy bread was in a shop at the entrance to Taitchsegass which was owned by Lithuanians. This was open to the Jews for only an hour or two before dusk, by which time the gentile Lithuanians had bought up most of the supplies. But until the ghetto had been completely fenced off, the Jews, in secrecy and in great fear, had bought farm supplies from the Latvian farmers who crossed the border in Taitchsegass on their way to the market square.

The day after the capture of Zhager, the Jews were ordered to assemble in the market square with Rabbi Riff at their head. They were given spades and brooms and taken to Count Naryshkin's estate, where they were ordered to clean out the stables and cowsheds. On their return, they were lined up in the market square and forced to

---

11 Ber Peretzman, Testimony taken by the Historical Commission in the Displaced Persons' Camp, Feldafing, 2 March 1949.

kneel before their implements. Anyone whose tools were not placed in a certain order or were not properly cleaned, was beaten. Rabbi Riff, being very tall, was then paired up with the shortest Jew, spanned into a cart and ordered to run through the shtetl. This caused great hilarity among the Lithuanians, who applauded enthusiastically. The Lithuanian partisans organised a daily ritual to further humiliate Rabbi Riff. He was made to stand in front of the assembly, and as each person walked past him, he had to spit in the rabbi's face. Those who refused were threatened with instant death. The rabbi commanded the people to carry out this order. The few who could not bring themselves to do so were shot.

On 25 June, a group of Jews was taken to a synagogue and told they were going to work in Latvia. Forty of them were then led away to a forest, where they were shot. The following day a Lithuanian teacher, Stasis Busis, together with the lawyer Krupsis, came to the synagogue and demanded another forty men. They joked that they needed them for dinner. With their arms tied behind their backs, they were led to the cemetery in New Zhager, where they were shot.

"The Lithuanian population of Zhager", Peretzman states, "had taken the law into their own hands. They attacked Jewish families, stole their possessions and tortured them cruelly."

A group of Lithuanians, he says, burst in the home of Mrs Broide and attacked her. She jumped from a second-floor window and broke her leg. Crying out in agony, she had been carried back into the house, laid down on her bed and murdered with an axe. This, he says, was just one of many such incidents.

At the beginning of July, all the Jews were concentrated in a certain part of the shtetl demarcated as the ghetto. They were allowed to bring some of their possessions with them. Gradually Jews from the surrounding towns and villages – Kurshan, Krok, Popilan, Yaneshok, Zaimol, Radvilishkis, Linkovo and others – whose menfolk had already been killed, were brought to the ghetto. Peretzman estimates that between 6000 and 7000 Jews had been in the Zhager ghetto at this time.

The ghetto was unguarded, and the Lithuanians had free run of it. They would burst in with horses and carts, load them up with Jewish property, then disappear, unchallenged. There was no authority to whom the Jews could appeal. An attempt had been made to form a committee, but they were completely without power. At night, the men were locked into the synagogues. Only women and children slept at home. At such times, the houses had been broken into, and the women and young girls taken out and abused. The food situation was dire, and many people starved to death.

Life continued in this way until Yom Kippur of 1941, when a group of thirty men from Einsatzkommando 3 arrived in Zhager from Shavel. They were accompanied by Lithuanian partisans. In the evening, the commander sent for a few prominent Jews and demanded gold, money and other valuables, assuring them that the Jews would be transferred to a place where they would be given work and would remain safe from harm. The commander also issued an instruction that all the men, women and children were to assemble in the market square the following morning at six o'clock. On the day of Yom Kippur most people gathered at the market square. A small number, suspecting an impending attack, attempted to hide their children.

At this point I quote from Jacob Kagan's testimony.[12] He had been in Zhager when the massacre took place.

Kagan was born in Krok, a small village not far from Zhager, which had a population of about 150 people. When war broke out, the inhabitants of most Lithuanian towns and villages immediately turned on their Jewish neighbours, Kagan writes. The priest in Krok, however, had protected the Jewish community, forbidding his congregation to rob or murder them. They were, however, expelled from the centre of the village to a poor district at the end of the village, where they eked out a meagre living by working for the local peasants.

---

12 Jacob Kagan, Eye-witness account, E1261 E/84.3.8.

In mid-August a band of armed men from the villages Zemel and Linhova appeared in Krok. They had already destroyed the Jews of their own villages, and were now participating in the murder of Jews from other towns and villages. They brought the Jews to the market-place where they were forced onto waggons and taken to Zhager under heavy guard.

On arrival, Kagan recounts, they were handed over to the local Lithuanian guards, headed by a native of Zhager called Statkus, a shoemaker, who had always had good relations with the Zhager Jews, and who spoke Yiddish fluently. He and his adjutant Eisgirdas, also a shoemaker from Zhager, counted the new arrivals, arranged them in groups, then crowded them into the synagogue in New Zhager, where they spent the first night.

The ghetto, Kagan writes, was divided into two parts. One was in New Zhager, all along Taitchsegass, the street that leads to the Lithuanian–Latvian border. It ran from the entrance to the market square, to the Struls' double-storey house at the other end, encompassing the Mill on the bank of the Shvete, and all the lanes leading down to the river. The second part of the ghetto was in Old Zhager, on the other side of the river. It included all the lanes running from the old cemetery to the river. Both ghettos were joined – or divided – by the river.

Kagan estimates that there were about 6000 people in the ghetto, most of whom were women and children. Many were survivors of fifteen or sixteen other villages whose men had already been killed. The rest were local Jews.

The ghetto had not been completely fenced. Kagan was in one of the fifty to sixty groups working on the fence. They worked long hours, every day of the week. The Lithuanian guards, he says, were not particularly cruel to them. Every evening at dusk, they had to report in front of the two synagogues in New Zhager. After a short roll-call, they were divided into two groups and assigned to the two synagogues where they slept. The guards locked them in.

"We slept fully clothed on hard benches," Kagan writes, "full of fears of the unknown. In this way our nights were passed. At dawn we were led out by a Lithuanian guard to our various jobs."

Only a few cobblers and tailors were allowed to work outside, returning to the ghetto each evening. The rest of the men were engaged in work like fencing and other kinds of manual labour. As they were separated from the women, Kagan did not know anything about their living conditions.

One of the men's jobs was to collect furniture and other household goods from Jewish homes, and pile them up in the market square. The German regional command in Shavel then sent in vehicles to take them away. These were the only Germans Kagan had seen in Zhager until the last few days before its destruction.

There were no internal Jewish organisations in the ghetto. It was run directly by Statkus, Eisgirdas and other local Lithuanians, none of whom wore uniforms. An informal relationship existed between the guards and several prominent Zhager Jews who, however, wielded little influence or power. By posing as a friend, by speaking Yiddish, and by reassuring the Jews that all would be well, Statkus staved off panic. In this way, he remained firmly in control. But he was vigilant. He and his helpers often concealed themselves inside the ghetto, to keep an eye out for untoward activity.

"There was a strong desire to live," Kagan says, "and we were seduced into believing that work would help us survive."

But they remained wary and seldom volunteered for work. In the first week of September 1941, Statkus called for fifty physically fit men to report in the market square the following morning for special work outside the town. As counting at roll-call was generally lax, the men sometimes did not return to the synagogue where they were locked in each evening after work. They were seldom caught out. On this occasion, however, the guards had been strict. Discovering that many people were missing, they beat up those present and forced them to bring out sufficient men to make up the quota. Kagan remained hidden.

The fifty victims had been led to the cemetery in Old Zhager where they were shot and buried in a mass grave. At the head of this murder squad, Kagan writes, had been two members of the local Lithuanian intelligentsia, a man called Palishmaushkas and Boyshek, a teacher of singing. This was revenge against the "Jewish Communists", Boyshek said, for the exile of his older brother, a fervent nationalist and anti-Semite.

When the fifty men did not return, there was great panic and unrest in the ghetto. Statkus, as usual, moved around from house to house in an attempt to reassure everyone that the men had been sent out on special duties. But when they did not return, everyone refused to go out to work, and the labour system broke down.

Jacob Kagan, in retrospect, believes this *Aktion* had been a deliberate ploy to kill the strong men in the ghetto, prior to the mass destruction which was to take place several weeks later.

After the initial shock and dismay, an uncertain calm descended on the ghetto, and life returned to "normal". About a week before the extermination, security around the ghetto was strengthened. Lithuanian militiamen from other places began to arrive, but they kept a low profile. Among them Kagan recognised men who had murdered in the villages of Zemel and Linkova. No one was allowed to leave the ghetto. Daily work stopped. Latvian farmers were not allowed to go through Taitchsegass on their way to the market. An atmosphere of fear and uncertainty descended on the ghetto. Rumours were rife that the closure of the ghetto was imminent, and that people would be moved elsewhere.

"No one", Kagan says, "believed they were facing the bitter end."

On the eve of Yom Kippur, a number of Sonderkommandos arrived from Shavel, where they were stationed. Until then there had not been a visible German presence in Zhager. All physically fit Jewish men were ordered to assemble in the market square the following day, when new working groups were to be organised. With the recent massacre in mind, Kagan and several others hid in the Strul house at the end of the market-place.

He learned afterwards that the situation had become chaotic when the Lithuanian guards tried to organise them into groups according to trades. Fearing an *Aktion* of some kind, the spokesmen for the Jewish community approached the commander, undertaking to collect jewels and other valuables from the Jews, on condition that the ghetto not be closed and they be allowed to live and work as before. The offer was accepted, the collection of valuables made, and duly turned over to the commander of the Lithuanian militia. The community was then ordered to assemble the following day for roll-call.

That night, the armed guards around the ghetto disappeared. This diversionary tactic worked. The Jews believed they were safe, and everyone appeared at roll-call the next morning, including Kagan. They were told they would be given better working conditions, and were ordered, once again, to arrange themselves into groups according to trades. And once again there was confusion as they moved about from group to group.

Manteiff, the Commander of the Einsatzkommando, was standing on the balcony of Dr Friedman's house, which overlooked the market square. He called for order, castigating the people for lack of discipline. The Germans, he said, could organise a large battalion in a shorter time than it took the Jews to form trade groups. He then called for young Jewish men who had served in the army to come forward to impose order. In their innocence, they obeyed.

"Soon we were standing in rows according to our occupations," Kagan writes, "facing the lanes and the alleyways that led onto the market square. A count was made and quiet descended on the square for a few minutes.

"Suddenly Manteiff blew a whistle, and the murderers who were concealed in the houses around the square, waiting for the signal, opened fire on us with machine guns. People fell over and died. The blood of the victims spilled over the cobblestones of the square. The murderers appeared from their hiding places and continued shooting and destroying. The few who tried to escape were caught and killed. Then the hunt began for those who were hiding. When they were found, they were shot. At the same time, local Lithuanians broke into the ghetto and looted Jewish homes. The screams of the victims mixed with the shouts of the murderers and the whimpering and groans of the dying. It seemed like the end of the world . . . By some miracle the bullets of the assassins did not find me. I was not hurt and managed to find a hiding place . . . I was the only one who escaped from ghetto Zhager."

Kagan, surprisingly, does not describe the resistance in the market square. Ber Peretzman, in his testimony, writes that, just as Manteiff blew the whistle, Alter Zagorsky, a resident of Zhager, shouted, "*Yidden, es iz schlecht! Laift!*" Jews, the situation is bad! Run! People panicked and ran in all directions, trying to evade the bullets. Zagorsky took out a knife and stabbed a Lithuanian partisan. They both fell to the ground, dead. Avram Ackerman, who was not armed, threw himself onto another Lithuanian partisan, and sank his teeth into his throat. He was shot.

When the resistance began, the Germans summoned help from Shavel, 70 kilometres away. Well-armed Lithuanian partisans arrived some time later, with guns and brandy. Those Jews who had escaped in the chaos and managed to hide were ferreted out and, together with those who had survived the shooting in the square, were thrown onto large trucks and taken to Naryshkin Park, where pits had already been dug. They were made to undress and stand at the edge of the pit, then mown down with machine guns. Ammunition, Peretzman writes, was not wasted on small children. They were grabbed by the feet, swung against the trees, their heads crushed, then thrown into the pit. Many were buried alive.

Peretzman also described how Rochel Mendelson (the teacher about whom Mierke had told me) went into labour at the edge of the pit.

"The murderers laid her down on the ground, allowed the child to be born, then killed both mother and child."

The resistance is recorded in one of the Einsatzgruppen reports found in the archives of the SS headquarters in Berlin after World War II. *Operational Situation Report USSR*, No. 55, dated 11 January

1942, states that efforts were being made to purge the Eastern Territory of Jews as completely as possible. Estonia was already *Judenfrei*. In Riga, Latvia, 2600 Jews remained, and in Daugavpils there were 962 Jews, all of whom were urgently needed for the labour pool. In Lithuania an effort had been made to purge the rural districts and the small towns of Jews. This was "an urgent necessity because Communist elements, particularly terror groups and parts of the Polish resistance movement, made contact with the Jews, instigating them to carry on sabotage and to offer resistance". The Jews are also accused of instigating anti-German feelings in originally loyal and cooperative Lithuanian circles. Describing the massacre in Zhager, the report continues:

"The Jews were particularly active in Zagare. There, on October 2, 1941, fifty Jews escaped from the ghetto which had already been cordoned off. Most of them were recaptured and shot in the course of a large-scale action which was carried out immediately. In the course of subsequent preparations for the wholesale execution of the Zagare Jews, at a prearranged signal, they attacked the guards and the men of the Security Police Einsatzkommando while being transported to the place of execution. Several Jews who had not been searched thoroughly enough by the Lithuanian guards, drew knives and pistols and uttering cries like 'Long live Stalin!' and 'Down with Hitler!' they rushed the police force, seven of whom were wounded. Resistance was broken at once. After 150 Jews were shot on the spot, the transport of the remaining Jews to the place of execution was carried through without further incident."

And in this manner, according to the reports of both victims and perpetrators, ghetto Zhager and all its inhabitants were destroyed.

As I read of the terror and the confusion in the market square, I visualise a short, elderly woman with her red-haired daughter among the crowd, clinging to one another as Manteiff blows his whistle. Or standing at the edge of the pit in Naryshkin Park, naked, as the Lithuanian shooters raise their rifles. Shmulke, with a face like my father's, appears in many places: among the fifty young men tricked into volunteering to fight the Germans, then massacred in the synagogue; or among the fifty young men shot by singing teacher Boyshek in revenge for his brother's exile; or among the men who offered resistance in the market square.

They then merge with the rest of the doomed innocents, and I realise that I shall never know how they died. But that has ceased to matter. They were all my family.

12

Quests

Naryshkin Park, 1920s. Maternal uncle Itze, second from right,
while a conscript in the Lithuanian Army.

Laden with taped interviews, documents, articles, and the terrible
testimonies of eye-witnesses of the Zhager massacre, I leave for New
York on the last lap of my search for "objective" history. YIVO is my
destination. Here, according to the chief archivist, I will find fifteen
folders of documentary material on Jewish life in Zhager, from 1919
to 1925, exactly the period I am researching. My parents had returned
from exile in the Ukraine in 1919, and left for Mexico in 1926.

YIVO's headquarters is situated towards the end of Museum Mile on Fifth Avenue. The organisation had been founded in 1922 by a group of Jewish scholars in Vilna who, with uncanny prescience, had begun collecting documents and other information relating to Eastern European Jewish culture. In 1940, the organisation had been relocated to New York. Before the Nazis looted the YIVO archives in 1941, Jewish archivists had managed to smuggle diaries and documents into the Vilna ghetto. After the war, three million books, thousands of photographs, newspapers, letters, Torahs and other artefacts had been rescued and added to YIVO's collection.

On the wall of YIVO's headquarters is a plaque stating that this building had once been the residence of Mrs Cornelius Vanderbilt. As I walk through the wrought-iron gateway into the black and white marble foyer, with its spiral staircase and crystal chandeliers, I am struck by the incongruity of the place itself and the purpose for which it is being used.

"We're moving to less ornate premises in Greenwich Village," Leo the archivist tells me. "The organisation needs larger premises and a link-up with an educational institution like New York University or Hebrew Union College. Much of YIVO's material is in a storehouse in Brooklyn at the moment. Don't be disappointed if you don't find what you are looking for," he adds. "People come here from all over the world to look for their roots. They rarely find them."

Half an hour later I am sitting at a desk in the library, going through the contents of two box files which contain fifteen yellow folders on Zhager. They are filled with faded documents of all shapes and sizes, in Yiddish, Hebrew, Lithuanian and English. There are thin brown envelopes with personal receipts and private letters; birth certificates, death certificates, marriage certificates, and journals divided into columns with names, addresses and occupations. In addition, there are official letters and documents, at the head of which is a logo of a knight on a rearing horse, raised sword in hand, with the words *Lietuvos Respublika* arched above him. It is the symbol of the independent Lithuanian Republic, circa 1922.

For the next week I arrive at YIVO when it opens in the morning, and remain at my desk until late afternoon, slowly working my way through the folders, photocopying documents for later translation. I set aside a few English letters, and glance briefly, despairingly, at the official documents in Lithuanian, Hebrew and Yiddish. I am beginning to recognise other researchers in the library, at least one of whom has sensibly engaged a translator.

I step into a time warp as I handle the faded documents and ledgers that attest to the fact that Zhager had once been a place where people had been born, married and died – natural deaths – paid rent, received help from charitable institutions, complained about taxes and sewerage, and registered to vote for the local Jewish Council. These are documents from the brief Golden Age of Lithuanian Jewry, when Lithuania had signed a League of Nations Charter ensuring minority rights, a time when there had been a Ministry for Jewish Affairs, and Hebrew street signs in Kovno.

Much of the correspondence is between the local Jewish community councils and various departments of the Ministry for Jewish Affairs. Birth, marriage and death certificates are in Lithuanian, Hebrew and Yiddish. Letters to the local community councils are in either Hebrew or Yiddish. A tattered post-World War I journal records names of those who received clothing and monetary aid from the community; faded personal letters crumble at the edges and crack across their folds.

Among the letters lies a blank ruled sheet, with a heading in the right-hand corner: "Rabbinas Izraelis Rifas, Zagare." From the office of Rabbi Riff, the tall, half-blind rabbi of Old Zhager – or was it New Zhager? – who, in 1941, had been humiliated, tortured then killed by Lithuanian militiamen. All that remains is his name on a blank sheet.

As a break from Yiddish and Hebrew texts, I turn to four letters written in English, which belong to a later period. They tell different but similar stories of the desperate rush to bring people out of Lithuania before World War II breaks out. On 21 October 1938,

Robert Bernstein, who owns a factory for men's and boys' pyjamas in New York, writes to Daniel Robins in Ohio, about his step-sister Mary Valencik, from whom he has received a "very pathetic letter".

". . . You must no doubt know of the difficulties they are living under, always in constant fear of Hitler and a German invasion of their territory. She writes me that you were good enough sometime ago to tell her that you would take her little daughter to live with you. As a result she went through a great deal of trouble and anguish in getting certain documents from the consul, in readiness for her little daughter to come to America as per your kind offer to her. Now she writes me that she has written you several letters but up to date she has not received a response . . ."

Three days later, Daniel Robins replies: "Let me assure you the matter of bringing our relative to America has not been forgotten by me. However, it has been extremely difficult to obtain definite procedures from the proper authorities. Thus far I have written several letters to the Hebrew Sheltering and Immigrant Aid Society of America, and have complied with all requests necessary in the matter. For your information, I have signed affidavits guaranteeing the support and welfare of this relative, which is vital in cases of this nature.

"The last correspondence I had from the above Society was 16 September, asking for additional information which they in turn will forward abroad. It naturally takes time and I feel we shall just have to be patient in the matter . . . I believe everything has been taken care of and just as soon as I hear from Mary and her daughter, I will take care of arrangements immediately . . ."

One gets an insight into the slow grind of the bureaucratic machine from two other letters concerning a woman called Chase Schwartz.

The first, dated 26 April 1939, is from the Hebrew Sheltering and Immigrant Aid Society, and is addressed to a Mr Samuel Newman, of Ohio. "In reply to your letter, please be advised that there is nothing that can be done to expedite the granting of a visa. These matters are regulated by the immigration laws and all persons must wait for their turn in the quota before receiving a visa. The Lithuanian quota is very small. A great number of applicants are on the list waiting to obtain visas to enter the United States. It will, therefore, take a considerable time before a person may expect to receive a visa . . ."

As the result of the apparent intervention by a member of the House of Representatives, Michael J. Kirwan, Samuel Newman receives a letter from the American Consul in Kaunas (Kovno) dated 23 June 1939.

"This office has the honor to inform you that it has received from the Department of State a copy of your letter dated 2 June 1939, concerning Miss Chase Schwartz (Chase Svarcaite), a registrant here for a nonpreference immigration visa.

"The records here show that the application of Miss Svarcaite has been formally approved, and that she is eligible to receive a non-preference immigration visa when a number under the Lithuanian quota is available for her use. As Miss Svarcaite did not register her name on the waiting list until November 4, 1938, and because of quota restrictions, it now appears that her turn will not be reached to be granted a visa until December 1939."

I search in vain for information about the fate of Chase Schwartz and Mary Valencik's daughter. Nothing in the files indicates whether they left Zhager before the German invasion.

My last day at YIVO is spent going through the remaining yellow folders, and taking photocopies of documents and letters for later translation. I come upon a journal headed "Voters' List for the Va'ad Hakehillah, 1923" in Yiddish, with the stamp of the ubiquitous armed knight on a rearing horse. Each page is ruled into five columns: surname, first name, age, street and number. I glance through it, and find the names of *landsleit* I have known. The name Yoffe occurs many times. Yoffe, I read: Hirsch, Rivka, Aryeh, Zelda, Itzchak . . . Shimon and Freyde! He is forty-six, she is thirty-nine. I cannot decipher the street name, but the number of their house is 1. The Yoffes' house had abutted the river; it was the first house in the street. An involuntary cry escapes me; the dates tally. Simon had been born in 1877, Freyde in 1884. She had been nineteen, he twenty-six when my father was born in 1903. Simon had been diagnosed with throat cancer towards the end of their exile in Berdyansk, and had died some years later.

Simon and Freyde have finally emerged from the mists that obscured their lives. I had never even seen photographs of them. In some mysterious way, this simple entry on a voters' roll establishes their existence for me. And their loss.

Leo hears my cry and hurries over. By now I am weeping openly. I show him the tattered journal with my grandparents' names.

"You are very fortunate. It is unusual to find such information," he says. "And I have found something else that might interest you." He hands me a buff envelope. "This is the only photograph we have of Zhager."

I draw out a photograph I have known since early childhood. It is of a group of young people lying on their stomachs at the crest of a hill – the Mill Hill. Among them are my uncles Itze and Leib. "Nature Lovers' Excursion" is written on the back of the photograph in a faded script.

When I take leave of Leo and the rest of the staff, I promise to ask Gerty Trubik's permission to send copies of Jack's Zhager photographs. Other people may one day identify an aunt, an uncle or a grandmother among them.

Before I leave New York, I meet with an American woman who was born in Lithuania, of Catholic parents. A mutual friend had put us in touch when he realised we were delving into our Lithuanian background from opposite ends of the spectrum. The woman, whom I shall call Bronye, had written to me soon after-wards, explaining what had led her to re-examine her Lithuanian past. Touched by her difficult task and by the honesty with which she was approaching her quest, I replied immediately, giving her the background to my own interest in Lithuanian and Jewish history. We arranged to meet in New York.

During our brief encounter, we establish immediate contact. She has brought with her a satchelful of books, among them *Lithuania:*

700 Years.[13] This, she explains, is the romantic, sanitised version of Lithuanian history that had been the basic historical text of her generation. It was only with the war crimes tribunals that the knowledge of Lithuania's collaboration with the Nazis began to percolate through to the younger generation in the US–Lithuanian community. Nazi supporters in Lithuania? Ghettos and massacres in mythic places like Kaunas and Vilnius? Unbelievable.

The full force of this erasure from history was to hit Bronye when publications and articles became too numerous to ignore. In the course of reading books on the Holocaust and eye-witness testimonies of Jewish survivors, she came upon an account of the massacres that had taken place in her own idyllic village. Until then she had only seen photographs of happy smiling people, and "of a me I don't even remember".

Thus began Bronye's unremitting search for "facts". She began collating two sets of histories, Jewish and Lithuanian, in an effort to reconstruct some sense of truth and reality of what had happened during World War II.

"After a year of visceral reading," she says, "the rage I feel at the betrayal by my father's generation is overwhelming. I just don't understand it."

After our meeting we began a correspondence which continues to this day. It seems an unlikely friendship. I had grown up with tales of the joys and sorrows of shtetl life and the terrible fate of the Jews at the hands of the Nazis and their Lithuanian henchmen. She had been nurtured on stories about the idyllic village of her birth, and the terrible manner in which her nation had been crushed by the Soviet government and their allies, the "Jewish Bolsheviks". I, the niece of a Communist, had lived among Jewish Lithuanians in South Africa most of my life. After spending a great deal of her childhood in Displaced Persons' Camps in Germany with her family, she had grown up in the tight-knit American Lithuanian community of the 1950s.

---

13 Gerutis (ed.), *Lithuania: 700 Years*, 6th edn, 1984.

Had my parents remained in Lithuania, I might be lying in the mass grave in Naryshkin Park with them. Had her parents not fled, hours before the Soviet army rounded up tens of thousands of gentile and Jewish Lithuanians for deportation, she would have spent her childhood and beyond in Siberia with her family.

Neither of us believes in collective guilt.

Bronye's material has been invaluable for my own research. The books, photocopies of articles by academics and historians, cuttings from newspapers, and translations from the Lithuanian press, provide a new perspective for me. They demonstrate how historians and scholars exploit erasure, denial or apologia to give a different slant to events. Not only are victims often transformed into perpetrators; these manufactured "facts" are passed on from one generation to the next as history, perpetuating destructive ancient myths and creating new ones.

In *Lithuania: 700 Years*, for example, there are only three brief references, in almost 500 pages, to Jewish Lithuanians, who had lived in the country since the fourteenth century, and who had constituted 7 per cent of the total population between the world wars.[14]

The first is a reference to foreign merchants and traders who had settled in Lithuania in the sixteenth century. They were "alien to the land-bound peasants in the rural areas. It was also around this time that the Jews began coming into Lithuania, mostly from German areas, forming the basis of what became in time the greatest center of Judaism in Eastern Europe."

In fact, the Jews had been in Lithuania at least since the fourteenth century. By 1388 Grand Duke Vytautus had officially endorsed the existence of the Jewish communities in Lithuania by granting them a charter which spelled out their legal and religious rights.

The second reference to Jews in *Lithuania: 700 Years* describes the Chmelnicki pogroms of the seventeenth century. "The main targets of this revolt were the Poles and the Jews. (The Jewish

---

14 Gerutis (ed.), *Lithuania: 700 Years*, pp. 73, 94, 292.

pogroms which resulted were surpassed only by the Nazi massacres of World War II.)"

The bracketed sentence refers to the slaughter of an estimated 100 000 Jews, killed over a period of ten years by the pogromists.

Only six lines are devoted to the Holocaust during which approximately 95 per cent of the 220 000 Jews in Lithuania had been murdered. "A cruel fate met the Jews of Lithuania. From the outset of the German occupation, they were killed wholesale and destroyed in every manner . . ."

It omits to say that Lithuanian killing squads had been willing collaborators of the Einsatzgruppen to produce this cruel fate. It mentions, however, that "A number of Lithuanians were punished for harboring fugitive Jews."

Bronye also sent me an 800-word print-out of Zagare's history from the Balzekas Museum of Lithuanian Culture in Chicago.[15] Most of it deals with Zagare's centuries-long battle against the Teutonic Order, which had been trying to convert pagan Lithuania to Catholicism. Jews are mentioned once, despite the statement that "most of the population was made up of Jewish craftsmen and traders" in the nineteenth century.

World War I is summarised in half a sentence. "World War I displaced about a third of Zagare's 14 000 inhabitants . . ." It does not say that only the Jewish Lithuanians had been "displaced", and that when they had returned from exile after the war, they found their homes looted or in ruins, their livelihood destroyed.

World War II is mentioned only to say that since the war, "many new public and private buildings have been constructed in Zagare".

Not only were Jewish men, women and children massacred by the Nazis and their Lithuanian auxiliaries. In this article they have also been expunged from Lithuanian history.

The Balzekas Museum, Bronye assures me, is least of all Lithuanian

---

15 Balzekas Museum of Lithuanian Culture. *Zagare*. Bibl. B. Uzumeckas, V. Buisas. "Zagares miestas," Siauliu metrastis, Simuliai, 1938. S. Suz.

organisations to blame for disseminating false information. Perhaps potted histories tend to be skewed. Or perhaps the writer of this history was more interested in the architecture of Zhager than in the fate of its Jewish population.

In the articles Bronye continues to send me, I observe that the word collaboration, when it is used at all, appears within quotation marks. "Adaptive behaviour" is how one apologist describes Lithuania's collaboration with Nazi Germany.

As I read her letters, I realise that in many ways it is easier to approach history from the victims' perspective. You feel anguish, horror, sorrow, anger, a terrible sense of loss. But if you are delving into the actions of your own people who might have been perpetrators or even bystanders, you are faced with one of three alternatives: to justify their actions; to take refuge in total denial; or to persist in searching for what actually happened, as Bronye is doing.

She is still finding it difficult to come to terms with the denial and neutralisation of Lithuania's Nazi past. Her way is courageous and painful. It threatens her close relationship with the community in which she grew up, and which remains of immense importance to her.

"[But] I have resolved," she writes, "that I will not be part of another reconstruction of a 'pretty picture' . . ."

I had not expected to find undisputed facts when researching the broader issues, yet was naively disappointed to discover that scholars, historians and academics were as much a part of the historical process as other individuals, and could rarely rise above it to give an unbiased perspective on history.

Can there, consequently, be no "objective" history? Are not some facts incontrovertible? What of the documents, reports, diaries, and testimonies by perpetrators and victims which point to the same facts? Like the account of the destruction of Zhager. Or the reports from the Wannsee Conference on 10 January 1941, at which Reinhard Heydrich, head of the SS Intelligence Service, outlined his plans for the "final solution". Or the Einsatzgruppen reports which meticulously list the massacres of Jews in towns and villages throughout Eastern Europe, specifically referring to the invaluable help they received from local inhabitants. Is it possible to misinterpret or deny such facts?

Historians, like their preliterate forebears the praise singers, pass on to the generations that follow them the names of their kings and the tales of their brave deeds, as well as the mores, beliefs and prejudices of their society. We are entreated to learn from history if we are not to repeat its mistakes. How are we to learn from our mistakes if we do not acknowledge them, if we falsify and distort history by denying its painful aspects? In this way, long-discredited myths live on, fuelling the prejudices of successive generations.

A whole generation of ethnic Lithuanians has grown up with a skewed view of the role Jews played in the history of the country. Where they appear at all in history books or in learned articles, Jews are portrayed as a troublesome minority, alien to the native population, a disloyal element which allied itself with the Soviet regime that oppressed the Lithuanian people. Their positive contribution to the country in which they lived for centuries is seldom acknowledged.

And when the massacre of 95 per cent of Jewish Lithuanians is not entirely ignored or denied, it is justified with the absurd logic that Jews were Communists, Communists oppressed and deported tens of thousands of Lithuanians, therefore Jews were responsible for these crimes. The genocide of the Jews, when it is admitted, is held to be a natural reaction to the suffering they inflicted on ethnic Lithuanians. The argument that the Jews had brought their destruction upon themselves by collaborating with the Soviet regime is too obscene to merit more than cursory mention.

With the material gathered from the archives of YIVO, Yad v'Shem and other sources, and the information Bronye has made accessible to me, I bring to a temporary halt the search for "objective" information. I can no longer delay my journey, my quest. It is time to go to *der heim*, the home of my forebears which no longer exists.

PART THREE

13

Vilna

Left to right: Leah, Freda, Ernest (standing), Misha, Hirshl, Assa.

"That's her!" someone cries out in Yiddish. "The one with the grey hair!"

Had I really waited that long to come?

They are standing in a group outside Passport Control, holding flowers. We embrace, strangers who have always known one another: Leah and her second husband Hirshl; their son Misha, his wife Assa, and their two sons; and Freda, the daughter Leib never saw, with her husband Yuri, and Ernest, their teenage son.

"Raizala!" Leah says, her eyes enlarged by unshed tears. Mine spill over. She scrutinises me at arm's length. "Gershon's mouth, like Leibke's."

The naming has begun.

We drive in convoy to Leah and Hirshl's flat, five in Yuri's battered car, the rest in Misha's. I sit in the back between Freda and Leah, who will not surrender me to the front seat. "She's only here for a week. Why only a week, Raizala?"

The hilly, wooded landscape is barely discernible through a mist of light drizzle. Freda, who once worked as a guide, tells me that Vilnius and some of its suburbs are built on and around an amphitheatre of hills which face onto the rivers Neris and Vilnia. Vilnius, she calls the city; Leah calls it Vilna. Vilnius, Freda says, is beautiful, especially the old city. The rest of the country consists of plains, with few elevations.

"Perhaps that's why some Lithuanians still believe the earth is flat," she says. "They were pagan till the sixteenth century, and worshipped oak trees. I myself prefer *birjoza, sasnai* and *yolke.*"

She gestures towards the forests of birch, pine and fir on both sides of the road.

Leah strokes my arm with one hand, the grey upholstery with the other. "Misha bought this car in Germany," she says. "He travels there to buy cloth."

Misha tells me he used to be a *hittelmacher*, a hatter, and earned about 3000 rubles a month, an average wage. After independence he set up a small workshop for the manufacture of trousers and skirts. Within a few years he could afford to buy a Wartburg for 300 000 rubles, the equivalent of $US2500. He is happy about the change to a capitalist economy.

Freda has reservations. Rent, transport and food prices, among others, have rocketed, and people are feeling insecure about their jobs. Her husband Yuri, an engineer, has had to take early retirement. Her own job has been cut to half time. They had bought their car, a Russian-made Lada, several years ago for 8000 rubles through the Department of Culture for which she works.

"Today we could not afford car. Only Yuri drives. I had accident, broke my nose and now I am nervous."

Freda speaks mostly Yiddish to me, interspersed with a few English sentences. She had studied English literature at the University of Leningrad, but rarely had an opportunity to speak. Contact between us is instantaneous.

"You speak Yiddish like English." She imitates the way I pronounce my o's. "I never heard such Yiddish before."

"And you speak Yiddish like a Cockney," I respond. "*Ich 'ob a 'oot,* I 'ave 'at. Are there no aitches in Russian, no definite or indefinite articles?"

"I 'ave big 'at," she clowns. "Most important, we understand each other. We speak from 'eart."

Leah and Hirshl live in the old quarter of Vilnius. The entrance to their building is through a stone arch which leads into a cobbled courtyard overrun by mangy cats. The odour of catpiss follows us up the wooden steps into a small, dark entrance, where it mingles with a dank, familiar smell. Later I am told that a corner of the entrance had been enclosed to build a toilet. Leah and Hirshl had found it increasingly uncomfortable to use the outdoor latrine in winter.

The front door, barely visible in the murky light, opens into a different world. We walk directly into a tiny, spotlessly clean kitchen, which has two doors. The one on the left leads into a small bedroom; the door on the right takes us into the living room, which is large and high-ceilinged.

"My boys were born in this room, on that couch," Leah says. "Freda was born four years earlier, in 1943, on a kolkhoz in Russia. But they all grew up together, in this room. Aleck, my youngest, now lives in Israel . . . But enough of that. First we eat, then we talk."

The table sags with tureens of borsht, mounds of boiled potatoes, pickled herring, chopped herring, gefilte fish, *perogen* and many other well-remembered dishes. I have returned to the source of

Litvak hospitality.

I marvel at the feast. "I'd been told there were shortages of every kind."

"It's Meishala, my Misha," Leah explains. "He's doing well, and for money you can buy everything."

Misha, a rotund, dark-haired man in his forties, with a merry twinkle in his eye, walks around the table, pouring iced vodka into small glasses. It has to be knocked back in one gulp, he tells me, after the salutation, "*Poyechali!*" – let's go!

"My mother told me Jews don't drink," I say as he fills my glass.

"*Azei gor,*" Leah sighs. Is that so.

Freda whispers that Hirshl had become a heavy drinker during the war, but had never become verbally or physically abusive. He would stagger home from work, lie down on the couch and sleep it off. It had been the central problem in their marriage.

Leah sings a ditty about an unrepentant drunkard who complains, from the grave, that the worst thing about being dead is that he cannot get a drink.

> *Az men't aruf gein oifen bashailem*
> *Vet men zoggen az a pyanitze likt do*
> *Vel ich entferren mit a troierikke shtimme*
> *Az do iz kain branfen nisht do.*
> *Vos hob ich gezindikt mit der mit?*
> *Ich hob getrunken branfen*
> *Un farbissen hob ich nit,*
> *Ich hob getrunken branfen . . .*

Freda translates the song for Yuri. "He comes from St Petersburg," she explains, "and speaks only Russian. Mathematics and chess are his strong points, not languages."

Ernest, Freda's son, whose first languages are Russian and Lithuanian, understands Yiddish because he is close to his grandparents. He learns English at school. Misha and his wife Assa understand, but can barely construct a sentence in Yiddish. Their sons, a nineteen-year-old and a boy of six, know no Yiddish at all.

"I never expected to meet Litvaks who couldn't speak *mamme-loshen*," I say.

"Mother tongue for our generation is Russian," Freda says. "Lithuanian is taught at school, but has been very neglected. Things will change with independence."

"Independence," Leah scoffs. "Who knows what independence will bring? In 1990 a gentile neighbour whom I've known for twenty years and with whom I've always spoken Russian, suddenly turned on me and said, 'Why do you Jews always speak Russian? Why don't you speak Lithuanian?' It was like a knife in my heart. 'The Jews who spoke Lithuanian', I told her, 'are lying in mass graves all over the country.'"

Misha, Freda and Ernest argue with her, in Russian. She dismisses them with a wave of her hand.

"My Lithuanian patriots," she replies, "who know so little about their own past."

Misha changes the subject. "Raizala, *du mein shvester*," he says in fractured Yiddish as he refills my glass. "*Ich trink, du trink*." I am his sister. He drinks, I drink. His wife Assa, a teacher of English at a primary school, speaks English haltingly.

"No practice," she says. She reads and writes with greater ease.

The family groans as Yuri begins a long, welcoming speech in Russian. Rozinchke, he says, our newfound sister . . . He is a short, balding man, with bushy eyebrows and a full, greying moustache. Translate! he constantly urges Freda.

Yuri is also the teller of jokes in the family. From time to time he jumps up, holds up his hand, and announces, "*Anekdot!*" As Freda is a good actress, the jokes lose little in translation.

The rest of the afternoon passes in a haze of Russian vodka and the warmth of my new-found family. The past that might have been my own, is yet to be confronted.

"Raizala," Misha says as he leaves, "say where you want to go and what you want to see. I will take you anywhere."

"Zhager," I reply without hesitation.

"Tomorrow we go to Zhager."

"We haven't had a chance to talk yet," Leah protests.

"The day after tomorrow we go to Zhager," Misha concedes.

I demur. I don't want to disrupt their lives; I had planned to hire a car. Everything's been arranged, Freda assures me. She has taken leave and Misha's son Leonye will mind the workshop. Neither she nor Misha has ever been to Zhager and they are eager to go. Leah and Hirshl insist on coming with us, though Freda fears it will open old wounds.

Hirshl slips away to sleep off the vodka, Yuri and Ernest leave to join a petrol queue in which they may wait for an hour. Freda rejects my offer to wash up.

"Mother wants to speak to you," she says, "when Hirshl is not around. After all these years, there are still sensitive areas in their marriage. His wife and child were massacred in Holocaust, and mother has never got over my father's death."

The living-room, warmed by the grey tile stove in a corner of the room, is now deserted. It is raining, and a hazy light filters through the orange lace curtains of the window that faces onto the courtyard. Leah and I sit on the sofa-bed in which her two sons were born. The table has been cleared and the linoleum-covered floor swept. A glass-fronted cabinet at the far end of the room holds a few ceramic ornaments, an assortment of drinking glasses, and photographs of Leah's grandchildren.

"All my treasures," Leah follows my glance. "Where to begin, Raizala, where to begin? I haven't been back to Zhager since 1946, a year after the war ended. It's nearly 400 kilometres from Vilna, but that's not the reason. I had to live in the present, otherwise I'd have gone mad. No, no. I need to talk. It's buried inside me like a cancer and eats away at me. What do you want to know?"

"Everything. Tell me first about my father's family, particularly about my grandfather Simon. He's always been a taboo subject. And all I know about Freyde is that she had a hard life and beautiful brown eyes. I know even less about her three younger children."

"The Yoffes," Leah says, "like most people in Zhager, were poor. Simon owned a cart and horses and used to drive people to Lettland. He could speak many languages. He knew all the customs officials and organised *propisks* and other papers for his passengers. A *propisk*? Nu. Friedke!" she calls into the kitchen, "what's a *propisk*?"

"She means passport."

"I heard he had another woman," I say.

"Another woman? I was too young to know about such things. But people did say that Freyde had a hard life because Simon had a *lubavitza*. I see you know what that means! Simon was very tall and good-looking. Leibke looked like him. Gershon was shorter."

Leah's family had lived in an apartment above Gershon and Leibke's barbershop, opposite the market-place. The large front room had been used as a knitting workshop, in which her parents, one of her brothers and three apprentices worked.

"When I completed primary school – even the poorest people learned to read, write and do arithmetic – I became an apprentice knitter. Leibke used to treat me like a little sister; he was six years older than me. He told me he was initially drawn to our home by the delicious cooking smells. We were all good cooks. Perhaps you'll have another *latke*, a small one, with cinnamon? No? You eat like a bird.

"I cannot remember a time," she continues, "when I wasn't in love with Leibke. I used to watch him stroll through Naryshkin Park with beautiful girls and I'd weep. I was too young for him. I was short, plump and pretty, and had a thick plait which hung halfway down my back." She points to a large photograph of herself on the wall behind the couch. "Perhaps if I had my hair bobbed I'd look older and Leibke would notice me. I went down to the barbershop and was greeted affectionately by Gershon. Leibke was busy with another customer. 'What can I do for you, Leah'la?' he asked, thinking my mother had sent me down on an errand. I was thirteen at the time. 'I want to have my hair cut, in a bob,' I said, turning very red. Everyone must surely guess why. 'Cut off that beautiful hair!' Gershon exclaimed. 'Go home, you *pisherke.* I'm sure your mother doesn't know what you're up to.'

"I burst into tears and ran upstairs. Leibke pretended not to notice what was happening. Later he came upstairs, as he often did, to have lunch with us. I hid away in the workshop. As he was leaving he sought me out, took my plait into his hand, kissed it, and said, 'Leah, don't change a thing about yourself. I'll wait for you to grow up.'

"We waited a long time. We were married only in June 1941, just before we fled into Russia. But that's another story."

I ask about Leib's political activities.

"I never knew much about that. Leibke had been in the Communist underground, together with my older sister Chana and his younger brother Faivke. All I knew was that they listened to illegal broadcasts from Russia at their secret meetings. They were waiting for the Revolution."

For the Jews, Leah tells me, the war had begun three years before the Germans invaded Lithuania. Hooligans would break windows in Jewish homes, tear out front doors, and scatter them all over the market-place. One day they attacked some young men who worked in the kosher abattoir.

"They never tried that again. The Jewish boys were used to handling large carcasses, and they made mincemeat out of them. But at the next Yahrmark, the annual fair which attracted people from all over the country, a gang of hooligans began throwing stones at the Jews. Everyone thought there'd be a pogrom. When they shouted 'Kill the Jews!', a cousin of mine, Chaim Beitler, his friend Kalmanowitz and a few other lads, stood up to them. My cousin picked up a heavy iron gate that was lying nearby, and threw it at them. The bandits ran away and things settled down for a few months."

Towards the end of 1939, Leah says, just before war broke out, Faivke had been confronted by three or four thugs in the market square. They pushed him around, called him a bloody Jewish Bolshevik, and slapped his face. Leib heard the row from the barbershop and came to Faivke's aid. He was also attacked, and during the ensuing scuffle, he knocked down one of his attackers. The police were called, and gentile witnesses blamed the incident on Leib. Jewish bystanders were ignored. Leib was arrested, charged with assault, and sentenced to two weeks' imprisonment. To humiliate him further, he was also sentenced to sweep the streets. He gave notice of appeal and was allowed out on bail.

"Leibke felt the sentence was unjust," Leah says. "He'd been defending himself and Faivke against hooligans, none of whom were charged. Leibke immediately phoned a gentile *nachailnik* whom he knew from his army days . . . You don't know what a *nachailnik* is? Nu, a *nachailnik* is . . . a *nachailnik!* Friedke!" she calls out. "Raizala doesn't know what a *nachailnik* is."

"Big officer, captain, something like that," Freda says in English. "*Mamme, zi farshteit nisht kein Russish.*" She reminds Leah I don't understand Russian.

"Who's speaking Russian? As I was saying. While Leibke was doing his military service, he made friends with this *nachailnik* who was also a Communist and who afterwards became the *nachailnik* of the jail in a neighbouring town called Akmejan.

"When Leibke explained what had happened, the *nachailnik*, whose name I've forgotten, told him to slip away when it got dark and come to Akmejan. As soon as he arrived, the *nachailnik* phoned the Zhager police. 'I've captured Yoffe,' he told them, 'and I'm prepared to hold him in the Akmejan jail. I know how to handle such people,' he assured them. The Zhager authorities were only too pleased to be rid of Leibke; feelings were running high in the shtetl. The *nachailnik* certainly knew how to handle Leibke. During the day he sat in an office in the Akmejan jail, reading, and at night he slept at the *nachailnik's* house."

Leib's friends devised a way of visiting him without arousing suspicion. They arranged a football match against the Akmejan team, and a few days later a group of Zhager "supporters" arrived in Akmejan with a large hamper of delicacies and drinks for Leib and the *nachailnik*.

"I was with Leibke in the jail from early morning till late afternoon," Leah says. "To show their gratitude, the Zhager team allowed Akmejan to win the match. Or so they claimed."

Aggression against Jewish Lithuanians intensified after the signing of the Nazi–Soviet non-aggression pact late in 1939. In the carving up of Eastern Europe between the Nazis and the Russians, Lithuania was expected to fall to the Soviets. Lithuanian nationalists vented their anger on the Jews. The Jews are Bolsheviks! they shouted as they raged through Zhager, smashing the windows of synagogues, breaking into homes, and beating up people. Jews were afraid to walk in the streets for months afterwards.

"There were very few Jewish Communists in Zhager," Leah tells me, "but the bandits took it out on all the Jews. It's true that Leibke, my sister and their comrades were very happy when their long-awaited Revolution came in 1940, without bloodshed. You should've heard them speak. Life would be safer and more just. There'd be work for everyone, proper schools, better housing, enough food, an end to pogroms. And the Iron Wolf hooligans would be driven back into the forest where they belonged.

"They believed in the Revolution like religious people believe in God. Leibke remained bitter about Gershon till the end. He spent his youth working for the Revolution, he used to say, then discarded his ideals for the gold of Africa. But Gershon had sense, Raizala. I might have been young and uneducated, but any fool could see that things weren't as simple as Leibke and my sister Chana made out. A new life is beginning, they said. Let me tell you what sort of life it was.

"The Russians arrived in Zhager in the middle of the night and set up their headquarters in the building where we lived, and where Leib had his barbershop. They brought with them boxes and boxes of books, pamphlets and other propaganda. Next day the people were summoned to the market square, and an officer announced from the balcony of our apartment – the very balcony from which I used to watch peasants setting up their stalls on market days – that

Zhager was now under Soviet rule. A single tank rolled through the streets of our shtetl. And that was the beginning of the Revolution."

The following day all shops and businesses, owned mostly by Jews, had been placed under the control of young commissars who allowed the owners only to give advice, not to handle money.

"But for most Jews," Leah says, "the coming of the Russians had been a relief. Firstly, the anti-Semitic bandits disappeared from town. We could walk in the streets again without fear. A few rich Jewish families were sent into exile – most of us were poor – together with well-off peasants who were accused of hoarding their produce. The *farbrente* Lithuanian nationalists, the extremists, were also sent to Siberia. Many of them escaped into the forests and they later helped the Germans kill the Jews. All the Jews are Bolsheviks, they ranted. My sister Chana was a Communist, Leibke was a Communist, Faivke was a Communist. But were my mother and father Communists? Was my seven-year-old sister a Communist? And all the others who lie in the mass grave in Naryshkin Park, were they Communists?"

"Don't upset yourself, Mamme." Freda comes out of the kitchen. "It's enough for today. Yuri and Ernest will be here any minute and I can hear Papa moving around in his room. Tomorrow we'll come here after showing Raizala around Vilnius and you can continue with your story."

"I just want to finish," Leah insists, drying her eyes. "You ask what sort of work Leibke was doing after the Revolution? He was a *perevotchik*."

"A translator," Freda says. "You're speaking Russian again, Mamme!"

"Nu. The Russians made him a *perevotchik* because he could speak and read Polish, Russian and Lithuanian. You see, they needed someone to deal with the refugees who were pouring into Lithuania after the Germans invaded Poland. In Zhager there was a camp for Polish students who had escaped from Vilna, which was still under Polish rule in 1939. Leib worked with the refugees for several months, then was transferred to the Voyen Kamat. What's a

Voyen Kamat? You're sure it's not Yiddish? Friedke, explain to Raizala what a Voyen Kamat is."

"Voyen Kamat is where you enlist to become soldier."

"Leibke wasn't in the army yet. He only worked there. His job was to speak to the peasants and write down how much land they had, and how many cattle and horses they owned. Who knows why they needed to know such things." Leah shrugs off my question. "*Ver veist.* He didn't talk much about his work, but I know it was very important. He was always making out lists, lists, and more lists.

"By now he didn't have such heavy family obligations. Shmulke, the youngest, was nearly twenty, and had taken over the barbershop. I taught his sister Bryna to knit, and she was working for the Yudaikin's son. They still lived with Freyde, who was old and sick. Leibke and I took her to a doctor in Shavel. I don't know what sickness she had, but her stomach used to get very swollen. Faivke and his family had moved to Shavel, and Henke eventually married a man from Riga. You heard about her love affair with Tanchel. An old story. Why do you think Leibke and I didn't marry sooner? First I was too young, then he had to look after his family. Gershon had sense. He married and left for Mexico. Not that I blame him, but the whole responsibility for the family did fall on Leibke's shoulders.

"And just when we could've married, the Voyen Kamat was transferred to Shavel, together with Leibke. He found work for me in Shavel in a Jewish knitting factory. I still remember the name: Mercury. He was proud that I adjusted to factory work so well. There's a song that describes how I felt about Leibke.

> *. . . Ich vel gain durch alle gassen*
> *Un vel shrayen, "ves tzu vassen!"*
> *Nor mit dir in einem zein . . .*

> I will walk through all the streets
> Crying "Washing to be done!"
> As long as I can be with you.

"But still we didn't marry. We couldn't find a place to live. I moved in with my pregnant sister Chana, her husband and their child, and Leib lived with Faivke and his family.

"Faivke's only child, a daughter, was a *kastainke*, she had chestnut hair. Like Bryna's. Not a redhead," Leah emphasises; "a *kastainke*. The first thing Leibke wanted to know after Freda was born on the kolkhoz, was the colour of her hair. With death stalking him, I ask you . . .

"Leibke had been in Shavel for about six months and I for five, when the war broke out. Things happened very quickly. Our world came crashing down. The Russians retreated as the Nazis overran Lithuania, and their supporters went into hiding or fled. And Leib's Revolution, for which he had waited all his life, came to a sudden end. It had lasted for just one year.

"So soon?" Leah says when Yuri and Ernest come into the living room. "Raizala, I need a year, not a week, to tell you what I've been through. Come for lunch tomorrow and I'll tell you the rest."

14

Whose Jerusalem?

Rose Zwi

The one remaining synagogue in Vilnius.

Freda and her family live in a housing estate about ten minutes' drive from the city centre. With Yuri at the wheel it seems much longer. He is a tense, over-cautious driver, and for most of the journey, he and Ernest argue heatedly, in Russian. Freda intervenes, and peace is restored by the time Yuri turns off the main road and chugs up a soggy ramp towards several rows of three-storey buildings. Each block is linked to the others by a grassy plot on which leafless trees huddle in clusters.

"*Liepa,*" Freda tells me when I ask the name of the bare trees. Lime. "*Liepa* is also name of month when flowers bloom. Next time come in July when smell of yellow *liepa* flowers makes everyone drunk."

The snow, she explains as we get out of the car, has only just melted, hence the muddy patches on either side of the paved path. She greets unsmiling neighbours cheerfully as we walk towards the apartment.

"Many artists and musicians live here," she says. "Because I'm cultural worker, I got apartment through connections at work. Connections", she adds, "is everything in our country."

"Is it hostility or unhappiness I am seeing in the faces of your neighbours?" I ask Freda. "Even the children look subdued."

"Life is hard this moment," Freda says.

"I know, Freda. But how do you, a Jew, feel about living in Lithuania?"

"All my life I am living here. I am Lithuanian, my friends and colleagues are Lithuanian. They know I am Jewish, I know they are Catholic. I am only Jew at work but it is not bad. I know what you are asking, Raizala. No simple answer," she says, leading me into the building.

Ernest and Yuri stagger in behind us, carrying my suitcase and hand luggage. Take as much as you can, I was advised before I left for Lithuania; they're short of everything.

The entrance to the building has a bleak, bunker-like look. We walk up two flights of rough concrete steps edged by a rusting banister. The walls are unplastered. Ernest opens the door and says, without irony, "Welcome to our beautiful home."

A short passage leads to a dining-room on the right. It is so narrow that it barely accommodates a small table, two stools, a bookcase and the couch that doubles as Ernest's bed. Floor coverings throughout the apartment are either linoleum or worn rugs. The walls and woodwork have not been painted for years.

The second room has just enough space for a double bed, a wardrobe and a chest of drawers. The kitchen is small, the bathroom even smaller, and the toilet is behind the front door, opposite the dining-room. I foresee problems.

Yuri deposits my suitcase in the lounge, which is large, carpeted, and furnished with a sofa-bed, a few armchairs, a small round table and a display cabinet, not unlike the one at Leah's house. A sliding door, curtained in pale orange lace, filters late afternoon light into the room. It opens onto a small cluttered balcony.

"I've been given the best room," I protest, but am talked down in Russian, Yiddish and English: I am their honoured guest and they only wish I had brought my husband and children. There is room for everyone.

"Something to eat, Raizala?" Freda offers. She laughs at my emphatic refusal. "I know. I begin to sound like mother. I get angry when she piles food on my plate. Those years of hunger. She's afraid I'll starve. Do I look starved?"

She does not. She is a five-foot-two-inch bundle of energy, seldom still. Her dark hair falls to her shoulders in a straight cut, with a fringe above her mischievous dark eyes.

Daughters of brothers who had been so similar in looks and character, in culture and world outlook, Freda and I seem worlds apart. We are yet to discover the depths of our connection.

After Yuri leaves for his weekly chess game with a colleague, and Ernest visits friends to show off his presents from the West, Freda and I begin a talking marathon which will continue throughout my stay. We have a lifetime to catch up on and many what-ifs to explore, including, what if Gershon had not left Lithuania in 1927.

"His letters were so warm, so, how do you say it – sympatish. He helped me understand mother. I was small when she married Hirshl and I was very unhappy. She told me always what a hero my father had been, how good-looking, intelligent, how musical. Who could compare? I think not even Leib himself."

"I also idealised him. I even named my oldest son after him," I tell her.

"And Hirshl was simple man. He worked long, hard hours in market to support wife and three children, and drank too much, to forget troubles. But he never shouted. Just came home after work and slept. 'You're not my father!' I told him; 'my father is dead.' He was very hurt. He treated me like daughter, even better than his own sons. But I longed for father. I wrote these things to Gershon. He was very understanding. He said I must not forget my father, but that Hirshl brought me up and was a very good man. Gershon was a tolerant man."

"Until I joined a left-wing Zionist movement and went to Israel at the age of twenty," I said.

"He wrote. He said he understood you wanted to make better world but you would suffer. He wanted to save you suffering."

"Like his father tried to save him," I say. I tell her about Gershon's foray into revolutionary politics while in exile in 1915. "It doesn't work. I suppose you have to make your own mistakes. Have you ever visited Leib's grave in Yelets?"

"No. I used to beg mother. First she had no money, then she had new family. Yelets is very far from Vilnius. There is no direct railway. And when I was older, I had different worries."

Freda had always loved the theatre. She had studied drama and literature at the University of Leningrad for four years, then joined a drama group in the Urals, where she acted and produced plays. Leah had been distraught; this was no life for a decent Jewish girl. Freda defied her for several years, then gave in.

"You know what mothers do. Get sick, weep, shout, make you guilty. When she was taken to hospital, I had to come home. After that life was complicated. Married, divorced, remarried, Ernest was born and I never went to Yelets. Nor did I become actress. Now I'm on stage as cultural worker."

For many years she had been a cultural worker for the Railway Workers' Union. She had produced plays, organised concerts, chaired debates and brought out musicians, singers and other performers from all over the Soviet Union: a dance group from Kazakhstan, a violinist from Leningrad, a ballet company from Moscow. In the last few years she has been doing the same work at the Palace of Culture for the police.

"From my limited brush with police," I say, "a shooting range seems more appropriate than a Palace of Culture."

"We also have very well-equipped gymnasium," she says. "But some police officers also come to concerts and theatre."

The Palace of Culture, she tells me, is open to the general public. People used to flock to performances, but since independence, things had changed. People are out of work, the price of tickets has soared, and they can no longer afford to bring out first-rate performers.

"We must make profit now," she says. "Something new for our country. So now we make dances for older people, discos for young ones, games evenings, and last week we had the full hall for hypnotist. People's culture. We feel insecure. Many colleagues have lost jobs."

Leah had told me, earlier, that Freda is on half-time employment. To make up the shortfall, she has taken on a cleaning job at her Palace of Culture. After each performance or dance, she changes out of her one good dress into overalls, sweeps up, scrubs floors, cleans toilets, and carts away the debris. Yuri, on an inadequate pension, supplements their income by working as a storeman in Misha's workshop.

It is almost 2 a.m. before we get to bed. My dreams are filled with disturbing images: Leah battling through the snow, with Freda, full-grown, on her back; my father, about whom I have not dreamed for years, fleeing from a burning village, calling "Wait for me, wait for me!" I run through a dark wood, stumbling over exposed roots, slipping on fallen leaves.

"Today we will show you Vilnius," Ernest tells me over a break-fast of fatty smoked meat, two kinds of cheese, black rye bread and a tin of Riga sprats, which Yuri bought at the market that morning.

They argue about where to start the tour of Vilnius. The Hill of the Martyrs, Ernest says. He is a Lithuanian patriot. Some of the thirty-seven churches, Freda suggests. Castle Hill, Yuri insists, to get an overall view of the city. As we talk, Ernest watches in bewilderment as I cut the thick layer of fat off the meat on my plate.

"That's the best part!" he exclaims.

"People in hot climates eat differently." Freda kicks him under the table.

"Weird," he says in English.

I wonder if there's a word for cholesterol in Lithuanian or Russian.

Our first stop is at Freda's Palace of Culture, a distinctly unpalatial concrete structure which blends perfectly into the dull grey morning. Ernest and Yuri wait in the car while Freda takes me up to a warren of offices on the second floor where she shares a cubicle with a co-worker.

"From here," she says with a wry smile, "we dispense culture to nation." On the ground floor we look into the large, well-equipped gymnasium where a few young men are working out.

"Everything is culture," she says as she leads me towards the theatre.

She stands centre stage, looking onto the large auditorium, arms outstretched, acknowledging wild applause from the phantom audience.

"I joke," she says as we leave the building, "but it was once my great dream."

From the tower on Castle Hill, we look down at church spires which rise above old, orange-roofed buildings; the cobbled, winding streets of the old city, the wooded hills that surround the city, and the rivers Neris and Vilnia which for centuries protected it from the crusading Knights of the Sword and the Teutonic Order. Below Castle Hill is Gediminas Square, with its tower and cathedral. Freda and Ernest vie in telling me its history.

"... and do you see that street? It's the main street in Vilnius. It's a mile long and it runs from Cathedral Square, which is 600 years old, to Parliament, where we'll take you later. The different occupiers of our country gave it different names: the Tsarists called it Tverskoi, the Poles, Michiewicz. First the Soviets called it Stalin, then renamed it Lenin Prospekt in the 1950s ..."

"And now," Ernest takes over, "it has proper name: Gediminas." Who apparently founded the city in the fourteenth century and made it the capital of the Grand Duchy of Lithuania.

"Every place in Lithuania has at least three names," Freda explains. "Follows history. For example, Zagare in Lithuanian, Zhagory in Russian, Zhager in Yiddish. Vilnius, Wilno, Vilna." The declension of a town, of a city.

Vilnius is beautiful. Vilnius, not Vilna, which no longer exists. As Ernest talks about Vytautus, Gediminas and other Lithuanian heroes, I wonder how much he knows about the history of Vilna, which for centuries had been the religious and cultural centre of Eastern European Jewry, the last of the Jerusalems of the Diaspora after Cordoba and Prague. I doubt whether that is taught in the schools. But he surely knows that Vilna, the Jerusalem of Lithuania since the middle of the seventeenth century, had been destroyed in the early 1940s when 70 000 Jews from the city and the surrounding areas had been slaughtered by the Nazis. They are buried in mass graves outside the city in Ponary, Ponar, Paneriai. A few plaques remain to testify to its former greatness. As we walk around the ramparts of the castle, I wonder in which direction Ponar lies.

Ernest points out the TV tower in the distance, surrounded by blocks of modern buildings, where a fierce brief battle had raged between Lithuanian patriots and the Soviet army just eighteen months ago. I am unmoved by Ernest's fervour; the phrase "Lithuanian patriots" has a chilling ring. Vilnius's beauty is dimmed, suddenly, by a cold drizzle and icy winds that drive us from the tower. The weather clears as we descend towards Gediminas Square.

The cathedral, Freda tells me as we make our way through crowds of worshippers, had been converted into an art gallery under the Soviet regime. The paintings are still hanging on the walls, but the cathedral has now been restored to its original function.

I watch, fascinated, as Freda buys a candle and adds it to the forest of leaping flames. "We need help, from anybody's God," she laughs as she catches my eye. I am relieved, agnostic that I am, that she does not genuflect or cross herself. I understand her pantheistic desire to propitiate the gods. But in this place, in this era? Are those fulminations against the "Christ slayers" that I am hearing from the pulpit?

It is a week before Easter, and as we walk through the streets of Vilnius, we see people with flowers queuing outside the Catholic churches, waiting to slake their deprived thirst for religion.

"Enough churches for today," I find myself saying. "Are there any synagogues left in Vilna?"

The last time I had been in a synagogue was six years before, at the marriage of a nephew. I am surprised, even alarmed, at my request to be taken to one. I'd like to explain to Freda that I am not religious, but wish to seek out those stiff-necked believers, the battered survivors, who never abandoned their God; he abandoned them. But I'm not much good at god-talk, especially in Yiddish, which is neither Freda's first language nor mine. I'd have to say something like, our people were massacred for no reason other than they were Jews. If religion is one of the elements that defines them as Jews, I will put aside my own disbelief and accept them on their own terms, even if they don't extend the same courtesy to me. I am a secular Jew, Freda, who identifies historically and culturally with my people, and feels no less Jewish for it. I say nothing.

As we drive towards the one remaining synagogue in Vilna, Yuri tells me, through Freda, that Napoleon is supposed to have stood before the Great Synagogue of Vilna which had been built in 1572, and said, "Now I understand why Vilnius is regarded as the Jerusalem of Lithuania."

"There's also a story about Napoleon standing before St Anne's church, with its intricate Gothic facade, saying he would like to place it on the palm of his hand and take it back to Paris," Freda adds.

In an effort to slough off a creeping depression, I tell the story about a lesser luminary, the Boer President Paul Kruger, who had been asked to officiate at the opening of the main synagogue in Johannesburg in the early years of the century. "I hereby inaugurate this synagogue in the name of our Lord Jesus Christ," he is supposed to have said. They laugh. I myself find a disturbing resonance in the story.

Unlike the other houses of prayer in present-day Vilnius, no one is queuing outside the one remaining synagogue. The building has a shuttered, abandoned look. Yuri, it seems, has a cousin who goes to shul. He will phone him this evening and ask when services are held. Only by appointment, it seems.

We walk through the narrow cobbled streets of what had been the Jewish ghetto. Gaon Street, I read; Jydu Street. Parts of the ghetto are crumbling, deserted. The rest is being gentrified. Gentilefied. Few Jews live here now. The Lithuanian government, Freda tells me, is in the process of putting up plaques on streets, squares and buildings, commemorating events in the tragic life of the Jews of Vilna. Better the plaques than the people. Until now only two plaques have been put up. She translates the one on the building in Rudiniku Street, which had housed the Judenrat in the ghetto.

On 3 November 1941 over 1200 Jews were sentenced to be exterminated in this courtyard.

The second plaque is on a building in Lydos Street.

On 7 September 1941 over 2000 Jews who were later killed in Paneriai, were rounded up here.

This is only the beginning, Freda says. The government is keen to impress the West and to dissociate itself from the past. But much remains to be done. She tells me about an old Jewish cemetery on the other side of the river which had been dismantled.

"They used headstones for paving and for making steps near a place where I was working. People have refused to walk there, Christians as well as Jews. But so far nothing has been done. A famous non-Jewish Lithuanian poet has said it is disgrace for our nation."

At Ernest's insistence I am taken to see the barricades which had been erected against the Soviet forces outside Parliament building, and then to the spot where crosses have been erected for those killed in the resistance.

By this time I am in a mood for neither Lithuanian patriotism nor the religious fervour which accompanies it. I am not warming to the severe-looking Lithuanians in the streets and in the church queues. I might have responded more warmly to their pagan ancestors who had worshipped oak trees.

I am perturbed by this reaction; I had prided myself on my tolerance. But perhaps too much troubled history lies between us to remain untouched by it.

Gentrifying the old Jewish ghetto, 1993.

15

Invitation to Kaddish

Leah and Hirshl.

Leah is expecting us for lunch. Or is it dinner? What does one call a four-course meal at five in the afternoon? Things will be less frenetic in Leah's apartment today. Misha and his son Leonye are at work, his wife Assa is teaching, and after our tour of Vilnius, Yuri has returned to work. There will be no Russian panegyrics and nothing stronger than mineral water to drink. I still have a lingering, low-grade hangover from yesterday's vodka.

When Hirshl takes his after-dinner nap, and Ernest goes off to visit a friend, Leah and I settle down to talk again.

"Where was I, Raizala?" Leah motions me to the birthing couch.

"You had followed Leib to Shavel where he worked in the Voyen Kamat, but couldn't get married because you didn't have a place to live. Then the war broke out."

"Then the war broke out. *Panika*. Such panic. People didn't know what to do, where to run. The night before we'd had dinner with Faivke and his family. Next day we left Shavel forever. Leibke was given a very big *grusavik* with a driver, and ordered to take all the important *utchotten* from the Voyen Kamat to Moscow. Of course she understands," Leah says when Freda throws up her arms in despair.

"My father," Freda comes to my aid, "was given very large truck with driver. He had to take all important military and other documents to Moscow before Germans entered Shavel."

"On the truck were forty children," Leah continues, "Jewish and Christian children from Lithuania and Latvia. They'd been stranded in a summer camp in Palanga when war broke out, and had been evacuated to Shavel. Don't ask me where their parents were, probably going mad with worry. Leibke was to take them to Riga, to a children's home. He rushed to my sister Chana's house. 'We must leave immediately,' he told her, 'the *grusavik* is waiting outside.' My sister was very upset, very angry. 'How can you desert me at such a time?' she cried. It was true. She was seven months pregnant, she had a six-year-old daughter, and her husband was out of town. 'Come with us,' Leibke pleaded. Chana and Leibke had been in the Party together for years, they were close friends. But she wouldn't leave without her husband and Leibke couldn't wait. The first bombs had already fallen, Shavel was burning, and the Germans were approaching. He had to get the documents out of Shavel. Imagine how I felt, leaving her, at such a time."

A great sob breaks out of her chest. She rejects the suggestion that we talk another time. The sky has darkened again, and sleet is powdering the bare trees in the courtyard. Hirshl joins us in the living room, which has been warmed by the tall, tiled wall stove.

"Hirshl also suffered, very much," Leah says.

He nods. He is eighty-one, a tall man who walks upright, his shoulders back. He takes a photograph out of a drawer. I expect to see his wife and child. It is a photograph of himself in army uniform, holding a horse on either side of him. He names them and draws his thumb over the surface, as though to remove a speck of dust.

"They saw me through the war," he says. "If not for them, I wouldn't be alive. I was in the army when my wife and child were killed, in Zhezmer, by the Lithuanians, not the Germans. Every year Misha takes us to *kaiveroves*, to the mass grave."

"Broken twigs after a storm," Leah says, wiping her eyes. "I can't cry any more. Where did we get the strength to survive? The will to live is strong. Too strong perhaps, so we do selfish things."

Leah heard later that the Jews from Shavel had been rounded up, the younger men and women put to work, the old and the sick shot. During the *Kinderaktion*, her sister Chana's six-year-old daughter, screaming with terror, had been torn from her arms and thrown onto a truck with other children. Chana, heavily pregnant, was beaten back with rifle butts as she tried to reach her daughter. She was sent to a concentration camp near Munich, the name of which Leah cannot remember. For a while her husband was a sanitary worker in the ghetto, then he too was killed.

"Later Chana gave birth to a son. A German nurse suffocated him under a pillow in front of her. How does one survive such horror? But she did. After the war she went to Israel where she eventually remarried and had another family. I went to visit her last year. She died only a few months ago . . .

"Nu. Shavel was being bombed and we had to leave immediately. In addition to the forty children, my cousin Chaim Beitler, his wife and their two children, and Faivke, his wife and child, were also on the truck. There was enough place for the rest of the family, so we drove straight to Zhager.

"In Zhager there was chaos. The Soviets had already retreated, and a Lithuanian *nachailnik* was in charge. My mother was half-crazed with grief. I didn't understand a word she was saying. My father told me that the previous day this *nachailnik* had asked for fifty young Jewish volunteers to train as partisans to fight the Germans. My two brothers, Mottala and Gedalia, were among those who volunteered. They were marched away, taken into the shul and shot. Mottala, who taught me how to knit. Sweet Gedalia . . . Now they lie in an unmarked grave in the old cemetery of Zhager. My mother refused to believe they were dead. She was waiting for them to return and would not leave without them.

"I didn't have proper identity papers, so Leibke insisted we get married. He didn't want to be separated from me. *Ech mir a chasene.* Some wedding. We went to the office and registered. None of our family was present."

She opens a box, riffles through a clutch of yellowing documents, and shows me the wedding certificate. "I can't read the date." She puts on her glasses. "Here, 25 June 1941. We were in Zhager for two days, from 24 June to 26 June.

"Next morning we persuaded my mother to come with us. 'Gedalia and Mottala are safe in the forest,' I lied. 'We'll meet again after the war.' She packed some valuables into a hollowed-out mattress and got onto the truck with my father and little sister. Freyde and her family were already on the truck.

"Yoffe's creating panic!" people shouted as we prepared to leave. Which people, you ask? Jews, gentiles, everyone. Some were jealous because we were leaving, others didn't trust Leib because he was a Communist. The rest didn't want to believe the Nazis were on their doorstep. 'Save yourselves,' Leibke pleaded. 'The Germans will be here within twenty-four hours.' But they wouldn't listen. 'Take no notice of Yoffe. He's creating panic,' they shouted. 'Now that the Soviets have run away, he's bolting too. Nothing will happen, don't run. Remember the Germans from World War I. Everything was *bitte schön* and *danke schön*. They were gentlemen, not like his Bolsheviks.'

"We drove up Taitchsegass towards the border. Other people joined us, on foot, on bicycles, on carts. But the border was closed, the boom was down. The same *nachailnik* who had shot my brothers and the other young men was standing there with his bandits, armed with rifles, and forced everyone to return to the shtetl. Everyone, that is, except me and Leib, the Beitlers and the forty children. Perhaps they were afraid the Russians would return.

"My mother, father and little sister; Freyde, Faivke, his wife and child, Brynke and Shmulke, were forced off the truck. The shouts, the cries . . . I can't begin to describe it. I sat, helpless, between Leibke and the driver. Don't look back, Leibke said. But as the truck started up, I twisted around. My father was carrying my seven-year-old sister Mashinke, who had some childhood sickness. 'Take her!' he shouted. 'At least take her!' The rest of them stood frozen, watching us drive away. 'Don't look back!' Leibke repeated, drawing me close. Don't look back . . . *Vi ken men dos aushalten?* How can one bear it?"

There is a long silence as the day draws in and the light fades behind the orange lace curtains. No one switches on the light. A drawn-out sigh emerges from the corner where Hirshl sits beside the tiled stove. "If I hadn't been in the army, I might have saved my wife and child," he mumbles.

"Riga was burning," Leah says when the silence becomes oppressive. "We had to sleep in a cellar that night. Next day we drove the stranded children to a home on the outskirts of Riga, then delivered the documents to the Party offices. The truck had been giving trouble and the driver said we wouldn't make it to Moscow. The Beitlers took a train into Russia, but Leibke refused to abandon either the truck or the driver."

The truck finally broke down and they took shelter in a forest. After a restless night, they woke to find the driver gone.

"What did we know about engines? Neither of us could drive. There we were, in the middle of a forest, bombs falling all around us, with a useless truck. We were in despair, didn't know what to do next.

But about an hour later, the driver turned up as though nothing had happened. He had gone into town to look for a part, he said. He repaired the truck, then told us he was not taking us to Russia, not even to the border; he was returning to Shavel. Leibke was devastated. He had known the driver for years. As the train was only leaving the following morning, and as it was not safe to wait at the station – the Latvian militia was killing and robbing – the driver took us to a nearby wood, threw our luggage off the truck, and drove away. It was pouring, we were wet, tired and hungry, bombs were falling, and part of the forest was on fire.

"What luggage did we have? A small suitcase with a few photographs, our documents, some clothes, and that mattress into which my mother had packed whatever valuables she possessed. She had left it behind on the truck when she was forced off. After Freda was born, I exchanged these things for a little bread, a cup of milk, an egg . . . My mother saved our lives. We couldn't save hers."

The following morning they pushed their way through a desperate crowd onto the train, and eventually arrived at Skoff, on the border with Russia, where Leib met a group of people he knew. After some discussion, they decided to go to a kolkhoz, a communal settlement, in Yereslav. Leah and another woman travelled on a waggon for one and a half days before they reached the kolkhoz. Leib and his friends had to walk. When the women arrived, they were given bread and milk, and slept on hay in the school building. The men arrived three days later, hungry and exhausted; they had lost their way. The group remained in Yereslav for a month, where they helped bring in the harvest. After spending several months on another kolkhoz, Leib enlisted in the 16th Lithuanian Brigade.

"We had been married for three months when he joined the army," Leah says. "I was pregnant. I never saw him again."

"Mamme," Freda says, "I can hear that wheeze on your chest."

Leah shrugs off Freda's concern. "We are going to Zhager soon and Raizala must know everything. It is forty-six years since I went back to Zhager. Freda was about three years old. Survivors usually returned to their shtetlech in the hope of finding family or friends. I found mine in the grave in Naryshkin Park."

Her cousin Chaim Beitler and his family, however, had survived. They, together with three or four others, had decided to resettle in Zhager. The men had been in the 16th Lithuanian Brigade and had fought in some of the bloodiest battles on the eastern front. Battle-hardened, distraught at the fate of their families, they returned to Zhager determined to avenge their deaths. By then, however, the main criminals had either fled or been sentenced by the Soviet government to long terms of imprisonment. The rest of the townspeople pleaded innocence. They had been appalled by the terrible massacre, they said, but to hide or help a Jew meant instant death.

"Not only didn't they help any Jews," Leah shakes with anger, "pogroms broke out before the Germans reached Zhager. Who killed my brothers, the Nazis or that Lithuanian *nachailnik* and his bandits? They were only too happy to be rid of the Jews. They moved into Jewish homes and took over their possessions even before the graves stopped heaving. They themselves described how the injured had been buried with the dead and how blood had spurted through the earth like fountains. The fire brigade had to be called in from Shavel to wash away the blood in the market square.

"'How can you live here?' I asked my cousin Beitler when I arrived in Zhager in 1946. 'How can you walk on this blood-soaked earth?' 'This is our home,' he answered. 'This is where our families are buried. Our houses have been returned to us by the Russian government, with whom we fought the Nazis. Living here, we'll be a constant reminder of our neighbours' guilt.'

"One of his group, Zlot, even became the mayor of Zhager. As for me, I walked around the shtetl in a daze. I did not want to remain a minute longer than I had to. I went to my home above Leibke's barbershop and knocked on the door. On my own door. The occupiers fell back in fright; they thought I was a ghost. 'Where are my knitting machines?' I demanded. They were so relieved I hadn't come to reclaim my house that they told me immediately. A woman who had worked for us had taken them all.

"I went straight to her house. Don't ask from where I dredged up the strength. I'm not usually so brave. But I was like one possessed. I didn't care what happened to me. The woman nearly fainted when she saw me. She denied she'd taken the machines and shut the door in my face. My cousin then took me to the *nachailnik* who asked if I could identify the machines, by name, or by description. My mind was a blank. The only thing I could remember was that the machine I worked on had a large label with roses, with *Dresden* printed underneath.

"The *nachailnik* went back to the woman's house with me. All our machines were there, crowded into a back room. Among them was the machine with the roses. When he said she must return that machine immediately, she began to cry. She had to finish off a garment on it, she said, and begged to keep it till the next morning. Fool that I am, I agreed. I got the machine back, without the needles or any of the working parts. By now I was exhausted, emotionally and physically. I did not complain to the *nachailnik*. Nor did I go to my cousin Beitler. Heaven knows what he would've done to her or to the machines. I hired a cart, put the machine on it and left Zhager. I've never been back."

Leah joined other survivors in Vilna. Small towns and villages, it was said, were not safe for Jews. For many months she struggled to support herself and Freda, living a solitary existence in a rundown room in the old quarter of Vilna. Mutual friends introduced her to Hirshl.

"Sole survivors of our families, in a strange town, without money or prospects, we decided, after a while, to marry. Hirshl managed to find needles and other parts for my knitting machine and repaired it himself. I started to work immediately. He got a job in the main market in Vilna, and we were seldom short of food again. We found this apartment where we've lived ever since. Our children keep saying we should move to a place with a bathroom and a proper toilet, but we don't feel like moving. We use the public bathhouse or take a tram to Freda's house . . ."

She is interrupted by the shrill ring of the phone. Freda stumbles across the dark room to answer it, while Hirshl gropes for the light switch. The bright glare shocks us into the present. After drawing the curtain, Leah stands at Freda's elbow, listening to the conversation.

"It's Misha," she says.

Freda is making reassuring sounds in Russian. After a series of emphatic da, da's, she puts down the phone.

"Misha can't leave the workshop for a full day until Thursday," she says. "Some cloth has just arrived from Germany and he has to plan production. I told him it didn't matter where we went first. He's got a whole programme drawn up. Trakai, Rasein, Kovno perhaps. And there's so much to see in Vilnius. The university, the folk museum . . ."

"Come for lunch tomorrow," Leah calls after us as we walk down the steps into the courtyard where wild cats are foraging for food and fighting over scraps.

The trams are crowded when Freda and I travel back to her apartment. We sway with the tram's movements, making physical, not eye, contact with the other commuters.

"I forget how much mother has suffered," Freda says. "I am not patient enough. Poor Hirshl. He has always to fight, how do you say it, the myth. Even now, when he is over eighty."

Yuri has news for us on our return. His shul-going relative has told him there will be a service the following morning. Someone is saying Kaddish for his father, and they have managed to raise a *minyan*, a ten-man quorum. We are welcome to come.

An invitation to Kaddish, a prayer of thanksgiving and praise for God which is recited by bereaved mourners. Kaddish should be said every day of the week in Vilna; there are legions of dead to remember. The problem is to raise a ten-man quorum.

Yuri says he will drive us to the shul on his way to work. He goes to bed; he has been up since dawn. Freda, whose sleeping habits have been shaped by her work, shows no sign of flagging; she is a night bird.

I plead exhaustion and am about to go to bed when Ernest brings out an old battered case from which he extracts a trumpet.

"Grandfather Leib's trumpet," he tells me. "When he died in war, his captain sent it to grandmother. She gave it to me. She hopes I will be musician, like grandfather. But I don't play so good. Also, trumpet must be fixed. I think maybe guitar is more easy. How is my English?"

"Good," I say, "considering you never have a chance to practise it on English speakers. Are you taught about definite and indefinite articles at school?"

"Every day. It is big problem for Russian speakers. Teachers have same problem. You will please correct?"

"If it doesn't interfere with our conversation. I am more interested in what you have to say."

He puts away the trumpet and promises to brush up his music repertoire. "You like Russian songs? I will make tape for you. My friend has recorder."

"My mother and father sang Russian and Yiddish songs."

"I will make present for you on grandfather's trumpet."

A night bird like his mother, he goes out to visit friends in the neighbourhood after assuring Freda he has prepared his lessons for the following day. He leaves behind a strong aroma of cigarettes.

"Yes, he smokes," Freda says. "It is my fault. I smoke, his friends smoke. They are only fifteen, sixteen. It is not easy to control him. Only with money. Yuri is very angry. He says I must stop smoking also." She shrugs. "I try, but it is too difficult."

I tell her that in the West people have been alerted to the dangers of smoking. It is banned in hospitals, cinemas and other public places.

"That is freedom? Here I think we have better freedom. We are even free to die from lung cancer."

That night my dreams are again vivid, frightening, and will

remain so, long after I leave Lithuania. I am always running through forests on fire, slipping on leaves, tripping over roots. Blood spurts up from the ground like geysers, horsemen hunt down fugitives. I wake each morning with a pounding heart, exhausted, reluctant to face another day, to hear of more calamities. I begin a countdown: two days gone, five to go.

16

A *Minyan* in Vilna

Interior of Vilna Synagogue, 1992.

The barbarians, miraculously, had not torn down the one remaining synagogue in Vilna. They may have needed it to stable horses. It is an attractive building of classic proportion, with a centre pediment flanked by two square wings. An acanthus-leaf motif runs along the outline of the building. Below the pediment, a large arch forms a portico with three recessed smaller arches, and on either side of the middle arch, two pillars, like giant torches, provide a stately entrance. A Magen David, sculptured in stone, is centred between arch and pediment.

Places of Jewish worship have come a long way from the portable Tabernacle of the desert.

At the highest point of the roof, behind the pediment, are the two Tablets of the Law, with the ten commandments in Hebrew. At the head of the second tablet is the sixth commandment, succinctly expressed: *Lo tirtzach*. Thou shalt not kill.

As we walk up the seven steps to the entrance, we hear chanting. The service is in progress. Freda, Ernest and I walk in quietly and sit on a bench near the door.

A chandelier and a few wall lights have little impact on the dark, musty interior. The Holy Ark, facing Jerusalem, is open, its embroidered velvet curtain drawn aside. The scroll has been carried to the *bima* in the middle of the synagogue where one of the congregants leads the prayers. There is no resident rabbi. The so-called Chief Rabbi travels to Vilna from England twice a year to officiate over the high festivals. The chanting and singing is familiar, but lacks the melodious vigour of the services I used to attend with my grandmother. The plaintive prayers echo through the decaying grandeur of the synagogue, out of tune, out of time, dissolving into the domed, arched and vaulted architecture, before they reach their destination, an empty heaven. The synagogue is filled with an absence. Fifteen kilometres from Vilna the former congregants lie in the mass graves of Ponar.

As I watch the twelve or thirteen men at prayer, their heads covered with skull caps or hats, their prayer shawls wrapped around their shoulders, their arms and foreheads bound with *tefillin*, I marvel at the tenacity of belief which gives the survivors the strength to pray to a god who has visited such calamity upon them. But even I, an agnostic, understand that to abandon Judaism, belief, is to confer victory on those who committed racial and cultural genocide.

"You and I should be sitting upstairs," I whisper to Freda, nodding towards the women's gallery beneath the grand arches.

"No one seems to mind. Except Yaacov, Yuri's relative."

She waves to a man sitting near the Ark. He turns away, frowning. "So holy. Now I remember why we hardly see him. Why are they wearing those funny little leather boxes on their foreheads and arms?"

"Those are *tefillin*." I am jolted into an awareness of the decades of cultural genocide in Eastern Europe. Women of my generation had known little enough about Jewish religious practices. We had been exposed mainly to the household rituals of our mothers, who, in the quaint language of the observant, are called queens of the home, but whose realm ends at the garden gate. Women may not even make up a quorum for prayers; God requires ten men for that. Although some women opted out of religious observance altogether, they had, at least, witnessed brothers or sons laying *tefillin* every morning in the period leading up to their bar mitzvahs, a practice many of them abandoned soon afterwards. Ernest, always eager to impart information, is uncharacteristically quiet. He probably did not pass through this rite of passage.

"The *tefillin*, those little leather boxes, contain prayers and excerpts from the Bible written on strips of parchment." I retrieve a few facts from my vestigial memories of religious rites. "One box is attached to a long strap which is wound around the left arm and points to the heart. The other is worn on the forehead. The idea, I think, is to observe the laws and customs of Judaism with our hearts and our minds."

"These things Soviet education did not teach," Freda confirms.

As the service ends, an elderly man – all the congregants are elderly men – approaches, and asks in Yiddish whether he can be of help to us. He introduces himself as Chaim. He has a long, wrinkled face and heavily-lidded brown eyes. Freda tells him I have come from Australia to visit family and to learn about the Jewish community in Lithuania.

Chaim shrugs. "What is there to know? Once we were a large, vigorous community. Today we live with our ghosts. Most survivors have left, the rest of us struggle on. We're getting on in years, we're weary, sick, and have nowhere to go, nobody to go to, no reason for going. Here, at least, we have a roof over our heads, even it if leaks. That's the whole Torah, told standing on one foot."

"That's not the whole Torah," says a tall, balding man with stern Slavic features whom Freda introduces as Yaacov, Yuri's relative. "You must not be so negative."

"Not that I wish it on you," Chaim says, a malevolent look appearing in his mild brown eyes, "but you and your committee should spend some time at the Jewish dispensary. Not as patients, God forbid, but to observe and speak to the people who stand in queues for hours to see the doctor. Old people, sick people, war veterans on crutches, camp survivors with all sorts of illnesses, widows supporting families, husbands caring for bedridden wives. Try telling them not to be negative."

"Life is hard," Yaacov agrees, "but we do what we can. We don't have enough funds."

"You do what you can," Chaim says, "for yourselves. Last week when I came to collect *matzo* sent to the community from abroad, I was told it had already been distributed. To whom?"

"There were limited supplies," Yaacov says.

Chaim waves dismissively and walks away.

Unlike Yuri, Yaacov speaks Yiddish reasonably well. He sits on committees run by elitist groups, Freda has told me. She and her family feel alienated from Jewish communal affairs.

"And what brings you here?" he asks Freda.

"Who, not what. My cousin. She wanted to see the shul."

"Very impressive," I say. "It reminds me a little of the main synagogue in Johannesburg. There it's also difficult to make up a *minyan*. For different reasons, of course. Most people have moved out of the city into the suburbs."

"As you say, for somewhat different reasons."

"My cousin", Freda tells him coldly, "is working on a book about the destruction of Lithuanian Jewry."

"Not quite," I protest. Freda's elbow digs into my ribs. I do not reduce the scale of my project.

Somewhat mollified, he sits down beside us. "This is a fine synagogue, built in 1903, but it does not compare with the magnificent Great Synagogue of Vilna which was built in 1592. People used to come from all over Europe to Vilna, the Jerusalem of the North, to pray in it. Destroyed, like everything else. Out of 160 synagogues and houses of prayer in Vilna, only this one remains. The hatters, the bakers, the coachmen, every guild and sect, had its own prayer house. You can destroy the buildings, but not the spirit. I understand Chaim's despair, but we must not give up hope. We are a small community, 6000 left out of 222 000. We must remain united, not give comfort to our enemies."

"Who are your enemies, our enemies?" I ask.

He hesitates. "Those who wish even fewer of us had survived."

"So there is anti-Semitism in Lithuania."

"The Lithuanian government claims there's never been anti-Semitism, and that before the Nazi occupation there hadn't been pogroms either. That's not so. Conditions might have been better for Jewish Lithuanians than for Jewish Poles, but there's no doubt that anti-Semitism did and does still exist. One only has to look at the newspapers. The mainstream Lithuanian press has been recycling all the virulent anti-Semitic myths of the past. We have protested against these distortions . . ."

"Very politely," Freda says.

"You have to go about things in a controlled manner, otherwise you create more anti-Semitism. Don't forget that the authorities have renounced the state anti-Semitism of the Soviet regime. We have Jewish schools and other institutions of learning, memorial plaques are being put up throughout Lithuania, cemeteries are being restored . . ."

"Like the Snipiskes Jewish cemetery, where the first burials dated back to 1487?" Freda says.

"That was levelled by the Soviets in 1950 for their Palace of Sport."

"But our government used the headstones for steps and paving and your committee's too afraid to open its mouth and protest."

"A few big mouths would come in useful," Yaacov says. "Join us."

Freda and Yaacov throw off the restraints of Yiddish and continue a heated argument in Russian, surfacing into Yiddish every now and then.

". . . I'm not calling the Lithuanians a nation of Jew-killers," Freda is saying. "I don't believe in collective guilt. That's the brush we're tarred with. Like – all Jews are Communists and all Communists are wicked . . ."

"Is it true," I ask, "that one of the first acts of the independent Lithuanian government has been to rehabilitate ethnic Lithuanians who'd been convicted of war crimes?"

"Yes," Yaacov says, "despite a law passed in May 1990 forbidding such rehabilitation."

"How did the Jewish community react?"

"By submitting affidivats and testifying that war criminals had in fact been rehabilitated. The Procurator-General's response to these affidavits has been narrowly legalistic. Those convicted, he said, had been tried and sentenced by troikas, special Soviet courts in which there had been a 'lack of due process'."

The rehabilitation had been accompanied by a payment of 5000 rubles – an average monthly wage is 350 rubles – and the return of property confiscated by the Soviet government. Confiscated Jewish communal property, however, has not been returned.

"We hope", Yaacov says, "that Lithuania's desire to draw near to the West and to demonstrate that the new Lithuania is democratic, will provide the incentive to clamp down on anti-Semitism."

By now everyone has left the synagogue. Yaacov gathers up the velvet bag which holds his prayer shawl and *tefillin*, and we follow him into the pale sunlight.

"A Jewish newspaper called *Jerusalem in Lithuania* comes out once a month," he tells me. "It's printed in English, Yiddish, Hebrew and Lithuanian. You might find it interesting. Tell Yuri", he turns to Freda, "that even an atheist can make up a *minyan*."

"Intelligent man," Freda concedes as he walks away, "but cold."

We walk along the winding streets of the old city, and through the cobbled courtyards of the Vilnius University. In the university bookshop where I buy a map of Lithuania, we crane our necks to admire the murals on the vaulted ceilings. Freda reads out the names of Lithuanian writers and scholars on wall panels. ". . . Simanas Daukantas, a famous historian . . ."

"My mother's family lived in Daukanta Gatve."

"We'll look for it when we go to Zhager," Freda says.

At Ernest's insistence, we visit the Ethnographic Museum. He leads me through the various halls, reading out the notes on Lithuanian history and prehistory.

"These hills are called Piliakalnis," he says, stopping at a display of photographs of ancient burial mounds from which earthenware, iron implements, weapons, iron necklaces, and armbands have been excavated. For him the mounds represent a heroic age in Lithuania's history. I am reminded of other graves, in other forests.

We walk through rooms with replicas of wooden houses with earthen floors, hand-carved furniture, and country pottery. The idyllic, sanitised past. The women, in national dress, are cooking over open hearths, the men are sharpening farming implements. Soon their sons and daughters will leave hearth and home and move to the towns where the crafts, trades and businesses are in the hands of Jewish, Polish and German minorities.

We enter a hall hung with banners; the era of fervent nationalism. A black and orange banner represents the Lithuanian unions of trade, commerce, industry and the crafts. Another banner promises that if all farmers unite, the country will be strong: *Ukininka Vienybe Tautos Galbyne!* A third banner says it all: *Lietuva Lietuvians!* Lithuania for the Lithuanians. Poles, Germans and Jews who have lived in Lithuania for centuries are not considered Lithuanians. *Lietuva Lietuvians!*

After Ernest makes an entry in Lithuanian in the visitors' book, ending with an approving exclamation mark, I write something like, "What about the minority communities in Lithuania who hauled the country out of the feudal age and who contributed to its culture?"

Half an hour later Freda and Ernest drop me off at the small, booklined flat of just such a contributor, Chatzkelis Lemchenas, a Jewish Lithuanian scholar. I bring him regards from his niece Dora, who lives in Sydney. He is a modest man who says little about his academic achievements and even less about his private life. Only after my return to Australia do I learn that as editor-in-chief of the *Russian–Lithuanian Dictionary*, he and his co-authors had been awarded the 1987 State Prize for outstanding contributions to Lithuanian culture. He is also the compiler of the *Short Russian–Lithuanian Dictionary for Schools*. A graduate of the Vytautas Magnus University in Kovno, Chatzkel Lemchem is recognised in Lithuania and in other countries as an outstanding lexicologist, philologist, translator and teacher. His book, *The Influence of Lithuanian on the Dialect of Lithuanian Jews*, is the only Lithuanian study in the field of Yiddish philology. A substantially revised and enlarged Yiddish-language version of this study, he tells me, is due to appear in volume 3 of *Oksforder Yiddish* within the next few weeks.[16]

When I mention that my family are from Zhager, he tells me that he was born in Popilan, but lived in Zhager for several years after World War I, together with his parents and other members of his family. He subsequently lived and taught in Shavel, Kovno and Wilkomir, where he met his wife Ela, a teacher of German. His parents had been killed in the Zhager massacre of 1941. He, his wife and their two sons, Victor and Azarye, had been incarcerated in the Kovno ghetto in July 1941. During a *Kinderaktion* in March 1944, both children, aged eight and twelve, had been taken from them and despatched to Auschwitz, where they perished in the gas chambers. After the Kovno ghetto was shut down in July 1944, Chatzkel had been transferred to Dachau, where he became prisoner no. 81180. His wife had been sent to Stutthof. Miraculously they both survived and were reunited in 1946.

---

16 *"Darbai ir polekiai."*

His thumbnail sketch of tragedy upon tragedy is related quietly, calmly. Only his eyes glisten behind his glasses. He has lived alone in this small flat since his wife died in 1979. Perhaps his love for the Lithuanian language and his dedication to his work help him transcend his private suffering. At the age of eighty-nine he is still making an important contribution to the culture of his country.

"Lithuania is my home, my country," he says when I ask whether he ever considers emigrating.

When Freda and Ernest call for me later that afternoon, I ask Freda the same question; does she ever consider emigrating?

"Too complicated," she says. "My brother Aleck lives in Israel. He doesn't encourage us They found work but it is hard to settle in. My parents are too old, Yuri will not find job, and what can Russian-speaking cultural workers do in Israel?"

"This is my place," Ernest says. "We have independence. It will be good here."

"What about that banner 'Lithuania for the Lithuanians'?"

"That is history," he says. "I am Lithuanian. I will show them I am Lithuanian. When you are going to Zhager?"

Ernest would like to come with us, but Freda does not want him to miss school. He has to prepare for exams.

"We're going in two days' time," Freda says, "when Misha is free. He is taking us to Rasein tomorrow. We need only half day for that. It is not so far from Vilnius."

"Raseiniai?" Ernest uses Lithuanian names. "It is not interesting. Just small town near Kaunas."

He does not understand why I want to visit a small town to which I have only a tenuous connection, and which, like most other shtetlech in Lithuania, is no doubt *Judenrein*.

"My husband was born in Rasein," I tell him.

"Why did not your husband come with you?"

"He has no wish to return to Lithuania. He was two years old when he left."

At a newspaper kiosk Ernest riffles through newspapers and

magazines and extracts an English edition of *Jerusalem in Lithuania.*

"Yaacov says this will be interesting for you. And I also will begin to read about our community. I am Jewish Lithuanian and maybe I know more about Lithuanian than Jewish. You think so?"

"I think so."

Ernest and I have established contact.

17

Lists

Rasein.

"I don't have to go to Rasein," I tell Misha at dinner that evening. "It's Zhager I need to see."

"I have always wanted to see Rasein," he responds, ladling more borsht and potatoes into my soup bowl, at Leah's behest.

"A remote place to which you have no connection? I don't know if there's even a memorial at which to leave a stone, a flower."

There is no dissuading Misha. "I call for you five-thirty tomorrow morning," he says.

As we are about to leave, Leah draws me into a corner of the room. "Did I tell you that I received three letters from Leib before he died? He never lost hope, you know. He believed in his ideals until the end."

Leib-preserved-in-amber, forever the lover, forever on the side of justice, an image she is unwilling to relinquish. She rejects Shlomo's notion of the defeated, disillusioned man.

Leib had lived his Revolution for only three years, most of them in the army, at a time of heightened patriotism. Exposed to civilian life under Stalin, would he have continued to believe? The only way to retain one's ideals, perhaps, is to die young.

"I remember every word of his last letter," she tells me. "'I lie here near death, yet I want so much to live. The Americans will open a second front and the war will end. We will win. And those who survive will live a happy life.'"

"You told me he was always compiling lists, of peasants' land, cattle and other possessions. Did he ever tell you what these lists were for?"

"I didn't ask. Leib was a *politruk*, a Party worker. He believed he was working in the best interest of the people."

Leib had certainly understood the implication of his lists. Collectivisation and the redistribution of land and wealth, after all, has always been the ideal of revolutionary movements.

"How did he feel about the mass deportations that followed?"

"We seldom talked politics. He thought I was naive. Friedke, you never give me a chance to speak to Raizala," she says when Freda insists on leaving. "Remind me to tell you about the other two letters, Raizala."

It is difficult to fall asleep tonight. Shadows of trees filter through the lace curtains, forming grotesque patterns on the wall, and the north wind soughs and sighs through the bare branches. I switch on the light and try to read. *The Destruction of the European Jews* is hardly bed-time literature. Neither is *The Einsatzgruppen Reports*. My travel guides, I told Freda when she asked what I was reading.

Twelve-fifteen. It is quiet in the apartment. Even Freda and Ernest, the night birds, are asleep. Only I lie awake in the dark, watching shadows on the wall. After all these years I shall soon be walking through the cobbled streets of what was once a shtetl, past the low wooden houses where our forebears had lived, imagining their lives, imagining their deaths. But why Rasein, a small town to which I have only a tenuous connection? Could I be propitiating the living, this time?

When my husband and I were living in Israel in 1949, we met his cousins Mordecai and Tova who had spent the war years in Ustlokchin, a small village in the frozen wastes of northern Russia. Their mother and my father-in-law had been siblings. She had married into the Perlov family which owned timber and flour mills in Rasein. When large numbers of friends and relatives had emigrated in the 1920s, the Perlovs stayed on; they lived well enough in Lithuania.

After the Soviet Union annexed Lithuania in June 1940, the Perlovs' possessions had been expropriated. Mordecai's father and uncle and their families were evicted from home and business, and their bookkeeper had been put in charge of the mill. Mordecai's family moved into the small house of his maternal grandparents, and for almost a year they waited in fear for the dreaded knock on the door.

It came on the night of 15 June 1941. They were given one hour to pack before they were taken to the railway station where the time-honoured cattle trucks awaited them. All along the way they picked up thousands of Jews and gentiles – the wealthy, the intelligentsia, the nationalists and other opponents of the Soviet regime. In the two months it took to reach their destination in northern Russia, many people died in the crowded, insanitary box cars.

Only the young and the strong survived the years in exile. There had been one source of work, logging, and only those who worked were entitled to rations. Mordecai's parents died from cold and starvation during their first winter in Ustlokchin. The fourteen-year-old Mordecai and his younger brother Jankel had had to dig a grave for them in the frozen ground. After five years in exile, Mordecai and his sister Tova made a hazardous escape, and arrived in Israel, via

Cyprus, in 1948. Jankel remained in Ustlokchin with members of his uncle's family. Successfully declassed and deracinated, he eventually married a woman from the Komi nation, with whom he had eleven children. When the siblings were reunited fifty years later, they did not even have a language in common; they were strangers.

Until Mordecai told us his story, we had never heard a first-hand account of the horrors of exile in the Soviet Union. Previous, and indeed ongoing, reports had been dismissed as anti-Communist propaganda. Mordecai's story had moved and confused us; it is disconcerting to have one's beliefs challenged in such a convincing manner. It was also the first time we had met anyone who considered the Soviet regime as evil as the Nazis'.

"If you hadn't been sent into exile," I had the temerity to say, "you'd have been massacred by the Nazis."

"The Bolsheviks did not intend us to survive either," Mordecai said.

Disillusion with the Soviet Union had been a slow, painful process for those who had hoped for a new and better society.

What must I look for in Rasein, I had written to Mordecai a few weeks before I left for Lithuania. The mill, he replied, stands at the entrance to the town.

I seem scarcely to have fallen asleep when Freda knocks on the door. "Misha's here. It's five-thirty."

Freda sits in front with Misha. "Wake me when it gets light," I say, dozing off on the back seat, exhausted after my restless night. They talk softly, waking me only at a misted lake on the banks of which they had spent many summer holidays. The next time I am woken is on the turn-off to the Ninth Fort, outside Kovno.

The Ninth Fort was the last of the fortresses built by the Russian Tsars to protect the city of Kaunas, Kovno. During Lithuanian independence, between 1922 and 1940, the Lithuanians had imprisoned Communists in its dark, damp cells. Later, the Soviet regime had used it to jail Lithuanian nationalists. Finally the Nazis had tortured and massacred 100000 people there, 70000 of them Jews.

They had called it Schlachtfeld, killing field. The Gestapo, with even finer precision, had named it Vernichtungstell Kauen, the Kovno extermination site. It had served as the slaughterhouse for Jews from Kovno, France, Austria, Holland and Belgium.

Our visit is brief. We walk up the wide, paved avenue that leads to the memorial at the top of the rise: three enormous sculptures of truncated tree trunks, half uprooted, leaning at different angles to one another, dwarfing the natural trees in the landscape. The museum is not yet open. Freda had been on a tour of the fort some years ago. Her guide, she tells me, had been a gentile Lithuanian woman who said she worked at the fort to help keep alive the memory of the terrible fate of Lithuanian Jewry, in which her people had played no small part.

By the time we return to the car, we are numbed by the horror of the place, and the icy wind which blows around it. We reject Misha's offer to drive through the city of Kovno. It is sufficient that we have been to the Vernichtungstell of its Jewish inhabitants.

Forty-five minutes out of Kovno there is a large road sign: *Raseiniai*. We have arrived at our destination. Misha drives slowly through the narrow side streets, avoiding the muddy shoulders, in a vain search for the mill. Nor do we find any low wooden houses and cobbled streets. Cottage-style houses with sloping tiled roofs, surrounded by bare young trees, line the streets. Occasionally an old wooden house, in a state of disrepair, is glimpsed down a narrow lane.

There are few people in the streets. Misha asks a woman carrying a large bottle of milk where we can find the mill. She was born after the war, she replies, and has never seen the mill. She knows an old woman who may remember the old days. She gets into the car and directs us to a dilapidated wooden house where an elderly, toothless woman in gum-boots is tinkering about in her muddy yard. Our guide explains what we are looking for. The old woman frowns, nods her head, and begins giving directions. Two younger women and a little girl come out of the house. The old mill, they tell Freda, no longer exists. It was destroyed by bombs, together with most of the town, at the beginning of World War II.

Misha asks a question in which I recognise the word *Zyde*. One Jew returned to Rasein after the war, the old woman says, but he left town many years ago. My mother is a little confused, one of the younger women tells Misha. He has retired and isn't seen much these days. She can take us to the apartment house where he lives.

We take leave of the woman with the milk bottle. Our new guide seems stern at first, but warms to Freda's lively chatter. She is smiling by the time we arrive at a large apartment block in a quiet street. She knocks on the door of a ground-floor flat, and once again I hear the word *Zyde*. The one Jew in town does not require a name. She leads us up to the third floor, and rings the bell. When a tall, refined-looking man with grey hair opens the door, she bids us farewell, refuses a lift home, and leaves.

"Avram Lazarsky," the *Zyde* introduces himself after Freda explains the nature of our visit. We had not intended to barge in on him, she says. We had not even been aware that there were any Jews in Rasein. He brushes aside her protestations. "It is not often that someone knocks at my door," he says in Yiddish. "You are very welcome."

We follow him into his small, simply furnished apartment. Freda and I sit on the couch. He and Misha sit opposite us at a table on which there is a neat pile of newspapers, a container with pens and pencils, and an ashtray.

"Do you smoke?" Freda eyes the ashtray hopefully.

He offers Freda and Misha a cigarette, but does not take one himself. He is trying to cut down, he says. Everything about him seems controlled, orderly, contained.

There are many framed photographs in the room, some on top of a glass-fronted cabinet which is stacked with books, the rest on the walls.

"As you see," he gestures towards the photographs, "I am surrounded by family. Those two young women are my daughters with their husbands. One is married to a Jew, the other to a gentile. They both live in Vilna. That", he points to a photograph of an attractive young woman holding a beautiful blond child, "is my older daughter at the age of five, with my ex-wife. And these", he points to a sepia-tinted photograph of two young women in cloche hats, "are my sisters. They were murdered by the Lithuanian auxiliaries in 1941, together with the rest of my family."

"How did you manage to survive?" Freda asks.

"*Ich bin arausgekrochen fun groob,*" he says. I crawled out of the pit. His eyelids redden.

"My husband's family is from Rasein," I say, looking at a photograph of the shtetl which hangs behind the couch. "They had a similar photograph."

We exchange names. He gives those of people from England who have come to visit the graves of their forebears. I know none of

Avram Lazarsky.

Sharon Zwi

them. I name my husband's family and their friends. He knows them all. He had been fifteen or sixteen when most of them had emigrated in the mid-1920s.

"The lucky ones who got away," he says without bitterness. "The rest were deported or slaughtered."

"Does the Perlov mill still exist?" I ask. "We drove around looking for it."

"Gone. Rasein was bombed on the first day of the war, on 22 June 1941. The town was destroyed. Your family would not recognise it now. It has been rebuilt. Only a few old houses remain."

I ask whether he would be willing to speak about his experiences. He shrugs. It sometimes helps to speak, he says.

Before the Holocaust, he tells us, there had been 2000 Jews in Rasein. Alerted by refugees from Poland, many had tried, unsuccessfully, to escape into Russia. Others sought refuge in the villages surrounding the town. Most were unable to escape.

"The local population attacked the Jews before the Germans arrived," he says. "The bandits entered houses, took what they wanted, beat up the men, raped the women. There was complete chaos in the town. People in the countryside were different. If not for them, I and the others who managed to escape would never have survived. It was the townspeople who fell upon us. We hardly saw the Germans. The Lithuanian militia ruled Rasein. It was they who carried out the murders."

The usual decrees had been issued: Jews were not allowed to walk on pavements, to come in contact with non-Jews, or buy food in the markets and the villages. At first they had to wear a white patch on the back and front of their outer clothing. Later they wore a yellow star. Bread was rationed, but Jews had to wait until the gentiles had claimed their rations, and often missed out on their share. The Jews had to clear the debris of the bombed buildings, and knock down walls that were still standing. The Lithuanian militia took pleasure in humiliating prominent members of the Jewish community. They had cut off or pulled out the men's beards, including that of the

Rabbi of Rasein. Doctors and teachers became special targets for torture. Many young women had been kidnapped and raped. Others, accused of being Communists, were arrested, and never seen again. He does not talk about the specific fate of his family, but glances from time to time at the photograph of his sisters.

All men between the ages of sixteen and forty-five, together with physically fit young women, had been imprisoned in a camp. The old people and women with children had been moved into a few houses in Nimokesht Street. They were forced to run and crawl, and to sing while they were being whipped. Later they were inspanned to wagons filled with bricks and stones, and made to haul them while being beaten.

"A group of 300 men, of whom I was one, were driven 7 kilometres out of town by the Lithuanian militia, and given shovels to dig a deep pit. We were stripped of all our clothes and personal possessions, and made to stand at the edge of the pit. Seconds before they fired, I fell into the grave. For hours I lay among the slain and the dying, drowning in their blood, listening to their groans, waiting for nightfall. By then the Lithuanian militiamen, stupefied by drink, lay snoring near the graveside. Another man and I worked our way out of the grave. We went off in different directions."

He dries his eyes and is silent for a while. "What can I tell you? I arrived in a village, naked, and the peasants clothed me and hid me. I spent my first winter in that village. Over the next three or four years, I lived in thirty-three different houses, hidden by poor people who didn't have much to give, but shared what they had. The peasants, as I told you, were different from the townspeople."

From an article on Rasein in *Yahadut Lite*,[17] I am later able to fill in the details of Avram Lazarsky's story. After the murder of the 300 men (298 as it turned out), the Lithuanian guards had returned to town, drunk and boisterous. They announced that they had taken the men to a place out of town to work, and they had come to fetch

17 *Yahadut Lite* (Hebrew), pp. 283–5.

money and additional clothing for them. Their wives and mothers immediately prepared special parcels, and handed them over to the Lithuanian guards.

A few days later, a Christian woman reported that she had seen freshly dug graves near a village 6 kilometres south-west of Rasein. At the same time, a Jewish tailor named Klamin was called to the Lithuanian commandant of the camp, and asked to restyle a man's suit to his measurements. The tailor recognised the suit as one he had made for his brother. He had been among the 300 men taken away.

After the truth was revealed, the Lithuanian guards openly boasted about the murders. They told how Jews from Zitkovan, Namokest and Shidlava had been killed at the same site and how the Rabbi of Zitkovan had cursed them, saying that God would avenge the spilt blood of the Jews. They laughed about the woman who had paid them to shoot her first so that she would not be buried alive. The old Rabbi of Rasein, Aharon Shmuel Katz, together with the doctor, teachers and other dignitaries of the community, had to dig their own graves. "They are doing some real work for a change," the Lithuanian guards had laughed.

As more and more people were massacred in the killing fields, the camp with the young people emptied out. Those who remained were transferred to Nimokesht Street, where they eventually met the same fate.

Between July and September 1941, 1677 Jews had been murdered. The mass grave is near Klanous, 2 kilometres west of the village of Kalnoi, which is 6 kilometres south-west of Rasein.

"None of my family survived," Avram says. "After the war I returned to Rasein – where else could I go? I got a job running a large cooperative. Then I married a Christian woman." He points behind him to the photograph of the woman with the blond child. "I had two daughters with her. Both are educated women. One is an engineer. My wife has left me. She is living in Kovno." He takes a deep breath, unable to continue.

Freda writes down her phone number and address, and invites

him to visit when he comes to Vilna. I too exchange addresses with him. He insists on making tea.

"What happened to the Perlovs?" he asks. I tell their story. "Bitter enough," he says. "But at least many of those sent into exile survived."

Avram Lazarsky has a right to say this, not I.

We take our leave of Avram, promising to keep in touch. We do not talk much on the way back to Vilnius. Misha reaches for a tape, but changes his mind. Nothing less than Kol Nidrei will do.

"Tomorrow," Misha breaks the silence, "we'll take a break. We'll drive out to a beautiful place, Trakai, where there's a medieval castle in the middle of the lake. You have to walk over a very long wooden bridge to reach it. And afterwards, we'll eat *kibinai* in a Karaite restaurant. We'll take Ernest with us. He loves *kibinai*. *Kibinai?* It's something like the *perogen* your mother probably made, a kind of meat pie, only much, much better."

"And in the evening I have booked for *Nutcracker Suite* at Opera House," Freda says. "We need strength for our visit to Zhager next day."

On the outskirts of Rasein where we had looked in vain for the Perlov mill, there is a sign *Raseiniai*, cancelled out by a red diagonal line.

"That's our way of saying, you are now leaving Raseiniai," Freda says. "No more Raseiniai."

"No more Rasein, you mean," says Misha.

I take a photograph of the sign. Mordecai will understand what that means.

18

Karaites and Khazars

Bridge over the natural moat in Trakai, 1992.

Photographer unknown

Our visit to Trakai provides a welcome if temporary diversion from the preoccupations that brought me to Lithuania. Ernest is our guide. He has been to Trakai often, as a student with his history class, and on summer excursions with family or friends. Freda, Misha, his wife Assa and I follow him across the long wooden bridge that connects the fortress to the mainland. The lake, a natural moat, had kept the Teutonic Knights at bay for centuries, Ernest tells us.

We enter the fortress with ease the Teutonic Knights would have killed for. As we walk through the draughty halls of the fortress, examining the martial artefacts of his Lithuanian heroes, Ernest tells me that Lithuania had once been a sparsely populated region of forests, lakes and rivers. By the fourteenth century, the Gediminian dynasty had become the leading military power in Europe, with an empire stretching from the Baltic Sea to the Black Sea, including Byelorussia and parts of the Ukraine.

"Gediminas was smart," Ernest says.

He was smart, according to Ernest, because he had gained great swathes of territory not by war, but by strengthening his ties with Russia through a series of political marriages. His daughter had been married off to the Duke of Tver; one son married the sole inheriting Duchess of Vitebsk; another the Duchess of Volynia, whose dowry included part of that state. In time, Gediminas's influence had reached as far as Smolensk, Pskov and Kiev.

"Russian geography", I tell him, "isn't my strong point."

"I will show you map," Ernest promises.

"Gediminas was certainly a strong man," I say. "Imagine wearing that armour, lifting that sword."

"Smart and strong," Ernest agrees. "Gediminas had capital in Vilnius and ruled from 1316 to 1341. He was Grand Duke. More important than other dukes. And grandson Vytautas is Great because in 1399 he defeated Tartars, and in battle of Grunwald in 1410, he defeated Teutonic Order, at last."

Ernest leads me through the internecine struggles between the descendants of the Grand Duke Gediminas. He loses me in the intricacies of the begats: Gediminas begat Algirdas and Kestutis, who begat Jogaila and Vytautas, who begat . . . Throughout this catalogue of begats runs the Order's unrelenting efforts to de-paganise – or colonise – Lithuania. After their defeat by the combined Lithuanian–Polish army under Vytautas's command, the Teutonic Knights beat their swords into ploughshares, and tilled the land whose people they had decimated.

Vytautas and Jogaila, after many power conflicts, were eventually reconciled. Jogaila was offered the Polish throne on condition that he agree to baptism, and marriage to the eleven-year-old Queen Jadwaga. He also undertook mass baptism of the Lithuanians. Vytautas, though baptised, was suspected of remaining pagan. He became the Grand Duke of Lithuania, and a close alliance had been established between Poland and Lithuania, leading eventually to complete union between the two countries.

This was not a good thing, according to Ernest, because the Lithuanian nobility gradually became Polonised, and Lithuania lost sense of itself as a nation. The nobles spent little time on their estates, depriving the peasants of an ethnic leadership. By 1795, however, most of Lithuania was ruled by Russia and the country had lost its independence completely.

"It was big mix," Ernest explains. "Landowners are Polish; peasants, Lithuanian; bureaucracy, Russian. That is why there is different name for same place. Like, Zagare, Lithuanian; Zhagory, Russian; Zhager, Yiddish."

"When did the Jews come to Lithuania? And where did they come from?"

Ernest does not know. Neither, at the time, do I. I learn later that they had come to Lithuania in two waves, the first from the south, the second, a century later, from the west. The migrants from the south had been drawn from major Jewish communities which, since ancient times, had lived in Babylonia, Persia, Bukhara and other Near East countries. Over the centuries, waves of conquerors had swept over these countries, among them the Khazars, a Turkic people. The Khazars had ruled over a vast territory on the Russian continent, and had been a balancing power between the Caliphate of Baghdad and Byzantium. Fierce warriors, they had been largely responsible for blocking the expansion of Islam into Eastern Europe.

What makes the Khazars unique, in the context of Jewish history, is that in about 740 C.E., their ruler (Khagan) Bulan, his court, and a substantial portion of the people, converted to Judaism. Little is known of the circumstances of the conversion. Historians and writers have offered disparate explanations for this and for the extent of Khazar influence on Jewish history. The Khazars' commitment to Judaism, however, seems to have been sincere. It was certainly enduring. Khazaria remained a country of Jewish dominion from the middle of the eighth century to the middle of the thirteenth century. Those who did not convert, remained Christian, Moslem and pagan.

Khazars and Jews: an intriguing combination. The little we know about the Khazars comes from Byzantine and Arabic sources, which describe a fairly complex civilisation. But not a line of the Khazar language has come down to us. Nor have any inscriptions so far been found. It is only single words, mostly proper names in Greek texts, that suggest they spoke a Turkic language.[18] The Jews, on the other hand, are defined by the Word, the Book.

Weakened by depredations on the kingdom from Viking–Russian raiders in the latter part of the tenth century, Khazaria was eventually overrun by Genghis Khan's horde in 1250. The Khazarians spread into the surrounding Slavic lands. As the conquering Lithuanian armies, under Vytautas's command, swathed a path through these countries in the fourteenth century, they came upon settlements of Khazarian Jews. Because of the Khazars' reputation as intrepid warriors – conversion to Judaism does not seem to have diminished their martial proclivities – they were invited to settle in border outposts in Lithuania, to fend off the Teutonic Order.

Fierce Jewish warriors protecting half-pagan, half-Catholic Lithuania from zealous Teutonic Crusaders: an image sufficiently bizarre to elicit an ironic shrug from latter-day Litvaks.

After the demise of the Khazar empire, significant Jewish immigration into eastern Europe from the south gradually ceased. During the fifteenth century, immigration came mainly from the west. Bohemia, Hungary, Silesia, Spain, Portugal, Italy and the

---

18 *Encyclopaedia Britannica*, vol. 13, p. 362.

Czech areas were either persecuting their Jews or expelling them. The Jews fled east, where they were welcomed for their skills.

In Lithuania, as in other countries in Eastern Europe, south and west met and intermingled, enlarging the Jewish gene pool, and creating what is known as Lithuanian Jewry. Thanks partly to Vytautas, therefore, an individual of Litvak origin is likely to have ancestors from all these communities.[19]

Vytautas also encouraged artisans, merchants and traders from all over his empire to settle in Lithuania. Russians, Tartars, Germans, among others, responded to the call. They were given charters which provided for tax exemptions, freedom of worship, and religious tolerance. Farmers were given land.

The Jews were granted their first charter in 1388, placing them under the protection of the Grand Dukes of Lithuania. The charter made provision for the Jews' personal and religious security, exempted synagogues and Jewish cemeteries from taxation, allowed them to live wherever they pleased, and even granted them the right to own land, which most other countries had not done at the time. It assured freedom of transit, permitted Jews to trade freely, and to work as artisans and craftsmen. The blood libel was proscribed, and the bearing of false witness punished. The testimony of a Christian, for example, had to be corroborated by a Jewish witness. Fines could also be imposed for a range of anti-Semitic actions such as throwing stones at synagogues, cemeteries, houses or other Jewish-owned property. If a gentile killed a Jew, his property and possessions could be confiscated.[20]

Despite periodic infringements of its ordinances, the charter formed the basis of the social, political, economic and legal life of the Jews of Lithuania from the fourteenth century until the disintegration of the Commonwealth in the eighteenth century.

Ernest may yet discover additional reasons for admiring Vytautas.

---

19 Schoenburg, *Lithuanian Jewish Communities*, p.8.
20 Greenbaum, *The Jews of Lithuania*, p. 8.

After our visit to the Trakai Fortress, we walk along the windy road towards the Karaite restaurant where we are to lunch. All Freda knows about the Karaites is that they are somehow connected with the Jews, and that they always have three windows along the front of their houses. She does not know when they came to Lithuania.

"Until recently," I tell her, "I even confused Karaites with Khazars. All I knew was that one of them had converted to Judaism and the other had broken away from Judaism."

I am later to learn that when Vytautas defeated the Tartars in 1392, a number of Karaite families had been among the Tartar prisoners brought to Lithuania from the Crimea. They settled mostly in Trakai where, for many centuries, they lived side by side with the Jews. Vytautas had called them Judaei Troceuses, the Jews of Troki.[21] Although they held many beliefs in common, and sent their sons to study with renowned rabbis in France and Turkey together with the sons of the "Rabbanites", as they called mainstream Jews, they did not consider themselves Jews. They even requested, and received, their own charter.

Karaism had its origins in Persia.[22] It began as a revolt against rabbinic Judaism in the eighth century and was not fully put down until the fifteenth century. From its earliest beginnings, it spread throughout the Jewish diaspora into every stratum of society. "Karaism" derives from the Hebrew word *karah*, to read; to read Scripture without the intervention of the rabbis. They rejected the Talmud as a conspiracy of the rabbis to separate ordinary people from the simplicity of the Five Books of Moses. For them the Torah was the sole source of religious law. When "modern" life conflicted with outdated laws, Karaite scholars created oral laws which differed from those of the "Rabbanites". Many Talmudic dietary laws, for example, were abolished, and the wearing of *tefillin*, phylacteries, was abandoned.

---

21 Greenbaum, *The Jews of Lithuania*, p. 8.
22 Dimont, *Jews, God and History*, p. 205.

There are many parallels between the sixteenth-century Protestant revolt and that of the Karaites. The main difference is that the Jewish rabbis managed to prevent a final schism in Judaism. Threatened by its spread, some of the finest rabbinic scholars set out to refute it, co-opting many acceptable Karaite ideas and reforming abuses. The Karaite revolt gradually dissipated, but it took almost seven hundred years before Karaism ceased to be a threat to conventional Judaism.[23]

But as we enter the restaurant, a two-storey building with a pitched roof and decorative log exterior, the history of the Karaites is as yet unknown to me. Spicy aromas float out from the wood-panelled interior. A dark-haired woman shows us to a table. The chef, her husband perhaps, makes a brief appearance from behind a wooden partition, then withdraws to his domain. Flushed with warmth and vodka, a group of Swedish tourists raise their glasses and say something to us in Swedish. We respond in Russian and English.

Misha orders various dishes: *chinaiki*, a potato and meat stew served in little ceramic pots, and *kibinai*, the famous Karaite meat pie. Soon we are as merry as the Swedes, whose drinking prowess impresses even Misha.

"In the seventeenth century," Freda says, "the Swedes came to Lithuania as unwelcome conquerors. Now they are honoured guests. You see, Raizala, time heals everything."

"You mean people forget or never know what happened. I'm all in favour of healing, but you have to know what the injury is."

"To the present!" Misha cries, lifting his glass. "*Poyechali!*"

"To the present!" we echo.

The afternoon melts away in a haze of warmth and good humour, which owes as much to the food and drink as to our delight in one another's company. Karaite food, unlike Leah's, does not resonate with memories of the past.

---

23 Dimont, *Jews, God and History*, p. 205.

Freda holds out a restraining hand, mimicking Yuri's call for silence. *"Anekdot!"* she says, straddling three languages with dexterity as she tells one joke after another. It is with reluctance that we eventually leave the restaurant; we must return to Vilnius in time for the ballet. Freda compliments the restaurant owner on the *kibinai*, and asks for the recipe. "Don't bother to cook," the woman takes up Freda's jocular tone. "Vilnius is close to Trakai. Come here to eat it."

Karaite separatism, I am later to discover, had spared the community from the Holocaust. Karaites, the Germans decided, had a non-Jewish "racial psychology". To confirm this theory, they had questioned three eminent Jewish scholars about the community's origins. To save the Karaites, all three had ruled that they were definitely not of Jewish origin. The Jewish experts perished in the Holocaust; the Karaites survived.

The Karaites, however, had not returned the favour. In some instances they had denounced Jews who posed as Karaites. They also provided German and Lithuanian authorities with community membership lists against which to check Jewish identity.[24]

Would it have made any difference to our afternoon in the Karaite restaurant had I known this? I cannot say. I might have decided that this was a new generation of Karaites (or Germans, or Lithuanians, or whoever) who were not responsible for the sins of their fathers. Or the food might have stuck in my throat. They may not even be aware of their own history, which does not mean they are free of culture-based prejudice. Ingrown prejudice, I am learning, is more enduring than history.

---

24 Greenbaum, *The Jews of Lithuania*, p. 159.

19

The Road to Zhager

Rose Zwi

Leib's widow, Leah, at the mass grave in Zhager, 1992.

We leave for Zhager at eight-thirty the following morning, three hours later than planned. Misha has had to issue cloth for the day's manufacture. He insists I travel in front with him; you'll see better, he says. Freda sits in the back between Hirshl and Leah. To start with, I see only leaden skies and the sleet which falls gently across the windscreen, dissolving on impact. The wipers are not working and

Misha does not have the necessary tools with which to repair them.

"Don't worry," he says cheerfully. "There's not much traffic on the road."

Within twenty minutes we are on the dual-carriage highway, travelling north. Built only five years ago, it is already showing cracks. Out of the mist, a road sign appears: *Ryga/Talinas*. Latvia and Estonia lie ahead.

The car is overheated. Misha turns down the heat and inserts a tape into the player. He hums and beats time on the steering wheel. Freda accompanies the singer in a deep, husky voice.

"You have a better voice than the singer," I say. "You should be on the stage."

"*Nor dos hot ir gefelt*," Leah responds tetchily. That's all she's short of. I remember, belatedly, her opposition to Freda's acting ambitions.

"Don't pour salt on my heart," Freda sings. The stirring Russian melody deserves less banal lyrics.

"There, to the left," Hirshl says as we leave the environs of Vilnius, "that's where my shtetl Zhezmer is. Was. You can't see it from the road. *Dort hot mein umglick getroffen*. That's where my tragedy happened."

Freda comforts him, kisses his cheek.

The countryside is flat. We pass clusters of thatched farm houses with sloping roofs, surrounded by fields of new wheat. Between them lie birch, pine and fir copses, remnants of ancient forests.

"*Birjoza*." Freda points to a copse of birches, their chalky trunks encircled by dark rings. "There are wonderful songs about *birjoza*. And those are *sasnai*. Pines, you say? We paint their cones at Christmas. And how do you call these trees? Firs. *Yolke*. And in spring *gandras* come to make nests on high roofs. Yes, storks. But we do not like that bird." She points to a crow standing on the branch of a leafless tree. She shudders. "It brings bad luck."

"At the moment, truck drivers seem to be their main victims," I say.

All along the verges of the highway, drivers hunch over the bonnets of their trucks, tinkering with stalled engines.

"It is very difficult to get proper tools and spare parts," Misha explains. "I'll stop at the next truck and ask if he's got the right-sized spanner to lend me."

Misha is in luck. He borrows a spanner, repairs the wipers, and returns to the car, shaking the sleet out of his hair. He turns on the engine and smiles broadly. The wipers glide across the windscreen in perfect unison.

"A few years ago I bought a dacha here," he points to some wooden houses along the banks of a river, "but I had to sell it to raise money for the workshop. The roads are empty now but in summer, high petrol prices or not, people still travel out to their dachas or to lakes and seaside resorts."

Ukmerge/Wilkomir, I read the road sign. Does Leah know the song about the philanderer from Wilkomir who is in love with three young women at the same time? Leah sings the song, delighted that I know it.

> . . . *Der bocher iz a Wilkomirer,*
> *Kaift a bulke fun a fihrer,*
> *Essen est er umgevassen,*
> *Leift noch maidlech in the gassen . . .*

"It's one of the few light-hearted love songs I know," she says. "Innocent days, when a broken love affair was a great tragedy. But when the pain faded, we could sing and laugh about it. I wonder what happened to the young man from Wilkomir?"

One of two things. He had either emigrated, in good time, to America or to South Africa, or had been rounded up by the Einsatz-gruppen which had followed in the wake of the conquering German army in 1941. They had moved with such devastating speed that they had entrapped and killed hundreds of thousands of Jews. They were swift, heavily armed and, most important, they could count on local support. At times they even had to curb the enthusiasm of their local helpers in order to put the killing on a "systematic" basis, in line with the squad's schedules.

In their rush to ensure that no Jew slipped through their net, they sometimes failed to eliminate an entire community in one *Aktion*.[25] Leaving the surviving Jews penned up in ghettos, under the diligent watch of their Lithuanian auxiliaries, they returned two, three, four, or even fifteen times, as they had done in Vilna, to complete the job. And as they carried out one massacre after another, they sent detailed reports back to the Chief of the Security Police and Security Service in Berlin, giving details of how many men, women and children had been slaughtered; where and how; the extent of local cooperation; the mood of the population, and the "work" still to be done. Teutonic thoroughness had helped document the greatest mass murder in history.

"That is your travel guide?" Freda asks as I page through Raul Hilberg's *The Destruction of the European Jews*, looking up the fate of Wilkomir's Jews.

"A very grim travel guide. It says here that it took four *Aktionen* to massacre the 4000 Jews of Wilkomir."

The further north we travel, the darker the skies become. The mist, the sleet, the empty road; the sodden fields, the copses of birch and pine, combine to form the landscape of nightmare. The singing has stopped, Leah's offers of food are rejected. We drive along in silence.

It is raining steadily as we follow the road into Ponevez, Panevezys in Lithuanian. The Germans had reduced the place to rubble in 1941. What we are seeing is a rebuilt town with neat three-storey buildings and tree-lined streets. My parents had known people from Ponevez. Like the Jews from Zhager and other shtetlech, they had organised themselves into a *Landsmanschaft* society in Johannesburg, held regular gatherings, and sent money back to the shtetl. In 1945 they disbanded the society. After six Einsatzgruppen *Aktionen*, there was no one to send money to.

The weather clears as we approach the town of Shavel, Siauliai,

---

25 Hilberg, *The Destruction of the European Jews*, p. 108.

which is also the name of the *guberna,* the province, in which Zhager lies. A large blue and white road sign indicates that road number A-216 lies ahead. The left turn-off leads to Zagare, 80 kilometres from Siauliai; the right turn-off takes you to Ryga, a mere 16 kilometres away.

Riga. The Big Apple of the surrounding shtetlech. From Zhager they had travelled to Riga to see a doctor, to visit family, to embark on a voyage. "I'm not going to Riga this time," I would have written to my parents, to my grandmother, to my aunt and uncles; "I'm on my way to Zhager." But there is no one to write to. The last surviving member of my maternal family, Hoda, whom I never called aunt, had died the previous year. But before she died, she drew a gem out of the darkening recesses of her memory. "41 Daukanta Gatve," she had said when I asked the address of her old home. Snatches of half-forgotten stories and songs race through my mind as we drive towards their *heim.*

"This is Shavel?" Leah asks, incredulous, as we drive through the city. "Half the city was on fire when we got onto the *grusavik* and fled to Zhager. Bombs were falling all around us. There was a lake on the

Road to Zagare, 1992.

edge of town . . . I don't recognise where Faivke lived, where the factory was, where Leibke worked in the Voyen Kamat. My sister was in the ghetto afterwards. Her little girl, together with other children, were snatched away. Her newborn baby was smothered . . . Here, in this town. And it looks so ordinary, just like any other town . . ."

"You shouldn't have come," Freda says, putting one arm around Leah, the other around Hirshl. "I knew it would upset you."

The scenery becomes increasingly rural as we approach Joniskis, Yaneshik in Yiddish. My mother used to sing a song of which I remember only the melody and the first two lines.

> *In di kleininke shtetala Yaneshik,*
> *Der trauer is zeier greis . . .*
>
> In the small town of Yaneshik,
> The sorrow is very great . . .

Leah does not recognise the song.

"But I can believe it," she says. "There was once an active Jewish community in Yaneshik, and where there are Jews, there is suffering."

As we drive out of the town, I see a street name on the wall of a wooden house: Zagares Gatve, the street which leads to Zagare. Thirty kilometres to go. We pass several hamlets mired in fields of black soil. The name Skaisgere flashes by. The village from which my uncle Bentze's wife had come; Hinde, the bride my maternal grandmother had sent to Mexico, to an unknown groom. The match had been an amicable arrangement between my grandmother, who lived in dread of Bentze marrying a dark-eyed Mexican Catholic, and Hinde's uncle, who had brought her up. Hinde had disgraced the family; she had fallen in love with a gentile Lithuanian, a *poyer*. A fine repayment, her uncle complained, for all his kindness. He had taken her in when her parents died. She had swept and scrubbed and brought water from the well; cooked, laundered and fetched wood for the oven. He had been delighted to marry her off, without a dowry, to a Jewish husband, even if he lived in the wilds of Central America. No local man, he told his wife when she demurred, would take a bride despoiled by a *poyer*, however beautiful she was.

There had been many kinds of sorrow in these little towns and villages.

We are approaching Zhager. We drive along a narrow tarred road with muddy shoulders, lined by tall, bare birches. The very road, unsealed, travelled by my grandfather Avram the Cucumber when he took his produce to town, and my red-bearded grandfather Simon when he transported his passengers to Konigsberg. The trees may not have been there, but the flat dark earth under slate grey clouds most certainly had. In this gloomy, late winter weather, it is unimaginable that spring will ever transform the sodden fields into tall green wheat jewelled with poppies and cornflowers.

Many years after my grandfathers had travelled here, peasants, silent and inscrutable as the landscape, must have watched the Shavel fire brigade speed along this road to Zhager, to flush away the blood of the massacred Jews from the cobbled market-place.

A rectangular road sign straddles a ditch: *Zagare*. Alias Zhager, *der heim*. We have arrived. I photograph the sign, first from a distance, then close up. *Zagare*. Black letters on white. All around us are bleak fields smudged with green, with clumps of leafless trees in the misty background. I record everything on camera. You can't rely on memory.

"This isn't Zhager," Leah announces. "When you come into Zhager, you go through the *vald*, the forest. And where is Naryshkin Park?"

"Perhaps we're still coming to the Park," Freda says.

There is nothing park-like in this desolate scene, only yellow winter grass and bedraggled pines and firs, weary from the weight of snow.

Fifty metres on, Misha pulls up at a blue rectangular sign on the right side of the road. Its arrowed end points towards trees on the far side of the field. *Fasizmo auku kapai, 0.2.* "Memorial to the victims of fascism," Freda translates. "You see these signs all over the country. Usually on the edge of forests where the massacres took place."

"This can't be Zhager," Leah insists. "The mass grave is in Naryshkin Park. Does this look like a park to you?"

No one contradicts her.

Misha turns the car onto a long narrow path, and we bump along the sodden field towards the memorial.

We come to a large area surrounded by trees, enclosed by a low wire fence. Three metal plaques soldered onto two iron posts stand near the gate. The top plate is in Lithuanian, the second in Yiddish, the third in Hebrew.

In this place on 2 October 1941 the Hitlerist murderers and their local helpers massacred about 3000 Jewish men women and children from the Shavel District.

Jews from Kurshan, Krok, Popilan, Yaneshok, Zaimol, Radvilishkis, Linkovo and other places had been slaughtered here, together with the Jews of Zhager. Local Lithuanians, former neighbours, had helped with the shooting. This is Naryshkin Park.

Leah shakes her head. Where are the beautiful shrubs and trees the Naryshkins had planted so many years ago? As a young girl she had strolled along its shaded paths, her heart breaking as Leib walked by with a girl on his arm. When the war is over, he had written from the eastern front in 1943, you and I will walk through Naryshkin Park. Three weeks later he was dead.

Before my parents had married, my father had walked here with his Russian teacher, and my mother had kept trysts with her faithless lover who sailed away to Africa. Young friends had posed against the dark foliage for a photograph by Shabselban, looking the camera straight in the eye, as though defying the fate that would make the Park their burial place.

Leah is silent, confused, as we get out of the car and walk down a paved path beside a very long garden bed. It takes a while to register that this is no garden bed; it is the mass grave.

"After the war, in 1945," Yehezkiel Fleischer had written in his testimony, "on the day after Yom Kippur, I went to the mass grave which stands in Naryshkin Park. It is 120 meters long and the width of two people. It is said 6000 people lie in the grave . . ."

To the left of the grave is a three-stepped concrete plinth on which a roughly hewn obelisk stands. I have seen two photographs of the memorial. The earlier one has a Yiddish inscription carved into the stone and is topped by a silver sphere. In the second photograph, the Yiddish inscription has been overlaid by a metal plaque which states, in Russian, that 3000 Soviet citizens, victims of fascism, had been massacred in this place on 2 October 1941. The silver ball had been removed, leaving a truncated pyramid at the apex of the monument.

We are looking at a modified version of the second photograph. The word "Soviet" has recently been gouged out. The two words of the original Yiddish inscription are barely visible: "Here lie . . ."

The obelisk is weather-worn, streaked with dirt and lichen. An icy wind soughs through the bare trees, freezing all emotion. We stand before the memorial in silence, dry-eyed. Freda rights a small plastic fir tree in a plastic pot which has been blown over. At the base of the obelisk Leah leaves a stone, her heart.

I have been photographing feverishly, my hands and eyes functioning independently of my thoughts and emotions. I must remember everything. I shall never return to this terrible place. The camera buzzes; the spool is full. I take a black and white film out of my bag and hastily wind it into the camera. Freda takes my arm as we walk towards the car. Ashen-faced, Misha walks behind us slowly, between Hirshl and Leah.

"Our forests are planted with such graves," Freda says. "I know some Lithuanians did terrible things under the Nazis, but if I'm to live here, I have to accept that there are good Lithuanians and bad Lithuanians. I'm a Lithuanian myself. At a particular time of my life I looked at people of a certain age and thought, what did you do during the war? But one can't live like that."

We notice, for the first time, a long brick building behind a row of trees. The sloping roof is topped by three helmeted chimneys, and halfway down the roof, in line with the ground-floor windows, are twelve attic windows, like dovecotes. Leah does not remember this building. Further along the road there is a notice: Department of Agriculture. Horse-breeding Centre.

"What I want to know is, if this is Zhager, where have all the trees gone?" Leah asks as we drive towards the town.

"Chopped down, mammele," Freda says, "with everyone else."

We all fall silent again. Houses and a church spire come into view. We have arrived in Zagare.

20

Zagare

Zhager 1920s. A bridge over the River Svete.

The sand road on which we enter the town is pitted with pot-holes. Misha swerves to avoid the muddy pools. The rain has stopped, but heavy grey clouds hang oppressively over the low wooden houses, most of which have TV aerials on their sloping, tiled roofs. The last house on a block has been converted into a shop. *Videos*, reads a large placard at its entrance.

"This isn't Zhager," Leah repeats.

"She doesn't recognise the video shop," Misha says.

"Mamme," Freda is losing patience, "what are you going on about? The road sign says Zagare, we have just been to the grave which is in Naryshkin Park. What other proof do you need? You haven't been here for forty-six years, things change, you've forgotten a lot."

But Leah is right. This isn't Zhager. It is Zagare. My parents would not have recognised it either.

"I have an address," I say. "41 Daukanta Gatve, where my mother's family lived. Let's try to find it."

Misha stops next to a poorly dressed couple standing on a street corner. The man is swaying, and lists towards his companion who is in no condition to support him. Their blotched faces and bleary eyes turn towards Misha when he asks where Daukanta Gatve is. They look at one another, shake their heads, and weave away. An elderly woman with a headscarf looks alarmed when Misha repeats the question. She hurries away without answering.

"They think we've come to reclaim property," Freda says.

A young man on a bicycle directs us to the municipal offices on the other side of the river.

There is an edge of hysteria in Leah's voice as we drive over the bridge spanning the slow-flowing river.

"That's not the bridge and that's not the Shvete!" she cries. "Do you know what the river looked like after the snow melted? Once, in spring, a young boy was carried away and drowned."

Jack Trubik's photographs show a wide, fast-flowing river. My uncles had told tales of daring swims in the Shvete. Now the river, clotted with weeds, flows languidly under the bridge. When Mierke, Leib's *geliebte*, returned to Zhager after the war, she had been told by a former gentile servant, that the blood from the market-place had flowed through all the little alleyways into the Shvete. All that blood, she had said, crossing herself. Now the river is drying out.

Yet another blood myth. And again the Jews are responsible. Only this time it's their blood. Pollution, that's what it is, I tell myself. Nutrients flowing off agricultural land into the river. Blue algae, green algae, whatever it is. Not blood. But I shudder as we drive across the bridge. *Svete*, a blue and white sign reads. Leah is very quiet as we park outside a white, double-storey building flying the Lithuanian flag.

I remain in the car with Leah and Hirshl when Freda and Misha go into the building. From a bag at her feet, Leah extracts hard-boiled eggs, thick slices of black bread, and a thermos with coffee. *"Der lebedikker muz essen,"* she says as she pours sweetened black coffee into plastic cups. The living must eat. I am grateful for the coffee. The egg sticks in my throat.

Freda and Misha seem to be away an inordinately long time. I get out of the car and look around. The car is parked in front of the municipal building which faces onto a square. It is longer than it is wide, an open space enclosed by shops and dwellings, with trees and flowerbeds on each side of a wide, paved avenue down its centre. The dark soil of the garden beds looks rich with the promise of summer flowers, and grass is beginning to sprout on either side of the walkway. This must be the town square. Small wonder Leah does not recognise Zhager. My family had never mentioned a town square.

Leah beckons anxiously from the car. She is not at ease. Neither am I. I photograph the square, drawing an angry mutter from a passer-by. There are few people in the street. Those who pass stare at us, stone-faced. Xenophobia? Hostility? I cannot interpret their expressions, but feel a sense of menace.

Freda comes bounding down the steps of the municipality building, followed by Misha. They are smiling. But instead of returning to the car, they speak to a thick-set man who is walking towards the square. Leaving Misha with the stranger, Freda walks quickly towards us.

"This is Zhager, mammale," she says. "But Daukanta Gatve no longer exists. Now it's called Cvirkos Gatve. The woman in the office realised we were Jews and was very helpful. 'There's only one Jew in Zhager,' she told us. 'If you're interested, I'll phone him.' As she picked up the phone, she looked out of the window. 'There he is,' she cried out. 'That's Isaac Mendelson! If you go down now, you'll catch up with him.'"

"Itzke Mendelson, that *zhulik.*" Leah frowns. "He was a wild boy. Ran around with all the *skotzim.*"

"Never mind what the signs say. Never mind what the woman from the municipality says. If that's Itzke Mendelson the *zhulik*, this must be Zhager," Freda teases. "He has invited us to his house."

Isaac Mendelson is a big man, with a broken, heavy nose, a Jewish Jean Gabin. He holds himself upright, feet slightly apart, arms loosely bracketing his sides, like a wrestler about to launch himself at his opponent. He acknowledges us with a nod, not a smile. There is a cautious look in his blue eyes.

"I was Leah Beitler, cousin of Chaim," Leah says. "I remember you as a young boy."

"I was seventeen when the war broke out," he says. "I escaped just before the Nazis invaded."

Leah introduces me. "Gershon Yoffe's daughter, Leibke's niece," she says. He shakes his head. He was born in 1924, two years before Gershon left Zhager. "She wants to know what happened to the Jews of Zhager. She's trying to understand . . ."

"Understand? Who can understand?" His eyes glisten, his face opens up. "But I can tell her what I know. And what I know is what Altona, my wife, told me. She saw it all. She's not Jewish," he adds. "Come to my house."

He lives in a ground-floor apartment in a two-storey block which faces onto the square. The entrance is through a lane at the side of the building. We pass a slim woman chopping wood in a yard opposite the building. She pauses only to give us a cursory glance, pats the frisky Alsatian pup who is tied by a long leash to a pole, then continues chopping. Children are playing with a ball further up the lane. We hear excited squeals and barks behind the door, and as we enter, two young dachshunds jump all over Isaac.

"*A choleria!*" Leah mumbles as she treads into dog shit.

Isaac is apologetic. His wife loves dogs. Usually they're well-behaved, but he had left them indoors too long. He picks them up and shuts them into the kitchen. Leah takes off her shoe and, holding it gingerly at a distance, follows Isaac into the living room. The front door opens, and the woman who had been chopping wood comes in. She takes in the situation at a glance, fetches a cloth, wipes the floor, takes Leah's shoe from her, and without a word, goes outside.

"My wife, Altona," Isaac says when she returns a few minutes later with the cleaned-up shoe.

She has a pleasant, lined face, short greying hair, and smiles gravely as we are introduced. "She doesn't speak Yiddish but understands everything. She even sings Yiddish songs. Most of her friends had been Jewish. She was a child when the war broke out."

He says something to her in Lithuanian and she goes out of the room. The living room is small, well-furnished, bright, and a large window looks onto the square.

"How pleasant to have a view onto the square," I say.

"The square?" A hollow laugh issues from Isaac's throat. "*Do hot men avekgeshossen Yidden. Dos is geven amol dem markplatz.*" Here they shot the Jews. This used to be the market-place.

I go to the window. People are standing around, talking. I imagine they are looking towards Isaac's apartment. Others are walking across the square. Leah joins me at the window. She is pale and her lower lip is trembling.

"Why didn't I recognise it? This building, the lane at the side, The lay-out of the rooms. Isaac," she says, "do you remember the Yoffes' barbershop?"

"Of course," he says. "It was next door. Faivke used to cut my hair. Shmulke was his assistant. I only met Leib later, in the army. This is 19 Turgaviette . . ."

"And we lived in number 18, above the barbershop. Friedke, Misha, this is where I grew up, where my parents, my family lived. And the market-place was opposite. This was the heart of the shtetl.

I used to watch the peasants setting up their stalls on market day. And from the balcony of our apartment . . . Isaac, where's the balcony?"

The building was renovated, he tells her, and the balcony removed.

"That's why I didn't recognise it! And my children think I'm already *aiberbottel*, growing senile. From that balcony the Russian officer announced that we were now Soviet citizens. But at least the Russians didn't kill us. The Nazis gathered everyone for the slaughter, and the Lithuanian bandits shot the Jews. Isaac, how can you live here?"

"I wouldn't leave Zhager for a million rubles," he answers defiantly. "This is my birthplace. My people are buried here. I want to be near their graves. I returned to Zhager in 1947 when the 16th Lithuanian Brigade was disbanded. I didn't have money, a trade, nothing. All I knew was how to shoot. And how to survive. Where could I go? Several other Jews were already living here. Your cousin Beitler, Zlot, a brother of mine. All dead now. I met Altona, we married, had three sons. *Zainen alle drai gemalt*. All three of them were circumcised. A rabbi came from Riga."

"How does a person make a living here?" Misha changes the subject.

"I own some land where I keep ducks, geese, chickens, a few cattle. A helper feeds them. And I trade in meat, fur, cowhide, anything. I am also a hunter. The forests are full of rabbits, buck and other animals. Tourists come here, specially to hunt. They pay good money. I once took a German hunting. I don't think he enjoyed it. When we were deep in the forest, alone, I told him I was a Jew."

Misha tells him he was trained as a hatter, but that he now runs a small clothing workshop. He would like to buy furs from Isaac.

"I'm not interested in selling anything until the currency has settled," Isaac says. "Money isn't worth the paper it's printed on." They exchange phone numbers and addresses.

"Aren't you a little nervous about living here," I ask, "a sole Jew, in a place where such terrible things happened? My impression is that after nearly fifty years, they're still looking over their shoulders for ghosts. Misha was advised not to sleep over in Zhager."

"Vilt ir zen vi a Yid lebt?" he responds. Do I want to see how a Jew lives?

When he leads me into a bedroom which faces onto the square, I expect to see a fine bedroom suite; Isaac has shown much pride in his material possessions. *"Proller,"* Leah had muttered as he was describing his business ventures to Misha. Boaster.

He draws the curtain aside to reveal a large gun in the corner. "That's how a Jew lives," he says.

"Why do you remain here?"

"Where's it better? At least here I know my enemy."

I cannot imagine living under such conditions. How real is the danger? His gun, after all, is part of his hunting activities. We return to the living room.

"I wasn't afraid of them when I returned from the war. I'd been through hell on the eastern front and knew how to protect myself." He bares his left shoulder; it is disfigured by deep scars. "Terrible battles. Half our division was killed. When I came back and learned what had happened to my family, I settled scores." He does not elaborate. "Before the war I used to play football with some gentile *yatten*, boys. They welcomed me back but warned that if I remained Isaac, the bandits would kill me. Change your name to Petrus, they told me. I didn't need their names, but they called me Petrus all the same. Now, they said, everyone will know they're not allowed to harm you."

"Did your friends name you Petrus, or did the priest make you Petrus?" Leah is quivering with anger.

"Mamme," Freda reproaches her.

"My friends, my friends," Isaac says. "They all know I'm a Jew. Everyone, from Zhager to Vilna and in Riga too. I go to shul in Riga on Yom Kippur. My wife sits upstairs and I sit downstairs. We buy *matzo* on Pesach . . ."

"Tzugeleikt a nomen," Leah says, tight-lipped. In the shtetl, someone close to death was given an additional name – *tzuleigen a nomen* – to confuse the Angel of Death when he came to call.

"How did you escape from Zhager?" asks Misha the peacemaker.

"On a bicycle. Many young people got away by bicycle. Beitler, Yoffe and the other Party people fled in a very big Russian truck. Others left by horse and cart. Along the road many were attacked by Lithuanian and Latvian militias. Their horses were taken away, their belongings stolen and they were shot. My family didn't have a chance. We didn't own a horse and cart, had no money . . ." He sits quietly for a while, furrowing his brow.

"Zhager always dealt in horses. There were many Jewish horse-dealers, *ferdbeiters.* Did you see that large building as you drove into Zhager? That was built by the Graf Naryshkin for his daughters. They used to hold indoor riding exhibitions for their friends. Now they breed horses there . . .

"I was telling you how I escaped from Zhager. A group of us left together, by bicycle. A Jewish tailor and two gentiles, the Mitskus brothers, each took a Jewish girl out of Zhager on their cross-bars. They saved their lives. Now the women live in Israel. The younger Mitskus became a lieutenant in the army. When he heard I was in the First Battalion, he came to visit me. He died recently in Vilna. I went to his funeral."

Count Naryshkin's stables and manège hall, now a horse-breeding centre.

Freda and Leah recognise the name. A good man, they confirm.

"The older Mitskus brother was hit by a sniper at the front, right next to me. The tailor was also killed in battle.

"We got out just in time. My mother and sisters . . . Nu. We got to Riga, under fire, and caught a train into Russia. Those with money went deep into Russia, into Tashkent. I didn't have money, so I went to a kolkhoz. I tried to enlist in the army, but they weren't yet taking people from Lithuania. My feet were swollen. I was starving. Berries I ate. That's all. There was a Jewish doctor from Riga on the kolkhoz with his wife and three children. 'Isaac, you'll die here,' the doctor said. 'Tell them you're from Lettland and go into the army.' As though you don't die in the army. But anything seemed better than dying of hunger. In those days I spoke Latvian like a native. I went to the enlisting office and was taken into the Latvian Brigade. I was injured in 1941 in a battle near Moscow." He touches his shoulder, his back and his leg.

"When I recovered, I joined the 16th Lithuanian Brigade which had 12 000 men, many of them Jews. We fought on the front, at Orel. It was snowing, we were hungry, conditions were terrible. They thought Jews couldn't fight, but I was already a battle veteran. I knew how to handle a machine gun. Many Lithuanian fascists deserted to the Germans. They gave them our position, told them there were many Jews in the brigade, and they bombarded us night and day. The Germans had superior firepower, but we fought until all our ammunition ran out. Then we were ordered to withdraw. Several hundred Jews died in that battle."

"Leibke Yoffe was at Orel," Leah says. "Did you know him?

"Who didn't know Yoffe? There was a price on his head. There were posters all over Zhager, offering a reward of thousands of rubles for his capture. I met up with him at Yasnaya Polyana. Also with Beitler, Blum and Zlot . . ."

"*Da! Da!*" Leah says. As happens often during Isaac's story, they break into Russian.

"Please! Speak Yiddish!" I plead. "I've heard at least three versions of Leib's death. What really happened?"

"Yoffe was killed in Orel, not in the town itself, but near Alexeyevka. He was buried in Yelets," Isaac says. "He was in Battalion 156 or 166 with Nunen. I was in 249 with Vilensky. Zaltsman was on the front with him. He told me what happened. It was very hot. After a big battle, he was very thirsty. *Hot er gevelt a trunk, hot er gevelt.* So he said he was going to look for water. Don't go, the other lads warned. But he went into the village, about 300 metres from where they were hiding. As he was drinking, he was shot by a German . . ."

"*Nyet! Nyet!*" Leah cries. "That's not how it happened, Zhukov told us . . ."

"Zhukov?" Isaac says with disdain. "What did he know? He wasn't a fighter. He was a shoemaker. Later they shot the three Germans who shot Yoffe. I saw all four of them, dead."

"He wasn't dead. He was injured," Leah says. "From hospital he wrote me three letters."

"He was injured here, I think." Isaac points to his back.

"*Da, da.*" Leah turns to me. "Afterwards I'll tell you what really happened. Everyone's an expert on Leibke's death."

Altona comes into the living room with a tray of tea, Nescafé, black bread and a large slab of cheese, which, Isaac tells us, is a speciality of Zhager. The dachshunds had been quiet while Altona was in the kitchen. Now they're barking again, scratching at the door. If she had known we were coming, Altona tells Leah, she would have prepared a proper meal.

"*Ich hob a gute vibe, hob ich,*" Isaac says. I have a good wife. Altona shrugs off his compliment with a wry smile. She cuts the bread, passes around the cheese, pours tea and coffee. She herself does not sit down. "*Bei unz in Zhager,*" Isaac continues in his idiosyncratic Yiddish, "*Kumpt men yedder yahr, kumpt men zuforren fun Vilna, fun Riga, flekt men kumen fuftzik, zechtzik machiness. Flekt di vibe meine avekkailenen a kalb un alle fleggen opessen, trinkin. Nor idster kumpt zuforren ein machina, tsvei machiness . . .*"

Fifty or sixty cars used to come from Vilna and Riga before Yom Kippur for the memorial service at the mass grave. Altona would slaughter a calf and prepare a meal for everyone. Very few people come these days, Isaac says, only one or two carloads. Most Jews have left the country. But those who come to *kaiveroves* still visit the Mendelsons, and Altona knows them all.

"She's a wonderful woman, Altona. She looks after me, keeps a clean home, cooks Jewish dishes, gefilte fish, *kneidlach*, whatever I wish. I never shout at her and she is never angry with me. And she helps me with my work. With everything. She was here right through the terrible times. Tell them what happened, Altona."

She sits down on a chair Isaac has brought in from the kitchen, and begins. "I was fourteen when the war broke out . . ."

21

Altona's Story

Isaac and Altona Mendelson, 1993.

Many of her friends, Altona tells us, had been Jewish, and as a child she had spoken Yiddish fluently.

"Now there's no one to speak to," Freda translates, "so she's forgotten a lot, but understands enough to know that Isaac has also forgotten Yiddish!"

Her mother had been a dressmaker. When she finished sewing a dress, Altona would take it to a small wooden house next to the river, where a young woman embroidered the cuffs and collars on a special machine.

"Henke! That was Henke!" Leah cries.

"I don't remember her name," Altona says, "but she had big dark eyes, a lovely face. She spoke softly, and worked quickly, well. Her mother was a short, fat woman. She was often sick in bed. No, I don't remember the other Yoffes, but I used to pass the barbershop almost every day."

As Altona describes her, Henke becomes a person in her own right, not a mere sister, daughter or lover: a gentle woman, sitting at her machine, smiling at the child Altona while she embroiders cuffs and collars for her mother, the dressmaker. Once this connection is made, Altona seems more at ease with us; we have the past in common. I show her and Isaac Jack Trubik's photographs. They recognise places, not people; they had been children when the photos were taken. Altona was born in 1927, Isaac in 1924.

Freda asks how the gentile Lithuanians had reacted when the Germans marched into Zhager.

"Most people were happy," Altona says. "They hated the Soviets who had deported Lithuanian nationalists and turned the peasants' land into collective farms. When the Germans arrived, the partisans came out of the forests and greeted them with bread and salt. The Germans, they said, would restore Lithuanian independence. But they didn't."

"How did they feel about the Germans' treatment of the Jews?"

"They said they were Bolsheviks who had sent their comrades to Siberia . . ."

"Or capitalists," Leah breaks in, "who had robbed the Lithuanian people. First they hated the Jews, then they looked for reasons. They didn't need the Germans to teach them to hate Jews."

"Mamme, let Altona speak." Freda puts a restraining hand on Leah's arm.

"My family and others," Altona says, "just wanted to live in peace. We were used to living with the Jews. We'd been neighbours all our lives. When the Germans arrived, notices were pasted on all the walls, signed by the chief of the Lithuanian partisans . . ."

"I knew him well," Isaac says.

". . . The Jews had to wear a yellow star . . ." Altona lists all the restrictions imposed on the Jews. "Not far from here, in the market square, was a shop where the Jews could buy bread only at sunset. By that time, most of the bread was gone. My mother used to buy bread for our Jewish neighbours until the other neighbours threatened to burn down our house. Things got worse very quickly."

Altona describes events which, with differences in detail, tally with the testimonies of the survivors. She tells of Rabbi Riff's humiliation, how he had been inspanned into a waggon filled with rocks, together with a very short Jew, and how they had been forced to draw the waggon through the town. The crowds, she said, had laughed, applauded and jeered.

"But even before the Germans arrived, terrible things had happened. The leader of the Lithuanian partisans asked for eighty young Jews to train for fighting the Germans. They were marched away and never seen again."

"They were shot and buried in a mass grave in the old cemetery," Isaac says.

"My brothers, Gedalia, Mottala," Leah begins, but cannot go on. "We arrived in Zhager in the truck a day after this happened."

"Who did the shooting?" Misha asks. "The Germans?"

"We hardly saw the Germans," Altona says. "They were in Shavel. The Lithuanian militia did it all. They were in charge of everything. They said this was revenge against the Jewish Bolsheviks who had deported their families. There were other cruel things. Dr Friedman and his wife were also killed. Prominent Jews were killed first."

"So were the strong ones who could have fought back when the massacre began," Isaac says.

In July, Altona says, the Jews were herded into a ghetto which had been set up on both sides of the river. Jews from surrounding towns and villages were brought into the Zhager ghetto some weeks later. Most of them were women and children; their men had already been killed. The Jews of Zhager realised what lay ahead for them, and they panicked.

"I read in an eye-witness testimony that a shoemaker called Statakus and his assistant Eisgertas had been in charge of the ghetto," I say.

"Statkus," Isaac corrects me, "not Statakus."

I show him and Altona a list of other collaborators named in the eye-witness accounts. Among them were members of the Zagare intelligentsia: Boyshek, a schoolteacher; Palishmaushkas, a teacher of singing, whose older brother, also a singing teacher, had been exiled to Siberia; Stasis Vosis, a teacher; Kropshis, a lawyer; the commander of the police, Smaitis; Janickis Gindwilus and two sons; Anton Trimkus; the teacher Busis, Mitrikis . . .

"I knew Mitrikis Vladis," Isaac says. "He was one of the main murderers, a shooter, like Statkus. He was sentenced to twenty-five years, but served only nineteen. His daughter went to Russia and paid a heavy bribe for his release. He returned to Zhager, a hero. When he was told I was living here, he said, 'How did a Jew get away?' Later he heard I'd been a soldier and was now a hunter. He never went out at night. When he began going to church, I went to the priest who knows me well, and told him what Mitrikis had done. How can you let such a person into church, I asked him . . . What did the priest say? What can he say? Money buys everything, everyone. Mitrikis's two sons and a daughter live in Zhager like millionaires. They go to Switzerland for holidays, they've got the biggest houses, the best cars. His daughter drives a Volga. People call it *Zydu machina*, a Jewish car. Everybody knows it was bought with Jewish blood, with the money Mitrikis stole from those he killed. *Er hot gepaigert mit dri menatten tzurik.* He died three months ago," Isaac adds. A beast *paigers*; people *shtarb*, die. "That he should have had such an easy death . . . I'll show you his house. It's on the way to the cemetery."

Isaac has taken over the narrative from Altona.

"I had a friend, a Lithuanian goy," he says. "He told me they had forced him to help dig the pits in the Park. He described how they shot the people, how they fell into the pit, and how they were covered with soil and lime. Then another lot was shot, and covered with soil and lime, and so on. Alive, dead, everyone was thrown into the pit. My mother and sisters among them . . .

"Even this was not enough. In 1943, when many gentile Lithuanians deserted from the 16th Lithuanian Brigade, one of them returned to Zhager. When he told those bandits I was still alive, they burned down our house.

"In Zhager," he says, "Mitrikis and Ikwildas were the chief murderers. After the war many bandits escaped to America, to Australia and to Canada. All they had to say was that they were anti-Communist and they were taken in with open arms. Ikwildas Edvardas, the chief of the Zhager partisans, escaped to Canada where he changed his name. Not so long ago, he returned to visit his two sisters who still live in Zhager. I'd known him since we were boys. One of his sisters came to my house and begged me to see him. 'If I see him,' I told her, 'I'll shoot him.' But let Altona tell you what it was like to live in Zhager during that period."

"It was impossible to live or sleep when these terrible things were happening," she says. "Only the bad people slept well. All normal people were distraught. We had gone to school with Jewish children, we had bought from Jewish shops, the Jewish shoemaker down the road mended our shoes. But we were threatened that if we sheltered Jews, our whole family would be shot. Everyone was afraid. Very few were brave enough to help."

"After the war," Isaac says, "I was told by a well-off peasant who lived just outside Zhager, that in 1941 he had hidden two Jewish brothers and their cousins, two girls. He had dug a pit for them, covered it with birch branches, and they lived in it for about a week. Then one of the girls went out in daylight to fetch water. A neighbour saw her. He reported this to the Lithuanian militia. All five were arrested. The peasant bribed his way out. The young people were shot. A good man, the *poyer*. He died about three years ago. I went to his funeral."

"We did not witness the actual massacre," Altona says. "We were warned to remain in our houses. But we heard the shooting, the screaming. It went on for three days, first in the market-place, later at Naryshkin Park. Afterwards we saw the blood in the market-place. It took days to wash away. I couldn't walk there. I always saw blood. Others felt the same. That's why they made it into a park, to cover it up. I still dream about it, even though it happened so long ago. I sometimes think we should rather have died with them . . ."

In Peretzman's testimony, I tell them, there is a description of the resistance the Jews put up before the massacre. The names Alter Zagorsky and Avram Akerman are mentioned. An Einsatzgruppen report confirms the revolt in the market square.

"It is good they resisted," Isaac says. "If I had been here, that's the way I would have wanted to die – fighting."

He suggests we walk over to Old Zhager where the Yoffes used to live, then go by car to the Old Jewish Cemetery and the other places which are not in walking distance.

Hirshl, who has been very quiet throughout our visit, says he will remain in the house. "And I have seen enough of Zhager," Leah says, "to haunt me for the rest of my life. We'll remain here and talk to Altona."

22

The *Heimen Shtetala*

Strul's Mill, Zhager, 1920s.

Photographer unknown

. . . vu iz di gesala, vu iz di shtieb?
Vu iz di meidala velche ich lieb?
Nisht do mer di gesala, nisht do mer di shtieb,
Nisht do mer di meidala velche ich lieb.

Where is the little street, where is the house?
And where is the girl whom I have loved?
Gone is the little street, gone is the house,
Gone is the girl whom once I loved.

We cross the bridge into Old Zhager, side-stepping puddles. The weather has cleared. Pale sunlight flickers over the turgid river, the bare trees, the cobbled streets and low wooden houses. In New Zhager the houses are larger, built of brick. Passers-by greet Isaac politely, casting a cursory glance over us. He acknowledges their greetings with a dignified nod.

Are these the people against whom he may have to defend himself with the rifle that stands behind the bedroom curtain? They look so grey, so depressed, so worn out. A group of men outside a pub stare as I photograph the shop where once my father's barber-shop had stood. And again I sense the hostility, the menace.

"If they leave me alone, I'll leave them alone," Isaac says. "They understand this is my home as well as theirs."

So they should. From the fourteenth century until 2 October 1941 there had been a continuous Jewish presence in Zhager. At the end of the nineteenth century, Zhager had had a population of 5500 Jews. They constituted 60 per cent of the total population. Today Zagare has a population of 3000 gentiles and one Jew. Isaac is the last of the line.

As I walk along the muddy streets of this depressed little town, it is impossible to evoke my parents' *heimen shtetala*, their home town. Nothing fits. Not their stories, nor their songs. I feel disoriented. In which direction did they walk to Naryshkin Park, or to the Mill Hill? On which side is the border with Latvia? Where did my mother go to choir practice, my father to his study circle? Where was the Kulturlige housed? Where was the *shul,* the *cheder,* the school, the bathhouse? There is no one left to ask. Isaac, twenty years younger than my parents, had grown up in a different era.

My parents had lived in a predominantly Jewish shtetl. Dogs had barked as they walked past the gentile houses on the outskirts of town; they had been strangers, trespassers. Isaac, on the other hand, had integrated into the larger community and spoken Lithuanian like a native. He had played football with his non-Jewish friends. In Leah's eyes he had been a *zhulik,* a rascal, who had run around with *skotzim.* Shlomo and Chana's close friend had been Ikwildas Edvardas, who had spoken Yiddish and had had many Jewish friends. That had not stopped him from becoming a mass murderer in 1941

History, in this town of dark secrets, has been buried with its dead. The parks and forests hide mass graves and places of death and destruction. A town square, fragrant with trees and flowers, covers the old market-place where Jewish blood had flowed over its cobblestones. Jewish homes had been taken over, destroyed or renovated. After half a century, strangers are still regarded with suspicion. Are they descendants of the dead, come to reclaim what is theirs? Do the dour-faced residents of Zagare sleep well at night, or do they still hear echoes of the shooting and the screaming? And as they walk across the town square under the shady trees, do their feet burn on the paving stones? And does the smell of blood still rise to their nostrils?

"The Yoffes' house stood here." Isaac stops in front of a grassy plot hugging the banks of the Shvete. A horse grazes under the bare trees, flicking flies off his rump. A cart lies behind the adjoining house.

In the backyard of the house which no longer exists, on the night before they had been driven into exile in 1915, Gershon and Leib had buried my grandmother's copper pots, brass candlesticks and pestle and mortar. On their return, four years later, they had found the house in ruins, the floors ripped up, windows broken, the roof tiles missing. And when my father had left for Mexico in 1926, Freyde and her children Brynke and Shmulke – Leib had refused to take leave of Gershon – had huddled together in front of their house, watching him walk up the road, out of their lives.

"The neighbours have pulled down the Yoffes' house," Isaac tells me. "They use the plot for growing vegetables and for their horse and cart. You say your mother's family lived at 41 Daukanta Gatve? It's called Cvirkos Gatve now. It's not far from here."

As we walk up the street, I see an old water pump near the kerb.

"Take a photograph of my old house if it's still standing," Gerty Trubik's brother had requested before I left for Lithuania. "It stood opposite the old *poomp*, in Daukanta Gatve."

"Could this be the *poomp* from the 1920s?" I ask Isaac.

He shrugs. "Perhaps. It's never used. Everyone's got running water in their houses."

I take a photo of the *poomp* with the houses in the background. I photograph everything: houses, cobbled streets, the river, trees; people, inadvertently. Later I shall fit the pieces together.

As we walk along Daukanta Gatve, now Cvirkos Gatve, I see gaps between the houses; 31, 35, 39. Number 41 no longer exists. A garden stands in its place. I photograph the empty space, my mother's home.

I ask Isaac in which direction the forest lies, the forest where he hunts. He points, but I do not know whether that is north, south, east or west. Could it be the same forest where once my grandmother and her children had gathered wild strawberries for winter preserves? She had never mentioned the hares, buck or other animals of the forest. Perhaps they live deep in its dark heart, where gatherers never venture. That is the preserve of the hunters.

The forest – the *vald* or its diminutive, the *veldel* – had featured often in songs of trysts and seductions, meetings and partings, some sad, some joyous.

> *Vi ken ich in finstern vald*
> *Fargessen di liebe tzu dir*
> *Dermon ich mir dein geshtalt,*
> *Ervekt zich a vaitik in mir . . .*

How can I in this dark wood
Forget my love for you
Your image appears in my mind
Awaking a pain in my heart . . .

And there was *"Margaritkes"*, a light-hearted song of seduction in which a young woman searches for daisies in the forest but finds, instead, a young man.

In veldel bein taichel, dort zainen gevaksen
Margaritkalach elent un klein
Vi kleininke zunen mit vaisinke stralen,
Mit vaisinke, tra lala lala . . .

Now the forest is scarred with graves. Hunting is more appropriate to it than the gathering of wild berries and *margaritkes*.

Freda takes my arm. "Where are you?" she asks softly.

Isaac is showing us the old bathhouse. It is a dilapidated old building, with two windows and a door at ground level, and two smaller windows, like close-set eyes, on the pyramid-shaped upper level.

"Before Pesach, they used to bake *matzos* on the upper floor. Now it's a storeroom. The bathhouse, downstairs, is still in use."

"What remains of the shtetl?" I ask.

"One synagogue. A shell. First they used it as a storehouse. Now they play basketball there. Everything was destroyed. After the war, I used to find Hebrew and Yiddish books on piles of rubbish, in abandoned houses, in woodsheds. I cleaned up the books and gave them to people who came to *kaiveroves*, to the memorial service, on Yom Kippur. The last lot I gave to the Shavel Jewish committee."

We follow him down a sandy road where a large white building, rain-streaked, crumbling, towers over the surrounding houses. It has a pitched roof and long, arched windows along its sides. Neglected though it is, it retains a certain dignity. Or so it seems to me. The reality is that this simple structure, once a synagogue, is now a basketball court. Its metamorphosis resonates bitterly with the fate of its former congregants. We look through the window. The rectangular shape of the synagogue has been marked out for basketball. On the wall facing Jerusalem, where the Holy Ark had been housed, a backboard and basket have been erected. The other goalpost is suspended on the far side, near the door. The arched windows cast long rays of pale sunlight over the wooden floors, highlighting the black markings. I cannot begin to imagine the community at prayer in this eviscerated structure.

"Is this where the eighty young men were shot?" I ask.

"No. That shul was burned down."

On the way back, Isaac stops in front of a double-storey red-brick building.

"This was the Jewish primary school where I gave the teachers a hard time." He allows himself a smile. "It's still a school today. Different children, different teachers."

Had my mother, my father, their sisters and brothers attended this school? There is no one I can ask.

"And this is where Rabbi Israel Riff lived," he says as we turn down a quiet street. Very little of the large red-brick house is visible behind the tall hedge that surrounds it. "He was the Rabbi of New Zhager. One of his sons was the Rabbi of Old Zhager. A giant of a man, the old rabbi. A good person. Everyone respected him. He was humiliated and tortured before they killed him."

Heavy clouds, driven by an icy wind, mask the sun as we walk over the bridge towards Isaac's house. Misha looks at his watch.

"Three-twenty," he says. "We should leave in about an hour. I'd like to be on the main road before dark."

"Next time come earlier. There's still a lot to see. Zhager isn't as small as you think," Isaac says as we climb into Misha's car. "First, let's go to the old cemetery."

"My grandfathers are buried there," I say. "Avram and Simon. They at least died in their own beds. I wonder if we'll find their headstones."

"Unlikely. Slow down," he says as we approach a large wooden house, painted yellow, on the outskirts of town. "This is where

Mitrikis's family lives. *Iz er geven der glavner schisher, iz er geven.* He was the main shooter. The one who was sentenced to twenty-five years and released after nineteen years. I told you. He died only a few months ago, a free man. He left his family a good Jewish fortune. Like a hero he walked around Zhager."

The road narrows. There is no room to manoeuvre around the pot-holes which Misha negotiates with care. The mud will dry as we drive along the highway later that evening, and Misha will labour mightily to dislodge it from the undercarriage and wheels. We are driving between fields. Some are ploughed, waiting to be sown; others are already tinged with green. Farm houses rise out of the dark fields, at one with the earth; smoke curls out of the chimneys. A scene of bucolic innocence, a country idyll. Is this where Isaac's peasant friend had dug a pit to conceal four young Jews? And if it is, this is also the place where a neighbour denounced them.

"That's the Christian cemetery," Isaac says.

To our right is a small, picturesque chapel, with orderly rows of crosses and headstones, surrounded by neat flowerbeds and trees. A woman wearing a headscarf plucks weeds from a grave.

Half a mile up the road we come to a smallholding where a farmer in dirty boots stands at his gate with a dog. Stiff and unsmiling, he acknowledges Isaac's greeting with a grunt as we walk past, kicks his growling dog, then turns back towards his house. His is an untended piece of land, unlike that of his neighbours. His house is in need of repair, and the farmyard is littered with rusting farm equipment. Isaac gives a dismissive shake of the head, then leads us towards a large mound, near the cemetery fence, over which weeds and grass run riot.

"This is where the eighty young men are buried," he says. For once Isaac seems uncertain of the facts. "Some say the young men were taken to the shul and shot. Others say they were shot on the banks of the Shvete. Still others claim they were brought to the cemetery, made to dig their own grave, then shot right here. But this is where they lie, without a stone to mark their grave."

Does Shmulke lie here? Or Leah's brothers? All we know is that eighty young men are buried here. They were the sons and brothers of those who lie in Naryshkin Park.

We follow Isaac over uneven terrain towards a bleak hillock, where a few trees sway and keen in the wind. It takes a while for the rounded dark shapes scattered in the yellow winter grass to metamorphose from antheaps into headstones. They lean at all angles; only a few have remained erect. The inscriptions are illegible, worn by time, weather and neglect. Lichen and moss pit their surface.

"The better tombstones have been uprooted for paving and building," Isaac says.

Jewish cemetery, 1993.

For a while we wander among the headstones, vainly trying to decipher a name, a year.

"It's time to leave," I say after a futile search.

We return to the house. Altona shakes hands and invites us to return any time we wish. If we phone from Vilnius, she will prepare a proper meal for us. She gives Leah a large white cheese wrapped in a snow-white napkin. The speciality of Zhager, she says. Leah embraces her.

"You are lucky to have such a wife," she scolds Isaac. "Take good care of her. You chop the wood."

Hirshl looks pale and weary. He is persuaded to sit in front with Misha. I photograph the Mendelsons standing outside their home, opposite the town square.

We retrace our way through Skaisgere, Yaneshik, Shavel, and reach the highway just as the last light fades from the sky.

"Isaac, that *zhulig*, thinks he knows everything," Leah says. "He wasn't even in Zhager when the Germans marched in. Altona knows. She's a good woman. I believe everything she says. Imagine, she used to come to the Yoffes' house to bring collars and cuffs for Henke to embroider. I might even have been there when she came. Who notices a young child? As for Isaac, he wasn't even in Leibke's battalion, yet he knows exactly how and where he died. I still got three letters from him while he was in hospital. Let me tell you how it happened."

23

The Death of Leib

Leib in the army.

After Leib and Leah escaped over the border into Russia, they spent a month on the kolkhoz in Yereslav, where they helped bring in the harvest, then two months on a kolkhoz in the Volgagrad district. By that time the Lithuanian Brigade had been formed. Leib enlisted immediately.

"To seek his death," Leah says as we travel along the dark, misty highway towards Vilnius. "There I was, pregnant, among strangers, unable to speak a word of Russian. *Dos is nisht tzu dertzeilen.* It was indescribable. I remembered how I had left my sister Chana in Shavel with a child of six, seven months pregnant with her second child, her husband out of town, bombs falling all around her . . . Nu. What can I say. A Russian woman on the kolkhoz took pity on me. She promised to help with the birth of my child."

Leib had been stationed near Moscow, where he played in the army band. Leah was not allowed to join him. It is safer for a pregnant woman to remain on the kolkhoz, the authorities decreed. To alleviate her difficulties, they sent her a document which stated that Yoffe Leib Simonovitch was in the Red Army, and that his wife should be given rations and other benefits.

"I've still got the document. I'll show it to you when we get home. It gives the number of his battalion, Artillery Battalion, NKO 249, and was signed by Colonel Sharkus on 11 June 1942. What do you think of that? I can't remember Friedke's phone number, but this is engraved on my mind. With this document I got a room of my own on the kolkhoz, milk and other rations, and a doctor came to see me from time to time.

"The birth was difficult. I was in labour for twelve hours. I had stitches, they became infected, I got a very high temperature and was sent to a hospital where I lay for weeks. Leibke was not yet at the front. He wrote many letters. The first thing he asked about was the colour of the child's hair. Such a question, at such a time. We were lucky to be alive, and he was relieved she was not a redhead.

"Leibke wanted to name the child after his mother, but as you can't name a child after a person who is still living, and as we weren't sure whether she was alive or dead, he asked me to name her Freda, not Freyde. I was surprised he cared about such things, not being religious. I had been very close to Freyde. I knitted her a grey cardigan, made sweaters for the younger children, and darned the family's socks on my knitting machine. Freyde always looked forward to seeing me. '*Ich kook aus di eygen biz ich ze dir,*' she used to say. If she wanted to know what Leibke was doing or thinking, she'd ask me. Not that I always knew. Although he loved his mother, he never confided in her. He was a very private man. And when she had to go to Shavel to see the doctor, she'd ask me, no one else, to take her. She loved Leibke and me very much, and we loved her.

"I sent him photographs of the baby. He was overjoyed. She's got my mother's eyes, he wrote. He died on 20 August 1943. He had known his child only through photographs.

"Is Hirshl sleeping?" she asks Misha softly. Misha nods. "After all these years, Hirshl still gets upset when I speak about Leibke."

The highway is eerily empty. Even the broken-down trucks are gone. Occasional headlights pierce the darkness, fix us in their glare, then swish by, intensifying the dark.

"By 1943 Leibke was at the front," Leah says, "in the Orel region. Terrible battles were going on. People were dying like flies."

Some months later, I was able to place Leah's story into historical perspective. The Germans, ill-equipped for winter, had been driven back from Moscow in 1941. They had begun a slow withdrawal to a line which ran north to south from Kursk to Orel to Medynitzhev, creating a 320-kilometre front. The Red Army, advancing from east to west, created a bulge in the German line west of Kursk, which threatened all German gains in the south. Hitler ordered the line to be held at all costs; the Kursk salient had to be eliminated. Six thousand tanks and four thousand aircraft had taken part in the battle for the Kursk salient. It was the biggest tank battle in history. By July 1943, over 3000 German soldiers had been killed, and 3000 tanks destroyed. The Red Army also suffered heavy casualties in men and equipment, but they had stopped the German advance; they were no longer on the defensive. North of the Kursk salient, the Russian army launched Operation Kutuzov against Orel, in order to dissipate the Germans' strength and to prevent reinforcements from reaching Kursk.

The 16th Lithuanian Brigade had been in combat in the Orel district since February 1943. The brigade had attacked the Germans at Alexeyevke. Riflemen and machine-gunners had charged on foot across the snow-covered plain. For two days the brigade had struggled against superior German firepower until its ammunition ran out and it was ordered to retreat. Isaac Mendelson had been seriously wounded in that battle. Despite their heavy losses, the brigade fought on until the last day of the war.

"Was Leib in actual combat?" I ask. "You said he played in the army band."

"That was in the beginning. Of course he was in combat. He was a *politruk*," Leah says.

"A political worker," Freda explains, "a commissar. He was a non-commissioned officer, a sergeant, and was expected to lead the men into battle."

"I'm losing thread of what I want to say. Ah yes, my terrible dream," Leah says. "Freda was just over a year old, and I wasn't sleeping well. *Es cholempt zich mir az di varabanas klappen, un the trubess trubenen . . .* I dreamed that drums were beating and trumpets were blaring, and a crowd of people were walking slowly towards me, carrying a dead man in an open coffin. On his chest lay his cap. I approached the coffin, but couldn't bear to look at the face of the dead man. I tore myself out of the dream, groaning and weeping. I told my dream to the Russian woman who had befriended me and she comforted me. Then I pushed the dream out of my mind.

"Two days later I am called to the kolkhoz office. A young Russian takes me into a room and tells me a notification has arrived for me from the front at Orel, concerning my husband. He reads it to me. In the course of military action, it says, Yoffe Leib Simonovitch had been wounded. He died from his wounds, and has been buried in the cemetery at Yelets, which is in the Orel region. I hardly hear what he is saying. I am back in my dream and the orchestra is screaming in my ears. But it is not the orchestra that is screaming. It's me."

Freda takes Leah's hand. "Enough, mamme," she says.

"I must finish, then I'll never talk about it again. As you know, Raizala, there are as many stories about Leibke's death as there are about his life. One man told me that after the battle, Leibke had been very thirsty and went to look for water. He stood on a mine and was severely injured. He had apparently begged this man to shoot him, but he couldn't bring himself to do it. He died soon afterwards. And today we heard Mendelson's version. Yet I received three letters from Leibke while he was in hospital! Does it really matter whether he was killed by a German mine, a German soldier, or a German tank? I myself believe Zhukov's account, the man Mendelson dismisses as a mere *shuster*. Shoemakers also have eyes and Zhukov was in Leibke's battalion. So was Zaltzman. And they both told the same story. All I wrote to Gershon was, Leibke was killed at the front. No other details. I wasn't going to tell him about the letter . . . What letter? First let me tell how Leibke died, according to Zhukov and Zaltzman."

During the heavy fighting in the Orel area, she says, the Lithuanian Brigade took a town called Alexeyevke. They then attacked Nikolsk, a nearby village, but were repulsed. When they launched a second attack, the Germans retreated. Leib then led a reconnoitring unit through the village, going from house to house in search of German soldiers. All the Germans have left, one woman assured them when they came to her house. By this time Leib and his companions were exhausted. They lay down in a shed where the woman kept chickens. It was hot and stuffy, and Leib could not fall asleep. He and two other soldiers went into the house and lay down on the floor, at the foot of the stairs.

In the middle of the night, German soldiers who had been hiding in the attic of the house crept downstairs, stumbled over the Lithuanian soldiers, and shot them. Two died instantly; Leib was seriously injured. A bullet had lodged in his spine. When they heard the shooting, the rest of the Lithuanian contingent rushed inside, and shot the Germans. Leib was taken to hospital, where he died several days later.

"It was from hospital," Leah says, "that he wrote the three letters I told you about. I received them after his death. They were written on 16, 17 and 18 of August. He died on 20 August. 'My head and hands', he wrote in the first letter, 'are in order. But I feel nothing from my waist down.' In the second letter he said how much he looked forward to being with me and the baby. 'We will live a contented life together when the war is over,' he wrote. '*Un du zolst tzugreiten alle gute zachen tzum essen: pomedoren, dinas, un fruchten fun yeder zort.*' Prepare good things to eat: tomatoes, melons, all sorts of fruit . . .

"I can't eat fruit without thinking of that letter," Leah says. "At the end he wanted only simple things from life, his wife, his child, good things to eat . . ."

"And the third letter?"

Leah takes my hand. "That letter was written to Gershon, in Russian. It was a long, angry letter, dated 18 August, two days before he died, and it summed up all the bitterness Leibke felt towards Gershon. My friend, the Russian woman, read it to me. I could speak Russian by then, but couldn't read or write. At the end of the letter Leib added a few sentences in Yiddish. I must have read those lines a million times. I used to read and cry, read and cry. '*Du zidst zich bei dir in shtub and trinkst a gutten kaffe, reicherts a gutten cigaret. Vos veist du fun leiden? Ich lig do nont tzum teit. Es vilt zich zeier lebben. Di Amerikaner vellen effenen dem tzveiten front, un di malchome vet zich endiken. Mir vellen gevinnen. Di vos vellen bleiben leben vellen lebben glicklech*'."

You sit in your home drinking good coffee, smoking a good cigarette. What do you know about suffering? I lie here near to death, yet I want so much to live. The Americans will open a second front, and the war will end. We will win. And those who survive will live a happy life.

"You can understand", Leah says, "why I never sent the letter to Gershon."

"Gershon would have been devastated," I say. "He thought of his family all the time and suffered very much. He blamed himself for their fate. Leib sounds so bitter, so angry. After all those years. Did he never get over his resentment of Gershon?"

"*A brivale di mammen*, Leibke used to say. Gershon should've written to his mother. That he resented most of all. You know how it is. People thought that if you lived in Africa, you found gold in the streets."

"My father struggled to make a living. We were never rich."

"That is my story, Raizala. I lived for the child after his death, struggling against starvation. It helped that I could sew. The kolkhozniks used to bring me *yupkes*, skirts, from which I made them jackets. By hand. I was paid with an egg, some butter, a loaf of bread. Eventually I became the kolkhoz dressmaker. I hired a hand-operated machine for which I paid two kilos of bread each week. And I sold off most of the things my mother had packed into the mattress. Not everything. Some I kept to remember her by: her candlesticks, the samovar, things like that.

"The war finally ended. I took leave of the people on the kolkhoz. A few of them, including my Russian friend, were also returning to their homes in different parts of the country. I packed my few possessions into a box and she addressed it for me. I couldn't write Russian. My box was sent off to the station with everyone else's luggage.

"I never saw it again. All my letters from Leibke, my mother's candlesticks, her samovar . . ."

"In another hour we'll be in Vilnius," Misha says after a long silence. "It's been a long day but I'm pleased you took us to Zhager, Raizala. Was it really Zhager, mamme? Or was it Zhezmer or Zhetel or Zaslai?"

"Mishala likes to tease me," Leah says. "Nu. *Der lebedikker muz lebben.* The living must live. Do you know the song about the cat's wedding? About all the animals who came to the wedding, and how the mice enjoyed themselves while the cats were away? Leibke used to sing it. I forget the beginning."

> *. . . A mazel far di kallah*
> *Hobben zich gevundert alle*
> *Di hun is gekummen mit di hindalach*
> *Un Zutzke mit tsvei hintalach*
> *Affile dem blinden Abke*

Hot men gebracht far a lapke
Un di groya meizlach
Hobben zich bavizen in di heizlach
Tra, tra, tra, un pitz, pitz, patz,
Heint hot chasene unzer katz,
Tra, tra, tra, un pitz, pitz, patz,
Iz dos a chasene far a katz!

"Mamme, now sing the one about the Jewish drunkard. Did you really believe that Jews don't drink, Raizala?"

Hirshl has woken up. "They drink, they drink," he confirms.

"I'm surprised they don't drink more than they do, with all their *tzores*," Freda says, leaning over and patting Hirshl on the shoulder.

The car echoes with snatches of song as, crying and laughing, we exhume the songs of the dead. Through the fog, the diffused lights of Vilnius appear on the horizon.

"*A bittern gelechter*, bitter laughter, and songs. That's what keeps us sane," Leah says.

Tomorrow I leave for Zurich to catch a connecting flight to London. When we reach Leah's and Hirshl's apartment, I embrace them, and as I begin to take leave, Leah looks at me, astonished.

"Do you really think we'd let you go without seeing you onto the plane?" she says. "Misha will bring us to the airport. Besides, I'm making *teiglech* for your son in London. You said he loves them."

Dough rings, I'll have to explain to Customs at Heathrow. Something like doughnuts, only smaller, harder, boiled in syrup till they're brown and shiny. Only Lithuanian Jews make them. You're probably not aware of how few of them are left. People, not the confection. Please, not in the bin. Don't ask me to put them into the bin. *Teiglech* are an endangered culinary species.

"Really, Leah, it's not necessary, please don't bother . . ."

"Even if it takes till midnight, I'll make them," Leah assures me. "What other way have I of showing you how happy we are that you came to visit us?"

I'll smuggle them through Customs. If caught, I'll plead ignorance, insanity, or both.

Freda and I enter the dark apartment. A note from Ernest informs us that Yuri has driven him to a friend to fetch a video. They'll be back by ten o'clock.

Neither of us is hungry. Freda puts on the kettle for tea, and I take my "guide" books and camera to my room. I might as well remove the completed Zhager spool from the camera and insert a new film, in preparation for the farewell at the airport the following day.

I open the camera. The film, hastily inserted at the mass grave in Naryshkin Park, has slipped off the sprockets; it hasn't moved. I have no photographs of Zhager.

Freda comes into my room with a cup of tea. She finds me sitting on the edge of the bed, camera in hand, motionless.

"What is it? Are you sick? You look terrible!"

I take the film out of the camera, hold it up, and allow it to fall to the ground in a long, dark spiral.

"Zhager", I tell her, "no longer exists."

24

Epilogue

A new roadside sign points to the Jewish grave in Naryshkin Park.

I returned to Lithuania in the summer of 1993; my quest was incomplete. I had sought out my parents' contemporaries, interviewed survivors, travelled to Zhager, spoken to the one Jew in that town of ghosts, and worked in libraries, archives and museums. But apart from Altona, I had not spoken to other Lithuanians who had lived in Zhager at the time of the massacre. The dour, hostile faces, and the air of menace that hangs over the town had made the asking of street directions sufficiently daunting. What would be their reaction to the question I have to ask:

How could people, who had lived side by side for generations, turn on their neighbours, or stand by as they were being massacred?

Had they really laughed and jeered when Jews were publicly humiliated? Had they protested when their Jewish neighbours were penned into the ghetto, starved, and harassed by rampaging militiamen? Was it indifference to their fate or fear for their own that had held them back? And when the Jews were finally driven to the slaughter, had a single shooter, at the edge of the gaping pit, lowered his gun and refused to shoot? And had these killers been excommunicated by their Church for the slaughter of innocents?

A report from Einsatzgruppe A, dated 16 August 1941, sheds some light on the last question.[26] Headed "Organisation of the Catholic Church in Lithuania", it states: "The attitude of the Church regarding the Jewish question is, in general, clear. In addition, Bishop Brisgys has forbidden all clergymen to help Jews in any form whatsoever. He rejected several Jewish delegations who approached him personally and asked for his intervention with the German authorities. In the future he will not meet with any Jews at all."

We are all made of the same stuff, I would say to anyone in Zagare willing to speak to me, and want to believe that ancient hatreds, revenge for perceived transgressions, fear of the stranger, greed and envy, need not plunge ordinary people into the depths of savagery. Tell something, anything, that will salvage my faith in people. Disillusionment in ideals is to feel bereft; loss of faith in humanity is to despair.

No one will speak to you, Bronye warned when I explained why I had to return to Lithuania. Lithuanian-language newspapers, she wrote, were warning Lithuanians against speaking to outsiders about World War II events. Friendly interchanges, they said, had been

---

26 Arad *et al.*, *The Einsatzgruppen Reports*, p. 90.

exploited to malign the Lithuanian nation. One Lithuanian newspaper had reviewed a recent German film about the return of a Jewish survivor to the town of her birth, Butrimonys. She had come in search of a former Lithuanian militiaman who had shot many Jews in the area. The townspeople's negative reactions to the woman are recorded on film. So is the survivor's meeting with the militiaman. Although he is totally unrepentant, he has been rehabilitated by the Lithuanian government. The Lithuanian reviewer called the film a "slander against our nation".

To ask questions is not to slander a nation. An entire nation cannot be blamed for the evil actions of some of its people. It reflects badly on that nation, however, when convicted mass murderers are released from jail, rehabilitated and given pensions; when the press is openly anti-Semitic, and when the Attorney-General can dismiss a case against a prominent Kedainiai farmer who had pulled up tombstones in the Old Jewish Cemetery and used them as a foundation for a cowshed. His grounds for dismissal were that the crime had been committed thirty years ago.

The past should not be forgotten, denied or covered up. Those who do not remember the past, it has been said, are condemned to relive it. Knowing and remembering might not have prevented the massacres in Cambodia, Bosnia or Rwanda, but the struggle to make sense of such catastrophes cannot be abandoned.

National pride, reluctance to confront an uncomfortable past, and the need for help from the West, has induced widespread amnesia in Lithuania. People have forgotten that they welcomed the German invasion in the mistaken hope that independence would be restored. Months before the German invasion, there had been constant contact with the Gestapo and the Eastern Command of the Wehrmacht. A leaflet issued in Berlin by the Lithuanian Activist Front, the LAF, included statements like, "The crucial day of reckoning has come for the Jews at last. Lithuania must be liberated not only from Asiatic Bolshevik slavery but also from the long-standing Jewish yoke." The right of sanctuary granted to the Jews by Vytautas the Great was to be abolished forever; no Jew would have citizenship rights; all "honest Lithuanians" were to take measures on their own initiative to punish Jews who had "persecuted" Lithuanians. "Let us prepare for the liberation of Lithuania and the purification of the nation," it states.[27]

On 23 June 1941, the day after the Germans invaded Lithuania, the LAF, made up of Nazi sympathisers, Lithuanian fascists and nationalists, set up a provisional government, and proclaimed a new independent state of Lithuania. It was headed by Colonel Kazys Skirpa, the Lithuanian Ambassador to Berlin, an admirer of Hitler, and representatives of major nationalist and fascist groups. Their impeccable Nazi ideals, however, were not rewarded with independence. On 17 July 1941, the provisional government was informed that Germany had no intention of allowing Lithuanian political independence. On 5 August, its activities were suspended, the LAF outlawed, and some of its leaders arrested. This soured the relationship somewhat, but did not prevent thousands of Lithuanians who had belonged to groups like the Iron Wolf, the Lithuanian Freedom Army, the Falcons and the Lithuanian Restoration Front, from volunteering for work in the Nazi murder squads.

The *Ypatinga Bura* – "the special ones" – had murdered about 70 000 Jews at Ponar, near Vilna. The 12th Lithuanian Auxiliary Police Battalion had killed Jews in Kovno and Byelorussia. In addition to these special units, Lithuanian militiamen had participated in the murder of Jews in more than 200 cities, towns and villages throughout Lithuania, slaughtering 95 per cent of Lithuanian Jewry. Such was their cruelty in Slutsk, for example, that Gebiedskommissar Carl had complained about the "wild execution of Jews" to Generalkommissar Kube of White Russia.[28] The 11th Lithuanian Police Battalion, he reported, had arrived in Slutsk with orders to wipe out the Jewish community. Jews had been severely beaten up before the

---

27 Greenbaum, *The Jews of Lithuania*, p. 304, quoting T. G. Chase, *The Story of Lithuania.*

28 Hilberg, *The Destruction of the European Jews*, p. 143.

mass shootings on the outskirts of town had taken place. Some of the Jews, wounded but not killed, had worked themselves out of the graves. Kube, in turn, had sent on this report to his superiors, adding that the burial of seriously wounded people, who could work themselves out of their graves, was a disgusting business, and that it ought to be reported to Goering and Hitler – who, no doubt, would have been greatly distressed.

Perhaps the Gebiedskommissar and the Generalkommissar were among the "decent fellows" Himmler referred to when he addressed the SS at Posen on 4 October 1943.[29]

". . . Among ourselves it should be mentioned quite frankly, and yet we will never speak of it publicly . . . I mean . . . the extermination of the Jewish race . . . Most of you must know what it means when 100 corpses are lying side by side, or 500 or 1000. To have stuck it out and at the same time – apart from exceptions caused by human weakness – to have remained decent fellows, that is what has made us hard. This is a page of glory in our history which has never been written and is never to be written . . ."

By this time Himmler had in hand grander and faster methods of annihilating the Jews which, presumably, would not offend the susceptibilities of his "decent fellows".

The Lithuanian, Latvian and Ukrainian auxiliaries might only have been part players in the genocide of the Jews, but without them, the brutal killings orchestrated by the Einsatzgruppen under Himmler's command could not have been carried out.

After reading Bronye's letter, I wondered if there was any point in returning to Lithuania. I had been to Zagare but had not found Zhager. The houses had been torn down, the gravestones over-turned, the bloody market square covered with concrete and trees. Within a decade the memorial in Naryshkin Park would have no visitors; the survivors were ageing and dying, and the younger

---

29 Shirer, *The Rise and Fall of the Third Reich: A History of Nazi Germany*, p. 1150 (Nuremberg Documents).

generation knew little of their past. The Yiddish and Hebrew inscriptions would be as Sanskrit to anyone who stumbled over them. Only the Lithuanian inscription would be read, then shrugged off; we are not responsible for our forebears' actions.

I might not get answers, I decided finally, but I had to ask the questions. So in the summer of 1993, I returned to Lithuania, this time with my daughter and younger son. They too wanted to make the journey to *der heim*, the home of our ancestors.

In Vilnius, the family receives us with flowers. It seems only yesterday, not fifteen months ago, that we last met. Hirshl is frail, Leah tearful, Misha and family are thriving. Yuri and Ernest break off an argument to say how happy they are that I have brought part of my family to visit them; next year I must bring the rest. Freda and I embrace; there is no need for words.

During a day of intense hospitality, Misha and Freda discuss an itinerary. A tour of Vilnius, a visit to Rasein and Trakai, and possibly a drive to Palanga, the famous coastal resort near Klapeida/Memel, where they used to spend their summer holidays.

"And this time we'll see Zhager properly," Misha says. "We'll sleep over in a hotel in Yonishkis, a short drive away, and travel in comfort, in the Mercedes."

I take Freda aside. "How can we go to Zhager in a Mercedes? The Einsatzgruppen, the German trucks . . ." An absurd response. Friends and relatives drive German cars, my husband's business car had been a BMW. The "new Germans", after all, had long taken their place among the world's democrats. Yet at that moment, driving a Mercedes into Zhager seemed obscene.

"Misha's so proud of car," says Freda, bemused. "He bought it cheap from Turkish worker in Germany."

I do not even know which German company had produced the gas vans or the vehicles in which the Einsatzgruppen had moved so swiftly from city to town to village, entrapping and annihilating every Jewish community in Eastern Europe. But I know something of the complicity of other German industrialists in the Holocaust. A group of fanatical SS leaders alone could not have carried out the mass killings. The Krupps had used slave labourers not only for their factories in Germany; they had also built a fuse factory at Auschwitz, where Jews had been worked to exhaustion, then gassed to death. I. G. Farben too had chosen this death camp to build a new synthetic coal-oil and rubber plant; slave labour was cheap, disposable and replenishable. Using the Zyklon B patent acquired from I. G. Farben, two German firms, Tesch & Stabenow and Degesh, had supplied tons of the cyanide crystals each month for the gas chambers. Entrepreneurs like I. A. Topf and Sons had built the crematoria at Auschwitz; Didier Works and C. H. Kori had also entered the lively competition for manufacturing furnaces for other extermination camps. Their correspondence with the SS bureaucracy, couched in impeccable business jargon, sounds like dialogue from an Ionesco play.

"We acknowledge receipt of your order for five triple furnaces, including two electric elevators for raising the corpses . . ."

Or: "Following our verbal discussion regarding the delivery of equipment of simple construction for the burning of bodies, we are submitting plans for our perfected cremation ovens which operate with coal and which have hitherto given full satisfaction . . . Heil Hitler!"[30]

Two days later we leave for Zagare with Freda and Misha. In the Mercedes. The grey skies of my previous visit have given way to soft sunlight, the soggy fields to swaying wheatfields. Poppies and corn-flowers glow like jewels through the wheat. Wildflowers carpet the verges of the roads and black-ringed birch trunks glimmer through the green forests. For a moment the mass graves are forgotten. Only the broken-down trucks and cars are a reminder of the earlier visit. With Leah's hamper in the boot of the car, we might be setting out on a picnic.

The talk is of Misha's business success, measured partly by the

---

30 Shirer, *The Rise and Fall of the Third Reich: A History of Nazi Germany*, p. 1158 (Nuremberg Documents).

unwelcome interest the Mafia has taken in it. In addition to his clothing workshop, he now has an interest in a food store, which is doing well. Misha is reluctant to talk about the call from the Mafia. Freda, however, tells us that three thugs had entered his office several months ago, dragged him into a waiting car, and roughed him up, promising less gentle treatment if he did not pay protection money each month. Misha brushes it off; the Mafia has become a fact of life in Vilnius. But his round, cheerful face suddenly looks drawn. He turns on the radio, and we hear the vigorous rhythm of a Russian pop song.

"Rasputin," Freda says. "Very popular singer."

The Mafia, in one form or another, has been around in this region for a long time.

At 7.30 a.m. we arrive in Panevezys/Ponevez. "The great actor Solaris lives here," Freda says. "He is known in all Russia. We have wonderful theatre in Panevezys."

The entire Jewish population of Ponevez had been massacred in six Einsatzgruppen *Aktionen* during 1941. Is there a single beautiful place in Lithuania which does not have a sub-text?

"Palanga," Freda says as we approach the road sign, "is about 200 kilometres from here. *Shlingarein*, we call it. Eat, children, eat, mothers say. You are on holiday and you must eat. Swallow it down, *shlingarein!* And of course, Mother has given us food for the journey. We shall *shlingarein* outside Shavel."

Knowing what lies ahead, our picnic in a field of flowers has an air of unreality. I do not trust this beauty; who knows what lies beneath it? Why had I imagined I could sail into hostile territory and ask those questions of strangers? I do not look forward to reaching our destination.

When we arrive in Yonishkes/Yaneshik, we cruise around, looking for a hotel. One of the two small hotels is closed for renovation. When Misha and Freda go into the second hotel, my children and I walk through the town. In the midst of new or renovated dwellings and shops, we come upon a neglected structure which retains some of its former beauty. It is a two-storey, red-brick building, and has a pitched roof with pediments at either end. Even before we see the Magen David, we guess it might have been a synagogue. The long, arched windows have been boarded up or bricked in, shutting out the light, blinding it to the suffering of its congregants. Passers-by regard us with curiosity, if not hostility, as we photograph the building. This time we're not taking chances. Each of us is armed with a camera.

A visiting sports team and their supporters have booked out the second hotel, Freda tells us. The nearest accommodation is back in Siauliai/Shavel, at least 67 kilometres from Zagare. Once again we shall only be spending one day in the town.

I have a feeling of *déjà vu* as we approach Zagare, only this time the fields and trees are a palette of greens, ranging from jade, emerald and lime to the grey-green of the fir trees. It is shot through with the red, blue, yellow and white of the wildflowers. At the roadside is a new sign, in Lithuanian:

In the nobleman Naryshkin's Park is the grave of Jewish victims of genocide.

The old sign, in Lithuanian and Russian, *Grave of the victims of fascism, 0.2,* has been removed.

We drive up the path towards the mass grave. The free-standing memorial plaques in Lithuanian, Yiddish and Hebrew have now been fixed onto the obelisk, replacing the Yiddish and Soviet inscriptions. We gather around the monument, beyond tears, beyond prayer. Freda places a bouquet of wildflowers on the plinth. Except for the lament of the crows, there is complete silence. The flowerbeds over the mass grave are in bloom. Lilacs out of the dead land.

Our next stop is at the cemetery where our ancestors are buried. A shield-shaped plaque on a concrete stele now identifies it as a historic site. To its left, three metal plates proclaim in Lithuanian, Yiddish and Hebrew:

Old Jewish Cemetery. May their blessed memory be for eternity.

Indeed. May their memory outlast the headstones, most of which have been knocked over or are missing. Those still standing tilt at gravity-defying angles, their inscriptions worn away or covered in dry moss. We walk warily through the weeds and wildflowers; we could be trampling over the graves of our ancestors.

It is mid-morning. We shall explore the town till one o'clock, when we are expected for lunch by Altona and Isaac Mendelson. As we do not possess a map of Zagare, Misha makes random decisions on direction.

"Raktuves Gatve," Freda reads as we drive towards the hills on the outskirts of town.

My parents had spoken about Raktuvergas, though I cannot recall in which context. They had never mentioned, perhaps never known, that the street had been named after a fortress called Raktuve. It had been built on a hill on the right bank of the River Shvete to protect its inhabitants from the depredations of the German Livonian knights. When the knights burned down the fortress in 1290, the inhabitants, who had lived in Zagare since the early thirteenth century, had been forced to withdraw deeper into Lithuania. Towards the end of the fifteenth century, the weakened Livonian Order had ceased to attack Lithuania, and Zagare had become a market town where trade fairs were held regularly.

At the base of the hills, there is an occasional low stele, erected by the Department of Archaeology. "Burial mounds of the Dukes of Zvelgaiciai," Freda translates. "Ninth to fifteenth centuries."

I had seen photographs of such burial mounds, *piliakalnis*, at the Ethnographic Museum in Vilnius, some of which date from the first century A.D. They had been built up by the Semigallians, an earlier Baltic people who had lived in the Zagare, Joniskis and Siauliai area prior to the arrival of the Lithuanians. The hills of Zhagar, my parents had called them. Burial mounds. White butterflies and flowers are everywhere.

Within minutes we are back in town. A chance turn-off takes us to the imposing structure that Count Naryshkin had erected for his daughters' equestrian activities. The Department of Agriculture now breeds horses there. We park the car under a tree, and walk towards the open door of the building. Ten horses are stabled on each side of a long hall with a beamed, wooden ceiling. Light pours in through the arched windows onto the wide, wooden passage between the decorative wooden stalls. Is this where Naryshkin's daughters had put their horses through their paces, or is there a larger arena elsewhere?

As we leave the stables, we see a woman sweeping up leaves a short distance away. Freda talks to her for a few minutes, then returns, smiling.

"All problems solved," she says. "The woman herself knows nothing about Zhager, but when I told her you were from Australia and wanted to know Naryshkins' history, she gave me the address of a teacher of history who will tell you everything. And if you want to see Naryshkin's Palace, it is there!" She points towards a copse of trees behind which a large white building glimmers through the leaves.

Count Naryshkin's palace. After World War II the palace was converted into an orphanage, then a school, and later a hospital.

As we emerge out of the small wooded area, we see a two-storey building of classic proportions, a stately manor house rather than a palace. The Yiddish word *haif* probably translates as mansion, the home of the feudal lord. But nothing remains of the legendary gardens which once surrounded the *haif*. They can only be imagined.

On the front door, a plaque in Lithuanian states that this white house is the palace of the Park. The building seems to be uninhabited. Except for the woman sweeping up leaves, there is no one in sight.

We go in search of the teacher of history. Misha, negotiating the uncharted streets of Zagare, eventually finds his way. In front of the house, birch logs are being unloaded from a truck. A woman with curly grey hair is showing the men where to put the logs.

When Freda and I approach her, she greets us with a friendly smile. Freda tells her that she lives in Vilnius, and that I am her cousin from Australia. We have been told that she is a historian, and as our parents were born in Zhager, we'd like to know more about their birthplace.

"You've come to the right source," she assures us. "My name is Victoria and I am a historian. I will be delighted to tell you whatever you want to know."

We arrange to return to her house in two hours' time, when she will have finished her household chores. I can hardly believe our luck. A friendly, outgoing resident of Zagare will be delighted to speak to us about Zagare; a teacher, to crown it, who has taught generations of Zagare residents the history of the town.

The Mendelsons welcome us like old friends. The apartment looks bright and cheerful, but I avert my eyes from the window which looks onto the square, once the market-place.

"Lovely flowers," Freda says.

"It is Isaac's name day," Altona says. "St Peter's day. All morning, friends have been visiting us with flowers."

When Isaac had told Leah, on our previous visit, that Christian friends had advised him to change his name to Petrus, Leah had cried out, "Did your friends name you Petrus, or did the priest make you Petrus?"

Who are we to question how Isaac choses to survive, Freda had upbraided Leah on the way home.

Altona has set the table with homemade sausage, cold meat, cheese, freshly-baked biscuits and dark rye bread. This time she sits down to eat with us, leaving the table only to make coffee.

Freda tells them about our meeting with the history teacher. We want to know more about the Naryshkins, she explains, and to ask a specific question of non-Jewish people from Zhager. Isaac shrugs. He switches to Lithuanian. I hear the word *Sajudis* repeated several times; independence. Victoria and her husband, it seems, are of a different political party.

For the benefit of my son and daughter, Isaac repeats the stories he told us on our previous visit. Although the Lithuanian militia had been the chief murderers, he emphasises, several ordinary people had risked their lives to save Jews. Essentially the Lithuanians are decent people, but it had been a time of madness. He speaks about the gangs of murderers who had moved around from shtetl to shtetl, participating in the massacres. They had recruited shooters from Zhager as well.

"We have had many guests since we saw you last," Isaac says, taking out his "visitors' book" from a drawer. It is a long sheet of paper, with the names and addresses of callers from America, South Africa and London. Isaac is becoming an institution, the keeper of memories. Who will replace him when he is gone? We add our names to the list of visitors.

After lunch we walk through the streets of what was once Zhager.

This time the people look relaxed and greet Isaac/Petrus with a smile. He seems comfortable in their midst. Had I imagined the hostility, the menace, of our last visit; had the gun behind the curtain been a dramatic gesture? Or was everyone feeling content because the *liepa* is in bloom? When Freda and I head off to our appointment with Victoria, Misha, with Isaac as the guide, drives my son and daughter around the town.

We are early and find Victoria in the backyard laundry. We insist she finishes her work. It is done, she says, drying her hands. She leads us into the house, which, she says right away, they had bought from Mr Zlot, the one-time Jewish mayor of Zagare. Ownership of property, it seems, must be established immediately; it is a sensitive issue in Zagare. On a round table covered with an embroidered cloth, is a vase with red flowers, newspapers and two pairs of reading glasses.

Victoria does not mind having our interview recorded, she tells Freda. She understands the difficulty of translating from Yiddish to Lithuanian to Yiddish and the need to have a back-up. It is a pity, she smiles at me, that we cannot have a direct conversation. Our grandson, she says when a boy of about ten comes into the room. He is spending part of the summer holidays in Zagare.

Victoria tells us she was born in Panevyzs and studied history first at Kaunas University, then at the University of Vilnius, where she met her husband Domas, a native of Zagare. At this point the native himself comes into the room. He has a pleasant face, and greets us with a smile. He indicates, however, that when he speaks, he does not wish to be recorded.

Victoria and Domas had returned to Zagare in 1952, where they worked as school teachers for forty years. Nineteen-fifty-two; eleven years after the massacre. Domas's family had probably been in Zagare at the time.

Freda tells Domas that our fathers had had a barbershop on the market square. Before he speaks, he indicates that the tape recorder should be switched off. Yes, he remembers the barbershop. Full stop. He has nothing more to say on that subject.

When had he left Zhager, Freda asks. In 1926, he says, and he returned in 1952, with Victoria. Many people had left for bigger towns after World War I, because the economic situation had deteriorated. Zagare remained a backwater because of its poor roads which become impassable in bad weather. After all these years, he says, there is still no direct rail link with the rest of the country. The nearest station is 25 kilometres away, in Yoniskis. He then sits back, and folds his arms across his chest. When it becomes clear that this is all Domas is prepared to say, Victoria takes over.

"I know a lot about the history of Zagare," Victoria says, "because of the documents I found in Naryshkin's Palace."

She tells us that the last of the Naryshkins had left Zagare for England in the winter of 1939. They never returned. After the war, the palace had been converted into an orphanage, then into a school and later into a hospital. Victoria had taught at the school for forty years. When she discovered documents relating to the history of the Naryshkins, nobody had shown interest in them. She later donated the documents to the Academy of Sciences in Vilnius.

The documents, Victoria says, relate mainly to the history of the Naryshkin family. Catherine the Great, grateful to the nobles who had supported her when she came to the throne, bestowed honours and land on them. Zagare had been given to Count Platon Zhubov, but as he had not wanted to live there, he had sold it to Count Naryshkin in 1850. Naryshkin, I had read somewhere, had been the grandson of Platon Zhubov and had inherited the estate from him. I say nothing. Who can argue with documents?

The last of the Naryshkins, though not a hunter himself, had built specially equipped rooms for his hunting friends. He himself had been more interested in astronomy. When Victoria came to the school, there was still a great deal of astronomy equipment lying around which was used for teaching purposes. The equestrian structure on his estate, she says, had been designed by the best architects in Lithuania. It was used in winter for manège, exhibition riding, and attracted riders from all over the Baltic countries.

An earlier Naryshkin had had a 26-hectare park laid out by an English and a French horticulturist, part formal, part wooded. The third-largest park in Lithuania, it had contained 113 different kinds of trees and shrubs.

Victoria exhibits a historian's delight in detail and statistics, and obviously has great respect for documents. This augurs well for the subject which we are yet to approach.

"Unfortunately many trees were felled during the Russian occupation," she says. "During the war, trees were cut down for heating, and recently, a hurricane destroyed trees. But since independence, the Park is being cared for again, and new trees have been planted."

I now understand why Leah had not recognised the Park of her youth.

"Ask when the Jews first came to Zagare," I say to Freda, leading gradually to the question I want to ask.

"The Jews came to Zagare in the nineteenth century," Victoria says, "because it was a large trading centre where they could make money." She speaks with confidence. After all, she had taught this history for four decades. "All the hotels and shops had been run by Jews. There was one particular hotel, owned by a man called Kvitzeinia, which attracted merchants from all over Lithuania. Not only did it have smartly-dressed waiters to attend them at table; the owners also brought in prostitutes from the other side of the River Shvete. These girls didn't live in the hotel. They only worked there."

We wait in vain for the kind of detail Victoria had lavished on the Naryshkins; dates, statistics, sources. But this is all she has to say on the subject. Is there any point in giving the historian a lesson on the history of the Jews of Zhager? It is too late, after all, to correct what her students have been taught: that the Jews had come to Zagare in the nineteenth century as traders and pimps in the hope of enriching themselves.

Victoria, I would have said if language and circumstances had permitted, there had been a settled Jewish community in Zhager by the sixteenth century. And they had not flocked to Zagare because it was a flourishing market town. It was their enterprise and hard work that had made its markets and fairs famous throughout Lithuania. In its heyday, Zhager had been known as a city of Torah and wisdom, and had produced many famous rabbis, scholars and writers: *Chachmei Zhager* they had been called, the wise men of Zhager.

Seventeenth-century documents – she respects documents – record that, in addition to importing salt and metals and exporting flax, grain, honey and wax, the Jews had leased the right to charge import duty from the government. Their occupations had ranged from artisans to tax farmers. By 1790, the market-place had been exclusively inhabited by about fifty Jewish families, who had owned thirty shops and taverns in and around the town. Mr Kvitzeinia and his smartly-dressed waiters may even have been among them.

In 1803, the market square had been paved, and at the request of the Jewish residents, the number of market days and fairs had been increased. As economic conditions improved, the Jewish population had expanded from 840 in 1766 and 2266 in 1847, to 5443 in 1897. It is recorded that in one year, towards the end of the nineteenth century, Jewish merchants had exported 4000 kronen worth of linen, and 1000 kronen worth of grain and wheat to Germany. They had also set up factories for processing bristles, candles, mead, wire and hides, and conducted a brisk trade in flax, grains, metal, wines and machines. The economy continued to expand until World War I, when the Jews were sent into exile, after which the fortunes of the town declined. It never regained its former vigour.[31]

In 1923, the tail-end of the brief Golden Age of independence, there had been about 2000 Jews in Zhager, constituting 40 per cent of the overall population. Before World War II, their numbers had declined to 1000, most of whom were either shopkeepers, artisans or vegetable gardeners. Their numbers had greatly increased, briefly, when Jews from surrounding towns and villages had been driven into the Zhager ghetto in 1941, and massacred shortly afterwards, with the invaluable help of Lithuanian auxiliaries. And today, as

---

31 Kagan, *Yiddishe Shtet, Shtetlech un Dorfishe Yishuvim in Lite*; *Yahadut Lite*; *Encyclopaedia Judaica*, pp. 362–90; Schoenburg, *Lithuanian Jewish Communities*.

you no doubt know, Victoria, there is one Jew in Zagare.

I like Victoria. She is friendly, warm, sincere. She does not know much about the history of the Jews of Zhager, but by now I have learned that historical sources are not easy to access, especially if you are not looking for them. However, I believe she will give me an honest answer to the question I have travelled so far to ask:

"How could people, who had lived side by side for generations, turn on their neighbours, or stand by as they were being massacred?"

She clutches her head and cries, "We must never forget it! The same happened in Panevyzs. Everywhere. It is difficult for me to say this, but the Jews were told lies. They were told they were being taken away to work. I cannot bear to speak about it," she says, covering her face. "The women and the children were beaten up and thrown onto lorries. The streets ran with blood. Streets of blood. People who saw this told me about it. Everyone was taken to Naryshkin Park where 3000 Jews were shot. Everyone must know what happened," she says. "I'll never forget it. How is it possible to shoot another human being?"

Everyone is quiet for a while. Victoria's grandson puts his arm around her shoulder. Domas says nothing.

"I am an internationalist," Victoria goes on, "not a leftist or a rightist, a fascist or a communist. I am an internationalist. It is very interesting for me to be speaking to Jews. As a historian I am very concerned with the reason for the murder of the Jews, and who committed the murders. But I do not have access to the archives which would give me the answers. Without documents, it is impossible to know. But as a historian and as a human being, I believe no one should forget what happened."

It is a pity Victoria does not have access to the archives. Without documents, she cannot tell who was responsible for the murder of the Jews.

Misha's car draws up beside the house. We had not realised how quickly the time had passed. We exchange addresses, shake hands with Domas and Victoria and thank them for speaking to us.

"So, did you get an answer to your question?" Isaac asks, when we later take leave of him and Altona.

"No," I say, "but I haven't given up trying."

Who will show visitors around after Isaac is gone? Whatever his reasons, motivations or rationalisations, he has played an important part in keeping the memory of the massacred Jews of Zhager alive.

Perhaps people will continue visiting the mass grave, after all; my pessimism may be unfounded. Or perhaps a fourth inscription in Lithuanian will replace the others on the obelisk in Count Naryshkin's Park:

We did not do it.

And/or:

It was their own fault.

Sharon Zwi

Exit from Zagare/Zhager.

Bibliography

Adler, Taffy. (Unpublished paper). History of the Jewish Workers' Club in Johannesburg.

Arad, Y., Krakowski, S. and S. Spector. (Eds). (1989). *The Einsatzgruppen Reports. Selections from the Despatches of the Nazi Death Squads Campaign Against the Jews, July 1941–January 1943*. New York: Holocaust Library.

Baron, S. W. (1957). *A Social and Religious History of the Jews, III* and *IV*. New York: Columbia University Press.

Browning, Christopher R. (1992). *Ordinary Men: Reserve Battalion 101 and the Final Solution in Poland.* , New York. Aaron Asher Books, HarperPerennial.

Darbai ir polekiai –. (1994). Thoughts and Aspirations: Marking the 90th birthday of linguist Chatzekelis Lemchenas. Vilnius: Jewish State Museum of Lithuania.

Dawidowitz, Lucy S. (1967). *The Golden Tradition*. London: Vallentine, Mitchell.

Dawidowitz, Lucy S. (1979). *The War Against the Jews, 1933–1945*. New York: Bantam Books.

Dawidowitz, Lucy S. (1989). *From That Place and Time: A Memoir*. New York: Norton.

Dimont, Max I. (1962). *Jews, God and History*. New York: Simon and Schuster.

Encyclopaedia Britannica. (1961). *13*.

Encyclopaedia Judaica: Lithuania. pp. 361–90.

Fedler, Solomon. (1969). *Shalecheth*. Johannesburg: S. Fedler & Co.

Gerutis, Albertis. (Ed.) (1984). *Lithuania: 700 Years*, 6th edn. New York: Manyland Books.

Gilbert, Martin. (1987). *The Holocaust: The Jewish Tragedy*. London: Fontana Press.

Gilbert, Martin. (1988). *Atlas of the Holocaust*. Steimatzky, Israel: Pergamon Press

Gilman, S. I. and S. T. Katz. (Eds.) (1991). *Anti-Semitism in Times of Crisis*. New York: New York University Press.

Greenbaum, Masha. (1995). *The Jews of Lithuania: A History of a Remarkable People, 1316–1943*. Israel: Gefen Publishing House.

Hilberg, Raul. (1985). *The Destruction of the European Jews.* New York and London: Holmes & Meier.

Hilberg, Raul. (Ed.) (1987). *Documents of Destruction. Germany and Jewry, 1933–45.* London: HarperPerennial.

Hilberg, Raul. (1992). *Perpetrators, Victims, Bystanders. The Jewish Catastrophe, 1933–1945.* New York: HarperPerennial.

Ignatieff, Michael. (1991, November). In the New Republics, *New York Review.*

Jerusalem in Lithuania. (1993, May–June). (5).

Kagan, Berel. (Ed.) (1991). *Yiddishe Shtet, Shtetlech un Dorfishe Yishuvim in Lite. Historical Biographical Sketches.* Brooklyn, New York: Simcha Graphic Associates.

Koestler, Arthur. (1983). *The Thirteenth Tribe.* London: Pan Books.

League of Nations. (1927, August). *Document for Protection of Linguistic, Racial and Religious Minorities by the League of Nations.* Geneva.

Lieven, Anatol. (1993). *The Baltic Revolution: Estonia, Latvia, Lithuania and the Path to Independence.* New Haven: Yale University Press.

Mendelsohn, Ezra. (1983). *The Jews of East Central Europe Between the World Wars.* Indiana: Indiana University Press.

Schoenburg, Nancy and Stuart Schoenburg. (1991). *Lithuanian Jewish Communities.* New York and London: Garland Publishing.

Shirer, William L. (1960). *The Rise and Fall of the Third Reich: A History of Nazi Germany.* London: Pan Books.

Suziedelis, Saulius. (1990, Spring). *The Military Mobilisation Campaigns of 1943–1944 in German-occupied Lithuania: Contrasts in Resistance and Collaboration. JBS, XXI* (1). Washington DC: US Information Agency.

Testimonies of Survivors: Yehezkiel Fleischer, Yaakov Kagan, Ber Peretzman. From archives of Yad v'Shem, Jerusalem.

Tory, Avraham. (1990). *Surviving the Holocaust: The Kovno Ghetto Diary.* Massachusetts: Harvard University Press.

Yahadut Lite (Hebrew). (1959–71). A History of 200 Jewish Communities in Lithuania. 4 volumes.

Yodaiken, Len. (1987). *The Judeikins: A Lithuanian Jewish Family in Dispersion.* Kibbutz Kfar Hanasi.

Zuroff, Efraim. Whitewashing the Holocaust: Lithuania and the Rehabilitation of History. *Tikkun, 7* (1).

If you would like to know more about Spinifex Press,
write for a free catalogue or visit our Home Page.

SPINIFEX PRESS
PO Box 212, North Melbourne,
Victoria 3051, Australia
http://www.spinifexpress.com.au/~women